The Jews in Colonial America

ALSO BY OSCAR REISS

Medicine and the American Revolution:
How Diseases and Their Treatments
Affected the Colonial Army
(McFarland, 1998)

Blacks in Colonial America
(McFarland, 1997)

The Jews in Colonial America

OSCAR REISS

McFarland & Company, Inc., Publishers
Jefferson, North Carolina, and London

LIBRARY OF CONGRESS CATALOGUING-IN-PUBLICATION DATA

Reiss, Oscar, 1925–
    The Jews in colonial America / Oscar Reiss.
        p.   cm.
    Includes bibliographical references and index.

    ISBN 0-7864-1730-7 (softcover : 50# alkaline paper)

    1. Jews—United States—History—17th century.
    2. Jews—United States—History—18th century.
    3. United States—History—Colonial period, ca. 1600–1775.
    4. United States—Ethnic relations. I. Title.
    E184.3512.R45   2004
    973'.04924—dc22   2003024606

British Library cataloguing data are available

Manufactured in the United States of America

On the cover: ©2000 PicturesNow.com

*McFarland & Company, Inc., Publishers
  Box 611, Jefferson, North Carolina 28640
  www.mcfarlandpub.com*

To the women in small Jewish
communities who work so hard to keep
Jewishness alive for their children;
and to their Christian friends,
without whose financial support
this would be more difficult

Acknowledgments

For this book as for my others, the sixth floor of the University of California San Diego Library supplied most of my information. As I reviewed my endnotes, I found many references to Jacob R. Marcus. To my mind, the volume of his output makes him dean of authors on early Jewish American history. I examined the historical magazines and books of the 13 original states. The pickings were minuscule, apparently because there were so few Jews. The *American Jewish Historical Quarterly*, with more than 100 years of publications provided much of the information used in this manuscript. In addition to these sources, I read Stephen Birmingham's *The Grandees*, which describes the Sephardim in America. B. Netanyahu's large tome *The Origins of the Inquisition in Fifteenth-Century Spain* has a wealth of information about the early history of Spain with particular reference to the Jews. My dear friend of half a century, Marvin Garrell, knew of my interest in this subject and recommended Paul Johnson's *History of the Jews*, from which I gleaned a great deal of information about the Hebrews of the Bible and about the emigration of Jews to the New World.

As I mentioned in other books, I have been constantly and gratefully surprised at the friendliness of the librarians. They often went out of their way to help me find material in the stacks. There must be something in their makeup that leads them into this profession. I wonder if the less friendly fall by the wayside before they get to the libraries. I want to particularly thank Lydia Ybarra, head of circulation at the UCSD Social Sciences Library. She bent the rules to allow this handicapped writer to do his research in the comfort of his home. I would also like to thank Nancy Relaford, day circulation manager at the UCSD Library, for her help in getting my endnotes in proper order and helping with accuracy.

Contents

Introduction

The eastern seaboard of North America below Canada was settled by Englishmen, predominantly from the Midlands. There was a sprinkling of Scotch and Scotch-Irish. These were all Anglo-Saxons. Protestant Saxons (Germans) came to escape the wars that devastated their homeland. The concept of primogeniture existed in Great Britain, and second (and third and fourth) sons had to leave the family farm. These were the people who migrated to America.

The Puritans were English citizens who came to these shores to avoid religious persecution. They set up a theocratic state. The fertile Puritans spread from Boston to all of Massachusetts, Rhode Island, Connecticut, and New Hampshire and were present in New Amsterdam and Long Island.

The Jewish minority was always minuscule in the colonial and federal periods. At the time of the American Revolution there may have been 2,500 Jews. The Jewish minority shrank to about 1,500 or less in the federal period. The federal period was one of recession because the infant United States could not trade with any of the European countries. The mercantilist concept still existed. International trade was the "heartblood" of the wealthy Jewish merchant-shippers. Perhaps a good number of these traders moved to the West Indies or back to Europe. Probably more important were conversion and intermarriage, with the loss of their progeny to the Jewish population.

The Wandering Jews

The concept of the "wandering Jew" was born when the Jews lost their homeland on the eastern shore of the Mediterranean. This loss started with the Assyrian conquest, followed by the Babylonians.[1]

By 531 B.C. there were more Jews living outside of Palestine than

1

within its borders. The Jews of Babylon were well treated and reasonably free. Babylon was conquered by the Persians. Cyrus, their king, offered the Jews the right to return to their homeland. Many preferred to stay and were the forerunners of an ancient center of Jewish culture.

The Persian Empire, in its turn, was defeated by Alexander of Macedonia. After his death, his generals divided his vast holdings. The Ptolemies controlled most of the Jews. The wealthy Jews were becoming Hellenized. The majority of the Jews simply accepted Greek rule and continued in their Judaism. In 175 B.C. King Antiochus Epiphanes seized the temple funds to finance his wars of aggression.

A Jewish revolt started when Matthias Hasmon killed a Jewish reformer in Modem. His five sons under Judas the Maccabee (Hammer) started a guerilla war. By 164 B.C. the Greeks were driven from Jerusalem. Three years later the Hasmoneans signed a pact with Rome. Judah became a client state of Rome in 63 B.C., and Herod was made king of Judah. During Herod's rule, the population of Jews grew to eight million and represented 10 percent of the population of the Roman Empire. Herod died in 4 B.C.

Most Jews were happy under Roman rule. However, a small group of Orthodox Jews, the Zealots, chafed under the Romans. They rose up against Roman rule in A.D. 66 and A.D. 135. Titus Vespasian with 25,000 troops enveloped Jerusalem and overcame the defenders. The Jews who survived were sold into slavery, and many of the men became gladiators.

More than a century before this maelstrom, Yeshua of the House of David was born. The temple priests, the Pharisees and the Sadducees feared his teaching and sent him to Pilate as a state criminal. Pilate convicted him for political reasons.

Saul (or Paul), a diaspora Jew, spread his religion to the diaspora Jews over the known world. The bifurcation of Christianity from its parent, Judaism, occurred around the time of the first uprising A.D. 66–70. After the revolt of A.D. 135 Judaism ceased to be a national religion, and the Jews lost their geographical country.

Jews in Europe

The Jews lived in the Iberian Peninsula before the growth of Christianity.[2] When the Visigoths accepted Christianity, they accepted the violent anti–Semitism of the true church. The Moorish invasion in 711 brought relief from the Catholic attacks. Under the Moors, the Jews were doctors, lawyers, architects, scientists and chemists. The Golden Moorish Age ended when primitive fundamentalist Moslems invaded Spain and destroyed the earlier Arab kingdoms (1146). The Jews fled to Christian Spain. The Golden Age of the Jews in Christian Spain began to tarnish when Pope Innocent III introduced the yellow badge to be worn on Jews' clothing. It was at this time, too, that stories were told of Jews killing Christian children to use their blood to make matzoh. Also, Jews were accused of poisoning wells, which many thought was the cause of the Black Death.

In April 1492, an order of total expulsion of Jews and Moors was delivered to the populace unless they converted. Fifty thousand Jews converted, and 400,000 left Spain. Many moved to Western Europe. Others were welcomed by the sultan of Turkey, and a large number moved to North Africa, Constantinople and Salonica. Another large group moved to Portugal. Those Jews who fled to the Turkish Empire were called "Sephardim," a corruption of the old name for Spain.

The expulsion from Spain enriched Portugal.[3] Unhappily, their stay was limited to five years. Prince Manuel of Portugal wished to marry a Spanish princess.[4] Queen Isabella forbade this union unless he evicted his Jews. Manuel did not wish to lose his newly found treasure and started a movement of enforced conversion.

The Inquisition was not directed against the Jews who refused conversion. Those Marranos, or New Christians, who practiced Judaism secretly were its targets. Those who were caught in their heresy were turned over to the civil authorities for punishment. The Marranos who refused to recant their heresy were burned at the stake. If they accepted Catholicism at the last moment, they were put to death mercifully with the garrot. It is believed the Franciscan and Dominican friars discovered 341,000 heretics. Of these, 32,000 were burned during the 300 years of Catholicism's existence in Spain, Portugal and their colonies in the New World.

The concept of expulsion was not limited to Spain. Jews were forced out of Vienna and Linz in 1421, Cologne in 1424, Augsberg in 1439, Bavaria in 1442, Moravia and Perrugia in 1485, Parma in 1488, Milan, Lucca, Florence and Tuscany in 1494, Navarre in 1498 and the Kingdom of Naples in 1541.[5] King John of England forced his Jews out in 1290, followed by France in 1306. They were actually welcomed in the recently captured Constantinople, where they helped create an arms industry. The Jews were invited into Poland by Prince Boleski in 1246. The Jews were permitted to establish an autonomous community in Poland. By 1648, 500,000 Jews lived in Poland.[6] They became the tax collectors for the nobility. In 1648, 1649 and 1656, a Cossack, Chmielnicki, united the Ukrainians, peasants and Crimean Tartars into a violent mob that attacked and massacred the Jews. In 1648, the Jews started a movement west across Europe to Holland, while a few found refuge in the German principalities.

In 1568, the seven Dutch provinces declared their independence and fought for 80 years until they became truly independent of Spain.[7] The Dutch recognized their dependence on trade for survival because they could not feed their large population. The Jews, with their trading networks in Christian Europe, Moorish North Africa and Western Asia, could help develop their commercial interests. As more Ashkenazi (German) Jews moved into Holland, the earlier Sephardic Jews recognized that they might cause a wave of anti–Semitism, which would endanger their hard-won place in Dutch society.[8] Menasseh Ben Israel was a leader in search of a release valve for the growing Jewish population. He turned west to England. The Puritans were more accepting of the Jews because they were "people of the book." Part of their doctrine involved the conversion of the Jews as necessary for the second coming of the Messiah. Menasseh went to England to urge Cromwell to repeal the expulsion order of the Jews. In 1656, 20 Marrano families entered England and reverted to their Jewish faith. They were inhabitants, not citizens, of Great Britain. Jews had complete freedom in economic activities. The leaders of England had a positive attitude toward these new dwellers. They were hard working, law abiding and capital producing members of society.

Many Jewish financiers came to England with William of Orange (who became William III in England). They helped develop the London Stock Exchange (also in Amsterdam) as well as the concept of bearer bonds and letters of credit. Jews were not permitted to own and work the land or join the guilds in the cities to which they gravitated.[9] Their only means of support was to lend money to the kings, nobility and commoners. The Christians could not lend money for interest after a papal bull in 1179, which threatened excommunication for usurers.

In Italy, after the sack of Rome, the popes owned a swath of land through the center of Italy. The condition of the Jews in Italy depended on the pope's encyclicals. In the Fourth Lateran Council, Innocent III ordered Jews and Muslims to wear a special badge, and they could not be employed in public places. At the Council of Treves (1227), no Jew could practice medicine, and at the Council of Baziers (1246) Jews had to wear a circular badge.

France, under the Carolingians (Charlemagne) welcomed the Jews, and they flourished.[10] This was short lived because they were expelled in the fourteenth century. Charlemagne's empire included much of present-day Germany, and Jews spread to the Rhine basin. The First Crusade (1095) brought German peasants traveling south to the Mediterranean to retake Jerusalem and kill the heretics. They found heretics in their midst. They turned on these people and massacred many Jews in communities along the Rhine.

In 1517, Luther posted his 95 propositions on the door of All Saints' Church at Wittenberg. Initially, Luther believed the Jews would join him against the Catholic Church. When they refused, he attacked them in his writings. He urged the Germans to burn their synagogues, prayer books and houses and force them to live in stables like the Romanies. In 1572, he had Jews banned from Germany.

By the end of the sixteenth century, Jews were permitted back into central Europe by the emerging German states. Prussia initially welcomed the Jews for their knowledge of trade and money. As more Jews entered Prussia, Frederick the Great issued anti–Jewish laws in 1750.[11] They were taxed at higher rates than others. More destructive was a law that said a Jewish family could keep only one of their children. The others had to leave Prussia.

Some would like to think Columbus's forebears were Jewish.[12] They claimed his family were Marranos who fled Spain for Genoa in the fourteenth century. There is no proof to substantiate that belief. The discovery of the New World was a relief valve for the Jews and Marranos who were constantly investigated by the Inquisition. Many went to New Spain. In the 1570s, there was a great migration to Brazil. In 1580, Spain and Portugal were united.[13] This opened up Spanish possessions to Portugal's new Christians, who moved into Mexico, Cuba, Buenos Aires and Peru.

The Marranos of Spain, to the third generation, were forcibly kept in Spain until Queen Isabella's death, when there was a massive migration to New Spain and to the Netherlands, where they openly reverted to Judaism. Many of them then crossed the Atlantic to Holland's possessions in America.[14] The Dutch saw Brazil as a great source of income and went to the northeast of that country (the only part settled by the Portuguese) and simply threw the Portuguese out. Many who were openly Jewish in Holland emigrated to Dutch Brazil and settled in Recife in 1630. By 1636 they had constructed a synagogue. In 1645, one-half of the whites in Recife were Jewish. Unhappily, their stay was of short duration.

The Jews in Northern Europe

William of Orange was elected Stadtholder.[15] William declared that no man should be injured for his faith or conscience. However, Jews could not serve in the trainband (militia), could not marry Christian girls, and were restricted from mechanical pursuits (guilds) and the retail trade. The toleration and wealth of the Netherlands caused an influx of poor Jews. The Ashkenazi Jews, fleeing the massacres in Poland, were often quite poor. By 1720, there were 9,000 Ashkenazi in Amsterdam. The rich Sephardic Jews recognized the need to get them out of Holland to England and the colonies in America.

The financial growth of Holland, helped in part by Sephardic Jews, caused many new Christians in Brazil and Portugal to move to Holland and become overt Jews.[16] However, many Jews remained in Recife. They were allowed complete liberty of conscience. The Jews and crypto–Jews welcomed the Dutch and fought in their armed forces. European Jews of all nationalities emigrated to Dutch Brazil, and new Christians returned to their original faith. The colony was recaptured by a fleet of 77 Portuguese ships. In January 1654, when Recife was retaken, most Jews and new Christians left for Holland. A fair number settled in the Dutch, English and French possessions in the Caribbean. Those Jews who stayed in the Caribbean went to Guiana, Curaçao, Barbados, and the French islands of Guadeloupe, Martinique and St. Domingue.[17] More Jews moved to the French colonies after the French and Indian War. It was the French Revolution that gave Jews in France and its colonies equality with the other French citizens (1791).

There were probably no Jews in Anglo-Saxon England.[18] Jews entered England with Flemish immigrants. After the invasion by William the Conqueror, their numbers increased, and they settled in the larger communities on the island. Half lived in London, and the rest in York, Winchester, Lincoln, Canterbury, Oxford and Northampton.

In 1144, William, a farmer's son, disappeared.[19] His body was found later. The Jews were accused of reenacting Christ's passion. It was claimed they used William's blood to make matzos.

In 1290, the king again needed money and seized Jewish property because they "broke his law against usury." The last 2,500 Jews were evicted from England after several usurers were hanged.

The Jews returned to England during Cromwell's protectorate. The fundamentalist Protestants (Puritans) believed the second coming of the Messiah was imminent.[20] However, by their interpretation of Deuteronomy and Daniel, this could not happen until the dispersal of the Jews was complete. They felt that allowing Jews into England would speed the Messiah's coming. In 1656, the Council of State allowed Jews to hold services quietly and to lease cemetery grounds. A Toleration Act in 1688 gave dissenters religious privileges which helped break the intolerance toward

Jews. In 1699, a Jewish child born in England had the same rights as other native-born subjects, and the Jewish child born in the colonies had the same rights as one born in England.

The trade and navigation acts passed between 1650 and 1663 kept all foreigners out of English foreign trade.[21] There were naturalization acts on the English books well before the trade and navigation acts. Prior to 1610, individual Jews could be naturalized by an act of parliament.[22] After 1675 naturalization was extended to those beneficial to the country and without the individual needing to receive the sacrament. In the colonies, resident aliens (Jews) could be naturalized by the legislature or governor of that colony. There were several forms and levels of citizenship in England and the colonies. A man could petition the king or the colonial governor for *ex donatione regis* letters patent to make him an English subject.[23] He became a denizen, a state midway between an alien and a naturalized citizen. The level above denizen was naturalization. The naturalized individual had equal rights to the native born with rights to property, inheritance and civic responsibilities. A third form of citizenship was "freeman of New York City." A freeman could carry on retail trade, serve in public office and become part of the electorate.

Perhaps the most significant piece of legislation for aliens living in the colonies was the Naturalization Act of 1740.[24] On June 1, 1740, George II issued "An Act for Naturalizing such Foreign Born Protestants and others Therein Mentioned, as Are Settled or Shall Settle in Any of His Majesty's Colonies in America."[25] The Jews could swear on the five books of Moses.[26] In 1763 parliament passed a Jew bill, which essentially gave Jews the same rights in England as they had in the colonies. However, the anti–Jewish violence that sprang up was so strong that the bill was repealed. Attempts were made to repeal the 1740 act, but these failed.[27]

The Jews Reach the New World

BRAZIL

In 1493, Pope Alexander VI (a Spaniard) decreed that Spain would have rights to land west of a line from the North Pole to the South Pole 370 leagues west and south of the Azores and Cape Verde. Portugal, therefore, could claim Brazil. Two boatloads of Jews and criminals were banished to Brazil every year after 1548.[28] New Christians joined them to escape the Inquisition. After the Dutch West India Company was chartered, a Dutch fleet conquered Bahia in 1624. However, the area was retaken in 1625, and at least five Jews were executed for their part in the seizure. A second invasion was more successful, and the northeastern coast of Brazil became a Dutch possession in 1630. The money required to outfit the attackers came largely from the silver fleet captured by Admiral Hein. In addition, large amounts were subscribed by six Amsterdam Jews who were directors of the Dutch West India Company.[25] Recife (northeast coast of Brazil) seemed like a more permanent community, and Jews flocked to it from Iberia, Holland, Middle Europe, the Middle East and Spanish colonies in America.[29] By 1643, 600 Spanish and Portuguese Jews emigrated from Holland, along with two rabbis. There were Jews in the Dutch expeditionary force that took Recife. The leaders of the expedition stated that Jewish soldiers on board the ships showed zeal and courage.[30] It is claimed that there were several thousand Jews in Brazil by 1645. They had a synagogue, schools and a cemetery. The Jewish population began to decrease after this peak was reached.[31] At its height, the number of Jews in Recife may have reached 6,000.

The early Jews were joined by Jews from Hungary, Poland, Turkey, the Barbary states, Spain, Portugal and Germany. Financially, things turned sour for the colony. There were three bad sugar harvests between 1642 and 1644. The Jews owned several sugar mills and were active in all branches of the sugar trade. The retail trade and brokerage houses were also owned by Jews. Poorer Jews were in the retail trade as well as the local slave trade. (They bought slaves from the large dealers, who purchased large numbers off the slave ships. They peddled slaves in smaller numbers to outlying plantations.)

The Jews in Recife were aware that the Portuguese Christians were becoming restive.[32] They warned the Dutch that the Portuguese would plan to retake this valuable outpost of their empire. The Jews in Amsterdam, warned by their trading associates, begged the Dutch to protect Recife. In 1653, the sword fell. A Portuguese armada under General Barreto approached Recife.[33] The Dutch could not protect their outpost because they were engaged in one of their naval wars with England to control the slave trade in the New World.[34] In January 1654, the Dutch lowered their colors. The Portuguese commander was surprisingly liberal to the Jews. He gave them three months to leave. The new Christians who had reverted were turned over to the Inquisition. The Jews of Recife had to find a new area of settlement. After the Portuguese reconquered Brazil, many Dutch Jews returned to Amsterdam. Still other Jews spread throughout the Caribbean and formed the nuclei of later Jewish settlements.

The Jews of Recife left Brazil in April.[35] Five months later some reached New Amsterdam. One wonders at the delay, since the trip by boat was only about six weeks. They may have been held captive in Cuba or Jamaica, at the time controlled by Spain, when their ship, the *Valck*, was blown off course. They sailed from Jamaica to St. Anthony in Cuba and took a French ship, the *Ste. Catherine*, to New Amsterdam. Although expelled from Brazil, the Dutch retained a foothold in South America in Surinam.[36] A large Jewish colony was planted there in 1651. Surinam was captured by the English, and more Jews followed them. In 1662, Lord Willoughby, governor of the territory, offered the Jews the same privileges as the English colonists. In 1667, Surinam passed back to control by Holland while New Amsterdam, taken three years earlier, passed formally to England by the Treaty of Breda. A large contingent of Jews left for Jamaica in 1670. Cayenne was the last piece of property owned by the Dutch in South America.

WEST INDIES

There was a large influx of Jews into Jamaica after Brazil was retaken. The island, under English hegemony, began to attract Jews after 1663. In 1670, the governor stated that no one was to be molested for religious reasons. The Jews became successful merchants and traders. This led to acts of anti–Semitism. In 1672, a petition by seventy-two merchants in Port Royal claimed there was an excessive influx of Jews. They claimed the Jews "eat us and our children out of all trade and make the town of Port Royal their Goshen."[37] A request for their expulsion failed.[38] Politically, conditions were turning against the Jews. In 1693, Jews could not keep Christian indentured servants, and they could be forced to carry firearms on the Sabbath.[39] In 1695, the assembly in Jamaica passed a tax on all residents with an additional tax on the Jews.[40] This was confirmed by the king's council in London. This was "an act for raising money for and towards the Defense of this island." The money was to be raised by taxes on slaves, horses, cattle, sheep and goats. The Jews had to raise an additional 750 pounds. If they defaulted, a £250 fine was added. At the end of the year, an additional tax of £1,000 was levied and was to be collected in one month.[41] Despite their financial oppression, Jewish immigration continued. It is believed that 1,000 Jews lived in Jamaica at the start of the eighteenth century, and by the middle of the century Jamaica had as many Jews as the thirteen colonies on the mainland.

Jews owned sugar plantations which were very successful. From this, they spread to the slave trade. In addition to using slaves on their plantations, they trained others to work as craftsmen and storekeepers. These trained slaves were hired out to others.

Barbados, the easternmost island of the West Indies, off the coast of Venezuela, was occupied by the British in 1605. The first uncontested evidence of the presence of Jews was a letter from Abraham Jacob to the Earl of Carlisle in 1628.[42] Jewish trading activity was suppressed by the strict enforcement of the navigation acts. In 1661, three Jews petitioned the king to allow them to trade.[43] The king's commissioners acted favorably on the petition. Other Jews followed and became active traders. David-Raphael de Mercado was listed as the highest taxpayer in Barbados in 1679.[44] By 1680, there were more than 200 Jews on the island.[45] As the Jewish population grew, they recognized the need for citizenship,[46] and between 1660 and 1700, 190 Jews were endenized.[47] The Jews were active in trade, and in one year (1679) six ships owned exclusively by Jews left Barbados.[48]

Finally, a note about English St. Nevis. The island is of importance to Americans as the birthplace of Alexander Hamilton and to the Jews because Hamilton received part of his education at a Jewish academy. Nevis was captured by the English in 1628.[49] In 1772, a hurricane drove out most of the Jews. The emancipation of the blacks in 1838 drove out most of the white population.

The Dutch occupied two islands in the West Indies, Curaçao and St. Eustatius. A Jew, Samuel Cohen, helped explore Curaçao and claim it for the Dutch West India Company.[50] By 1651, there were almost 100 Jews in the capital, Willemstad. It had the largest, richest Jewish population in the eighteenth century in the New World. In 1732, the synagogue Mikve Israel (Hope of Israel) was build. It is still in use today and is the oldest surviving place of Jewish worship in the Western hemisphere.[51]

The island of St. Eustatius was taken by the Dutch in the eighteenth century.[52] It soon had a large, prosperous population of Portuguese Jews who had emigrated from Amsterdam. During the American Revolution, it became an important stopover for blockade runners. There were about 100 Jewish males on the island, and they favored the Americans. They were important in smuggling supplies and munitions to keep the revolution alive. After Yorktown, the British turned their wrath on St. Eustatius. The Dutch turned the island over to English Admiral Rodney. The island was eventually returned to the Dutch.

The Jewish position in the French islands of the West Indies was short and unhappy.[53] Some Jews who left Brazil settled in Martinique despite the fourteenth-century decree that expelled them from France. They and the Dutch Protestants were forced to leave and migrated to Guadeloupe. The Jews on the French island of Haiti, along with other whites, fled the slave insurrection, which started in 1780. Many of these colonists came to Philadelphia and brought the devastating yellow fever epidemic, which brought the capital of the new United States to a standstill.

The Danes were also involved in claiming islands in the West Indies. Danish Jews settled in St. Thomas when it was taken by the Danes. By the mid–nineteenth century, there were about 500 Jews in these Danish islands.

The Jews of Mexico had a very unfortunate history. After Cortez conquered Mexico, there was a large influx of "new Christians." These were Jews and their descendants who accepted baptism in order to stay in Spain after the order of expulsion. Those who were forcibly converted were called *anusim*. The Spaniards called them "marranos" (pigs).

The first persecution of the Jews was carried out by the grand vizier of the Dominican Order.[54] The Inquisition in Mexico during 300 years of Spanish hegemony tried many miscreants beside Judaizers. About 16 percent were lapsed Catholics. Other offenders were tried for fornication, bigamy, blasphemy and Lutheranism. Some Franciscan and Dominican friars were condemned for soliciting sexual favors. Those Judaizers who were not killed lost their possessions, served prison terms, and were expelled from Mexico. The impoverished Holy Office in Mexico City grew rich in 1640 as a result of trying marranos, then confiscating their cash, goods and real estate. From 1640 to 1649, a total of three million pesos was seized. Most went into the pockets of the judge-inquisitors. They purchased real estate at prices they themselves set. Judaism was exterminated in Mexico by the end of the seventeenth century.

I

Jews in the Middle Colonies

New Netherland was a territory taken and occupied by the Dutch West India Company. By rights of discovery, North America belonged to Spain, but Spain could not hold the territory. The French occupied Canada, the English had colonies on the eastern seaboard south of Canada and north of Spanish Florida. (The country immediately north of Florida was bestowed later.) The Dutch occupied the area that would become New York, New Jersey and part of Connecticut up to Hartford. The Swedes were on the Delaware River with several forts, but had few men or munitions to hold them. Later, Peter Stuyvesant was sent to remove the Swedes and occupy their territory. He did this by showing a naval force, and the Swedes capitulated. Most of the Swedish inhabitants remained on the South River (Delaware River) because the terms of capitulation were excellent.

In addition to England's worries about Spain, New Netherland was a thorn in England's side. It separated the English colonies and was a serious competitor in the slave trade. What the Dutch did to the Swedes, the English then did to them. They took the area without firing a shot, but we will discuss this more later on.

After the Dutch West India Company seized the northeast coast of Brazil, many Dutch emigrated to the area. At its height, the area was said to have 5,000 Jews, many of whom were wealthy and had many slaves and plantations. The Portuguese and the Brazilians then recaptured the territory.[1] Those Marranos who had reverted to Judaism were considered heretics and were held for the Inquisition. The Jews who had never converted to Catholicism were free to leave. In 1654, 16 ships filled with Dutch Protestants and Jews left Brazil. Many returned to Holland, but some stayed in the Dutch possessions in the Caribbean. One ship, the

Valck, was blown off course and was picked up by a Spanish privateer.[2] At this point, its history becomes murky. Some historians say the ship went to Jamaica, which was still in Spanish hands. Others say the *Valck* was sunk, and the passengers were told they would be sold as slaves in the Mediterranean. More "heretics" were sent to the Inquisition, and the rest were allowed to leave. A French bark or brigantine or man-of-war, the *Ste. Catherine* (or *St. Charles*), captained by Jacques de la Motthe, became involved. Some reports describe him as a privateer who fought the Spanish ship and removed the passengers.

The Jews passed from Jamaica to Port St. Anthony on the western tip of Cuba, a Spanish possession. It is not clear how they went from one area to the other. Some claim the Jews went from Recife directly to Cape St. Anthony, found a group of Jews planning to go to New Amsterdam, and begged to be taken along. Another description tells of Jews taken on the *Ste. Catherine* and carried directly to New Amsterdam. Whatever the preliminaries, the small group of Jews were picked up by the *Ste. Catherine* and contracted to pay the captain and crew 2,500 guilders for twenty-three Jews.[3] There were thirteen children, six women and four men. Two of the women were widows. The heads of the Jewish families were Asser Levy, Abraham Israel de Piza, David Israel Faro and Moses Lumbroso. The widows were Judith Mercado and Rieke Nunes. The price charged by the captain was three times the usual cost. The ship made its way to New Amsterdam and tied up a few days before the Jewish New Year, (Rosh Hashonah). Because the Jews could raise only 900 guilders of the amount contracted, they were put off the ship without their tools and belongings. The captain brought action against the Jews to the court of burgomeisters and scheppens (landowners and sheriffs).[4] The case is known as "Jacques de la Motthe, Master of the bark *St. Charles* contra divers Jews," September 16, 1654 (or September 9, 1654).[5] De la Motthe was permitted to auction their possessions to raise the 1,600 guilders still owed to him.[6] The sale was set for September 14, which permitted the Jews to celebrate their New Year on September 12 and 13. The inhabitants of New Amsterdam were sympathetic to the Jews and offered ridiculously low prices for the merchandise.[7] They then returned their purchases to the Jews.

The captain brought his contract to court, and the judges ordered that two Jews, David Israel and Moses Lumbroso (or Ambrosius), be placed in jail until the debt was paid.[8] The court ordered the captain to post 40 (or 50) guilders for court costs and to pay the cost of feeding the prisoners (16 stivers per day). Meanwhile, Mr. Pieterson (a Jew who had arrived from Holland prior to the *Ste. Catherine* or *Charles*), examined the contract between the Jews and the captain.[9] He discovered that the ship's officers and crew were involved in the contract. Pieterson talked to them and convinced them that the next ship from Holland would have the money and would leave it in New Amsterdam. Because the crew was waiting in the Dutch city, they were not earning any money. They agreed to Pieterson's plan for receiving what was owed them, and the Jews were let out of jail. Whether or not the sailors received the money is unknown.

Who was Simon Pieterson, and what was he doing in New Amsterdam? Pieterson and Jacob Barsimson (and perhaps a Mr. Jacob Aboab), all Jews, were given passports by the company in Amsterdam to evaluate the colony and to find ways to increase its population.[10] The passports protected them from the governor. Pieterson and Barsimson arrived on *de Pereboom* (*Peartree*) on August 22, 1654. The third man, Aboab, stole goods from the others and jumped ship at the Isle of Wight. Barsimson sued the captain, Jacob Jansz Huys, for not protecting his property. (One gets the impression this was a very litigious society).

After their problems with de la Motthe, the Jews next faced the ire of a virulent anti–Semite, Governor Peter Stuyvesant, and also the minister of the Dutch Reform Church. Stuyvesant petitioned the governor of the Dutch West India Company to "expel these blasphemers of the name of Christ."[11] He warned that Lutherans and Papists would soon follow. The governors were advised by several Jews in Amsterdam that the Jews in New Amsterdam could not return to Spain and Portugal because of the Inquisition. It was also pointed out to them that Jews were defending Dutch interests in Brazil with their blood and possessions. Furthermore, the English and French were allowing Jews in their colonies, and New Netherlands needed people. Finally, and most important, there were Jews who were principal shareholders in the company. In a letter in the spring of 1655, the governors ordered Stuyvesant to allow the Jews to reside in New Amsterdam.[12] Perhaps as a balm to his injured pride, they advised him that the Jews would not be allowed to worship their religion openly. "So long, therefore, as no request is presented to you to allow such a free exercise of religion, ... you will be doing well to refer the matter to us in order to wait thereon the necessary orders."[13] Furthermore, because the poor were not to be a burden on the community (composed of 400 Gentiles), they were to be supported by their fellow Jews.[14] The Jews were advised to live together in Jews' Alley. Not to be put down, Stuyvesant wrote to the directors on June 10, 1656, that the Jews had complete freedom to trade.[15] "Also they have many times requested us the free and public exercise of their abominable religion, but this cannot yet be accorded to them." But because the directors knew they needed immigration to sustain a colony and that any restriction would halt the flow of bodies, Stuyvesant's letter fell on deaf ears.

Dominie John Megapolensis of the Dutch Reform Church, minister of the Dutch Gentiles in Rennsselaerwyck, who later became a minister in New Amsterdam, wrote to the Classis (head of his church) in Amsterdam on November 11, 1654.[16] He described the Jews (Barsimson and Pieterson) who came in the summer to trade. Later, other Jews came, and they were healthy but poor. The minister claimed his church had spent several hundred guilders for their support (probably an exaggeration). He claimed the Jewish merchants would not support the poor Jews. At this time in New Amsterdam there were only two other Jews who had arrived a few weeks earlier. These men were investigators for the company and could not afford to support 23 countrymen. It should be noted that one of the obligations of the church was to support the poor (any poor) in the colony. On March 18, 1655, Megapolensis sent another letter after several more Jews came to New Amsterdam. "These people have no other God than the unrighteous Mammon, and no other aim than to get possession of Christian property ... by drawing all trade to themselves. These godless rascals are of no benefit to the country, but look at everything for their profit... For as we have here Papists, Mennonites and Lutherans ... also many Puritans and Independents and many Atheists ... it would create a still greater confusion if the obstinate and immovable Jews came to settle here." The Classis in Amsterdam described the letter to the governors, who were mostly concerned with trade and guilders, and their response led to the Order of Toleration (1656). They ordered that any group, even Quakers, must be allowed to practice their religion "as long as he behaves quietly and legally, gives no offense to his neighbors and does not oppose the government."

In the spring of 1655, five wealthy Jews came to New Amsterdam.[17] These were Jacob Henriques, Abraham de Lucena, Salvador Dandrada, Joseph D'Acosta and Jacob Cohen. On November 29, 1635, they petitioned for the right, like other inhabitants, to trade on the South River (Delaware) and the North River (Hudson) as well as other places under the jurisdiction of the government. The director general and council (in New Amsterdam) met and voted on the petition. Stuyvesant, allied with Dr. La Montagne (doctor for the community), forced a denial of the petition. However, "yet having been informed that the suppliants have already shipped some goods, they are for the time being allowed to send one or two persons to the South River in order to dispose of the same, which being done they are to return hither."

Although Salvador Dandrada petitioned to purchase a house, "the premises herein is for pregnant reasons denied."[18] After he was turned down on January 13, 1656, the seller (a gentile) asked the council to pay him the purchase price of 1,860 guilders because they refused to transfer the house to Dandrada. The house was again put up for auction, and another person purchased it. However, the Jews petitioned that since they were taxed for fortifications (they had paid 500 guilders for the improved fortifications), they had a right to own real estate. This was permitted by the directors in Holland for Jews resident in that country. The council in New Amsterdam presented the case to the directors in Holland. In a reply of June 14, 1656, the directors admonished the local council to obey their previous orders to immediately allow Jews to trade. (It should be remembered that Dandrada was a wealthy Jew, and the directors in Amsterdam hoped that he and the others would become involved in international trade. They knew the Jews had connections, frequently relatives, in different parts of the world.) The Jews were admonished not to open retail shops. However, on March 15, 1656, "inasmuch as Jews and foreigners are as much encouraged as a *burgher* or citizen, it is resolved that the same be taken into consideration in full court." After this, Jews could open retail stores, and eventually specialized in liquor, tobacco and furs.[19]

Prior to the freedom to enter the retail trade, Abram De La Simon opened a store and kept it open on Sunday.[20] Apparently, he had recently come from Portugal to Holland to New Amsterdam. He did not understand the Dutch language and was unaware of the laws against Jews in retail. Simon was arrested and ordered to pay a fine of 600 guilders. In addition, the authorities hoped to use this offense to evict all Jews from New Amsterdam. This failed again, because the Jews represented warm bodies and international connections.

A minor stumbling block to the Jews involved Asser Levy (Van Smellen).[21] In 1657, he tried to become a burgher. This was at first rejected, but he received it later that year (in April).

When several Jewish families came together, their first communal thought was to purchase land for a sanctified cemetery. After two years, in 1656, they were permitted to buy land for this purpose.[22] The year before, their petition for a cemetery was turned down. The directors in Amsterdam became aware of a need for a cemetery (which was on a par with being permitted to live there) and notified Stuyvesant in a letter on April 26, 1655. They would have liked to fulfill his request that the new territories should not be "allowed to be infected by people of the Jewish Nation," but after reconsidering they believed it would be "unreasonable and unfair especially because of the considerable loss sustained by the nation ... in the taking of Brazil" and also "because of the large amount

of capital which they still have invested in the shares of this company."
They decided "that these people may travel and trade to and in New
Netherland and live and remain there, providing that the poor among
them shall not become a burden to the company or to the community.
You will now govern yourself accordingly." Despite this stinging letter to
Stuyvesant, the Jews were forbidden to build a synagogue, but they were
allowed to hold services privately.

In a petition the directors received in January 1655, from Portuguese
Jews living in Amsterdam were complaints of difficulties of Jews trying
to get passports to go to New Amsterdam. A similar letter was sent to
the directors in New Amsterdam explaining the Jews' losses in Brazil. (It
should be remembered that the rich Sephardic Jews tried to get the poor
Ashkenazi Jews out of Holland). The petition further pointed out that
New Netherlands was large, and the more Jews that left, the better it
would be for Holland. They would pay taxes and excises and import necessities. The petition maintained that the states general had always protected
the Jews on the same footing as others and that the company granted land
for free to those who wanted to go. How (the petition asked) can you deny
them the same privileges?

Stuyvesant and his council looked for more ways to harass the Jews.
It was decided that all men except Jews, aged 16 to 30, were to serve in
the militia.[23] Those who did not serve had to pay 65 stivers per month
(about $1.20). The Jews could not join and therefore had to pay the tax.
Asser Levy and Barsimson petitioned to be in the *trainband* (militia)
rather than pay the tax, which they said they could not afford. They were
advised to pay the tax or leave the community. At this time, Indian troubles increased, and more bodies were needed to stand guard on the
fortifications. The Jews were then admitted to the militia.

Stuyvesant said the Protestants would refuse to serve in the militia
alongside the Jews. This, too, proved to be a lie, perhaps because of the
additional need for warm bodies. When the directors in Amsterdam
ordered Stuyvesant to evict the Swedes from the South River, he called
for recruits: Asser Levy volunteered, only to be turned down. Another
demand fell on the population of New Amsterdam. The Indians were
becoming restive, and the fortifications needed strengthening. All individuals were taxed according to their estates.[24] Five Jews were each
assessed 100 guilders. A total of 210 people raised 6,305 guilders. While
Jews represented one-thirtieth of the population, they paid one-twelfth
of the total raised (Levy and Barsimson were taxed six guilders each).

The problems faced by the community as a whole seemed to relax
some of the difficulties suffered by the Jews. On April 9, 1657, the local

council notified the population that they could apply for *burgher* rights.[25] Two days later, "Asser Levy, a Jew, appeared in court: requested to be admitted as a *burgher*: claimed that such ought not be refused him as he kept watch and ward (*tocht en wacht*) like other *burghers*; showed *burgher* certificates from the City of Amsterdam that the Jew was a *burgher* there. It was decreed, as before, that it cannot be allowed, and he should apply to the Director General and Council." The leading Jews appealed to Stuyvesant and the council both to give Levy *burgher* rights and not to deny other Jews. In their petition, the Jews claimed that they bore and paid all *burgher* burdens and that Jews in Holland received the *burgher* certificate. Eventually Levy, followed by four other Jews, received *burgher* status. It is believed that Stuyvesant was disturbed by the number of complaints against him to the directors in Amsterdam, and he finally acquiesced to the Jews' requests.

Levy bought a house at auction in Albany for 1,709 guilders to be paid in beaver skins (1661).[26] This piece of real estate made him a *burgher*, so he could go into business (in furs) in Fort Orange (Albany). Shortly before his dealings in Albany, Levy was appointed as a butcher for the community of New Amsterdam. This was an important position in the community, but especially for the Jews, who needed properly slaughtered animals. Levy was excused from slaughtering hogs. It seems that Levy's fortunes turned at this time. He built a slaughter house with a partner, Garrett Roos. Before Levy's death, his trading network extended from Albany to Gravesend, Kingston, Newtown, Flatbush, Gowanus and Staten Island. He sold supplies to fur traders, lent money, represented Dutch merchants in New Amsterdam and sold liquor. He either gave or lent money to the Lutherans to help build their church in 1671. He owned land in several parts of New Amsterdam.

The number of Jews slowly increased in New Amsterdam in the 1650s, so that there may have been 60 Jews at the end of the decade.[27] They carried on religious services in a private home. A *Torah* was sent from Holland, but it was returned in the 1660s for lack of a congregation. Early in the 1660s, the Jewish population started to decrease. Whether the decline was due to the constant irritation by the community's Dutch leaders or the lack of commerce, the Jews started to search for greener pastures. Some returned to Holland, while others went to Newport, Curaçao, Surinam, Barbados and later to Essequibo (Guiana).[28] Many of the original 23 left along with the wealthier Jews who had followed them to New Amsterdam. Solomon Pieterson converted and Barsimson disappeared. Levy remained. It is not known how many others, if any, remained with Levy.

In October, 1664, the British sent a man-of-war to New Amsterdam, and the Dutch capitulated without a shot being fired; on October 21, 1664, Levy swore allegiance to the king of England.[29] On the tax list in 1665, he was assessed two florins per week for the support of British soldiers stationed there.[30] Just as Levy had sued and sent letters of complaint to Holland, so he did with the British. His name appeared frequently on court records, mostly as plaintiff, but occasionally as defendant, in civil cases. To preserve his rights, he sued anyone of any station. On the tax list of 1674, his property was valued at 2,500 florins. Under the English, he dealt frequently with Christians, and his honesty and integrity were recognized by them and the leader of the community. He was executor of many wills written by gentiles.

Levy's reputation spread to other colonies. A fine ordered on Jacob Lucena in Connecticut of £20 was lowered to £10 because Lucena was a Jew and supposedly did not have the same moral standards as the Puritans. It was lowered to £5 as a token of respect to Levy. When Levy died in 1680 (or 1684), he left an estate valued at £553. Asser had a son (also named Asser) who married Margaret Levy in 1684. Like his father, he was frequently involved in civil court proceedings. A grandson, Asser Levy, was an officer in the New Jersey forces in the Revolution. (This progression of generations is questionable. Other documents deny that Levy had children. The Levy in the American Revolution reportedly descended from his sister's line.)

The conquest of New Netherlands was confirmed in the Treaty of Breda of 1667.[31] An act in England under William IIII replaced all colonial laws repugnant to the laws of England and made English laws applicable to the American colonies. It must be remembered that England had no legal relationship with the Jews for 400 years. Although Jews started to trickle in to England from Holland ten to 15 years prior to the conquest of Holland's possessions on the eastern seaboard, the Jewish settlement in England was never sanctioned by law. However, England had its complement of anti–Semites. Lord Coke proclaimed that Jews were infidels and perpetual enemies and had no right in English courts. This concept was overruled in English courts but not in the courts of the British West Indies. In 1673, the Jews appealed to Charles II for relief, who ordered that all acts and proceedings against them were to be stopped. In 1685, 37 Jews were indicted for not attending the Anglican Church, but James II put a stop to the farce. In 1723, parliament recognized the Jews as the king's subjects and permitted them to take the oath of abjuration without the "true faith of a Christian."

Meanwhile, in America, New Amsterdam's name was changed to

New York to honor the Duke of York, who would become James II.[32] A charter of liberties and privileges was adopted by the colonial assembly under Governor Richard Nicolls. This document extended religious freedom to all Christians (1665). "No person shall be molested, fined or imprisoned for differing in judgment in matters of religion who profess Christianity."[33] Governor Edmund Andros omitted Christianity in his declaration of 1674. Everyone could practice their religion as long as they did not disturb others in the free exercise of their religion. The next governor, Thomas Dongan, declared that liberty of conscience is given to those who believed in Christ. Three years later he omitted the requirement of belief in Christ.

Despite the freedom of conscience, Jews still could not practice their religion openly. When the duke of York succeeded his brother, Charles II, to reign as James II, he instructed Governor Audros to "permit all persons of whatever religion, freedom of worship." However, a petition to build a synagogue was rejected by the New York legislature. Three years prior to this rejection, in 1682, the Jews were permitted to purchase land for a cemetery.[34] In May 1682, Joseph Bueno, representing the Jewish community, purchased land from William and Mary Merrit "in trust for the Jewish Nation." A year after this, a relative of Bueno named Benjamin was the first Jew to be buried in the new site. Ten years after the land purchase, a French traveler, Lamotte Cadillac, noticed a house of worship for the Jews (1692).[35] In 1695, Pastor John Miller drew a map of New York City and located a synagogue. However, this was a private house rented by the congregation for services from John Harpor at £8 per year. Finally, in 1728, three Jews acquired land on Mill Street for a synagogue. The land cost £100 plus a loaf of sugar and one pound of Bohea tea. Funds were obtained from local Jews as well as from congregations in Europe and the West Indies to construct the synagogue. The building was 35 feet long and 21 feet high and was consecrated in 1730. After its completion, the Jews built a school and a meeting place for synagogue officers. A home for the "minister" was purchased from Cornelius Clopper, Jr. The first minister to use the new temple was David Mendez Machado, who came from Portugal to England to Savannah and then New York.[36] There was a succession of ministers until Gershon Mendez Seixas was appointed in 1766. He was the first leader born in the colonies (1745). No fixed dues were required for membership. Money was collected from donations and reading the Torah. The hazzan (minister) received £50 per year, the *shohet* (ritual slaughterer) £15, and the sexton, £2, 4 shillings. Money was set aside for charity. At the dedication there were 37 members, of whom 15 were Sephardic and 22 Ashkenazi. The ritual was Sephardic.[37] In 1797, the seal for the corporation was designed, and eight years later the constitution of the congregation Shearith Israel was adopted. Land was purchased for cemeteries as the old ones became filled. All evidence pointed to the fact that this would be a permanent site of the "Jewish nation." They joined the Dutch and French Calvinists, who were established in 1628, the Evangelical Dutch Lutherans in 1657, the Quakers in 1672 (or 1696) and the Protestant Episcopal in 1697 to become the fifth settled religion in New York.[38]

As the Jews moved inland and away from the synagogue, Jewish ritual became difficult to observe. In an attempt at control in 1757, the New York congregation declared that "whosoever for the future continues to act contrary to our Holy Law by breaking any of the Principal Commandments (eating forbidden meats and trading on the Sabbath) will not be deemed a member of the congregation, have none of the *mitzvoth* [religious functions] of the synagogue conferred on him, and when dead will not be buried according to the manner of their brethren."[39] The synagogue held a monopoly on the control of Kasruth (ritually prepared food) since it was the synagogue leaders who prepared and guaranteed that the meat was kosher. The preparation of matzoh and other holiday fare, however, was in the hands of the religious community.

All Jewish philanthropy was centered in the synagogue. Approximately ten percent of the budget went for charity: boarding of the needy, help to widows and orphans and money to transport itinerants to the next community. Part of the budget also went for maintaining the cemetery. In prayer, the congregation was led by a hazzan, who was a layman with a good voice and some knowledge of Hebrew. (He was not a rabbi.) In problems of ritual, the community turned to a learned layman. Occasionally, a rabbi might pass through, usually seeking funds for the poor Jews in Palestine. Problems of ritual and law were saved for these rabbis to solve.

At the time of the outbreak of the Revolution, the Jewish religious center was fairly large. On the synagogue lot there was the temple, the community center, home of the hazzan, home of the caretaker and the ritual bath.

The Jews of New York and other communities worked, socialized and intermarried with the gentiles. The Sephardim were more prone to intermarriage because they dressed and spoke like their English neighbors. Some Ashkenazis intermarried, and their children were lost to the Jewish community. Sephardim and Ashkenazis rarely intermarried. Proselytizing among the Christians was forbidden, but some Christians converted to Judaism. In earlier societies in Europe, the church and state were intertwined. In America, because church and state were separated, the state government assumed many functions that the congregation's leaders had controlled when they were a state within a state (ghetto). Therefore, the leaders of the congregation had less control over individual members. The activity and authority of the congregation now depended on the good will of the members.

During this period, Jews were not particularly interested in higher education.[40] There were few Jewish doctors, lawyers or teachers. Boys needed to know arithmetic, calculation of percentages and an intimate knowledge of the business they were to follow to compete in the outside world. There was a concept of Jewish learning to keep the religion alive for future generations. The Yeshivah (religious school) had developed after the destruction of the temple 1,700 years earlier. Boys attended the Yeshivah to study the Jewish texts because the sages warned that a community without schools would and should perish. Jewish education was based on a knowledge of the Bible, the Mishnah (whose percepts are taken from the Pentateuch), and the Talmud (the body of Jewish traditional law). The Sephardim had been isolated from Jewish principles and knowledge for generations in Spain and Portugal. (They were the Marranos who avoided all overt acts that might suggest a relapse.) The Crypto-Jews remembered less and less of the religion of Abraham and instead did things by rote. The Ashkenazis kept their religion throughout their travels and travails in Europe.

Freedom of conscience and with it freedom from massacres and pogroms was of prime interest to Jews and other minorities. Once they were assured of the protection of life and limb, the second problem was how to make a living. Under the Dutch, Jews could not be involved in the retail trades or in the mechanical crafts. After the English occupation, Saul Brown (his Portuguese name was Pardo, which meant "brown") petitioned Governor Dongan in 1685, stating that his trade was interfered with by the Dutch laws.[41] The governor referred his petition to the New York city council, which declared that no Jew was permitted in the retail trades, but that Pardo could be involved in wholesale trade if the governor permitted. The concept of selling retail meant that the individual needed property to carry on his business. Under Dutch law, owning property brought burgher rights.

There was no English law one way or the other concerning retail trade by Jews, and under English hegemony, Jews could become retailers. They also became goldsmiths and silversmiths and engaged in other mechanical arts as well. Jews also became soap makers, distillers, butchers and day laborers. The whole Dutch concept to keep Jews out of the retail trades may have been an attempt to force them into intercolonical trade. The Dutch felt that all Jews had relatives all over the Caribbean, the English colonies and Europe. After the turn of the century, Jews could receive denizen rights and become retailers, wholesalers and merchant traders (on the seas).[42] In New York city records, Solomon Myers, a denizen, was a shopkeeper. Jacob and David Pardo were described as retailers. Jews recognized the need to protect their position and sought some form of citizenship.[43] The lowest form of citizenship was denizen, and above this was naturalization. The highest level in New York was the freeman, who could carry on retail trade, hold public office and be part of the electorate.

Some Jews, particularly the Sephardim, did become involved in international trade. They required citizenship because of the navigation acts of 1650 to 1663. These acts kept aliens out of the mercantilist system. With citizenship, they could trade with the interior and all colonies on the seaboard. They carried agricultural products, slaves, rum, fur and some manufactured goods. The Jews also became purveyors to the British armies in the constant warfare with the French in the eighteenth century. This brought great wealth to these suppliers if and when the English parliament paid their bills. The openness and freedom to engage in commerce brought new Jews to New York. By 1700, there may have been 100 to 150 Jews in a population of 5,000.[44] In 1730, when the synagogue was dedicated, there were 75 Jewish households with about 225 Jews. At the outbreak of the Revolution, there were 400 Jews in New York. On the tax lists, Jews paid a higher percentage of the total than was expected from their numbers. This implies they were better off than their neighbors.

In 1740, a Swedish visitor, Peter Kalm, wrote in his diary: "[T]he Jews possess great privileges. They have a synagogue and great country seats of their own property, and are allowed to keep shops in town. They likewise have several ships which they freight and send out with their own goods. In fine, they enjoy all the privileges common to other inhabitants of the town and province."[45] As the eighteenth century came to a close, Jews were able to accumulate large estates. In his will, Joseph Israel Levy (1789) left £100 to the Portuguese synagogue, £50 to the Jews' college in Jerusalem and £25 to the poor on the day of his funeral.[46] He left little to his siblings, but to Sarah Israel Levy, his daughter, he left nine houses. Everything else went to this wife, Polly.

Early in their stay in New Amsterdam and New York, many Jews considered themselves as transients. Therefore, they were not interested in acquiring the right to vote, to hold office or to try for equal rights. However, their attitudes changed as they accumulated an estate and recognized that New York would be their permanent home. They needed citizenship and eventually the right to vote and hold office. In 1731, three Jews held appointive office.[47] Mordecai and David Gomez were interpreters to the admiralty and supreme courts (they spoke Spanish), and Rodrigo Pachecho was colonial agent to parliament. In New York City, Jews could be elected constables to enforce the law. This was an unattractive and unsafe position. On October 14, 1719, Moses Levy paid £15 as a fine to be relieved of this duty.[48]

Jews were not permitted to vote in New York until the Revolutionary constitution in 1777 gave them all the rights of other citizens. However, they did vote earlier in the century. In 1737, Cornelius Van Horn complained to the legislature that Adolph Philippe was elected with the support of Jews.[49] The legislature resolved that since Jews could not vote for members of parliament in England, they could not vote for representatives in New York. This proclamation was gradually forgotten, and by 1761, there was a formal awareness that Jews voted.

Pennsylvania

After William Penn accepted the Quaker religion from George Fox, he made a voyage to the Netherlands and Germany to acquire converts to the new religion. He preached toleration of all religions and described the effect of the persecution of the Jews. Penn believed this kept them from turning to Jesus. In Germany, he felt the sting of intolerance.[50] In a letter to the graf of Bruch and Falchenstyn, he claimed the Quakers were held back by his soldiers and had to sleep in the fields. He asked why the soldiers let the Jews through when they had crucified Jesus while the Quakers did not crucify Him.

There were four themes in Penn's papers: (1) a strong support for religious liberty in the scriptures (he could point to countless references); (2) religious liberty, which was supported in English common law, was essential to good government; (3) religious liberty was good economics (a government that guaranteed religious liberty prospered); and (4) he could point to authorities in the recent and long past who favored it (except for Catholics).[51] He changed his course when James II, a Catholic, ascended the throne in 1685. Toleration of all people was one of the cornerstones of the "holy experiment" in Pennsylvania. Catholics and Jews could worship openly in Pennsylvania, but they could not hold office.

Everyone who believed in God received complete religious liberty. He believed strongly that Jews could be converted to Christ. In the appendix to *The Harmony of the Old and New Testament*, a book by John Tompkins in 1694, Penn wrote "A Visitation of the Jews." He urged Jews to respond to the "Universal Light Within" and join the "Christian Fellowship of Friends." Penn wanted Jews to convert because of his concern for them. Penn showed that Christians accepted the Old Testament; why should the Jews not accept the New Testament? In his lifetime, Jesus performed his miracles in front of audiences made up mostly of Jews. Penn believed strongly that God destroyed the Jewish temple in Jerusalem because the Jews told the Romans to crucify Jesus, and His blood would be on their hands. Finally, he believed that Jews had the "Divine Light" within them and should follow it to Christ.

In the start of most English colonies, the leaders received a charter from the king and took the land as though it was unoccupied. Penn brought the Indians together and purchased the land from them. Perhaps his strong positive feelings toward the Indians and the Jews was because they were of the same stock. "I am ready to believe them [the Indians] of the Jewish Race, I mean of the stock of the Ten Tribes and that for the following reasons; first, they were to go to a land not planted or known, which to be sure Asia and Africa were, if not Europe; and he that intended that extraordinary judgment upon them, might make the passage not uneasy for them, as it is not impossible in itself, from the Eastern-most parts of Asia to the western-most of America. In the next place, I find them of like Countenance and their children of so lively Resemblance, that a man would think in the Dukes-place or Berry-street in London (that they were Jewish).... [T]hey agree in rites, they reckon by Moons; they offer their first fruits ... their Mourning a year."[52]

The Quakers suffered from severe intolerance in the new English colonies. In Puritan Massachusetts, Quakers were hanged for their beliefs. Yet, in Quaker Pennsylvania during the colonial period there was no molestation of Jews, deists or Unitarians, and the Jews were accepted into fashionable circles.[53] In 1682, the leaders of Quaker Pennsylvania stated that "all persons living in this province who confess and acknowledge the one Almighty and eternal God ... shall, in no ways, be molested or prejudiced for their religious persuasion ... nor shall they be compelled, at any time, to frequent or maintain any religious worship place or ministry whatsoever."[54]

There were Jews in Pennsylvania (or Delaware) before Penn came to America.[55] Three Jews, Abraham de Lucena, Salvador Dandrada and Jacob Cohen, requested of Peter Stuyvesant's council the right to trade along the South (Delaware) River. They were permitted only to send two men to dispose of stock that they had previously shipped there. In 1655, they sent Isaac Israel and Isaac Cardoso to the Delaware River Valley.

They reached Fort Casimir (originally built by the Swedes). At the time, there was a treaty in effect between the traders and the Indians to give the Indians more goods for their furs. The Jews did not sign the treaty because they were refused the right to trade by Governor Stuyvesant. In 1656, the directors in Amsterdam ordered the governor to allow Jews all of the rights in trading given to others. Therefore, Jews had free access to the Delaware River. In 1657, Isaac Mesa (or Masa or Mara) signed a treaty with the Indians to give them fair trade prices. A small settlement upriver called Wicaco was where Philadelphia now stands. It is conceivable that Jews were temporary residents in the area. On February 14, 1657, an Isack Masa was in court suing Jan Schaggen.[56] Masa claimed that Schaggen had sold him a hogshead of bad tobacco. Four months later, an Isaiah Mesa appealed a case against a Swede. In the account of this case, the appellation of "Jew" was not written after his name. In 1656, an Isaac Israel brought a suit against Hammen. Isaac Israel was probably not Jewish either. Many non–Jews had typical Jewish names, and these complainants were probably Mennonites.

Jews were probably living in the center of the colony since the mid-seventeenth century as Indian traders and moved east to Philadelphia later in the century.[57] Other Jews traveled down to Philadelphia from New York and Newport. They also came directly from Holland, England and central Europe. The predominant group were Ashkenazi, but they followed the Sephardic ritual in prayer. A number of Ashkenazi came from Prussia. Frederick II, to limit the number of Jews in his state, allowed Jews to have only one son. Other sons had to leave.

After the turn of the century, a Philadelphia business directory listed a Jonas Aaron. In a ledger of William Trent, a merchant, there was an account with Jonas Aaron in 1703.[58] There was no definite evidence he was Jewish, however. Between 1706 and 1719, in a receipt book of Thomas Coates, a Quaker, there is evidence of his business dealings with six Jews from New York and the West Indies. A Joseph Monteyro sold Coates "mellassoz" (molasses) as well as a bag of cotton. A Jew, Eleazor Valverde of Barbados (1706), dealt with Coates. In 1708, Samuel Peres sold cotton and other commodities to Coates. Isaac Miranda was the first definite Jewish inhabitant of Pennsylvania, but he later converted to Christianity.[59] Miranda settled in 1715 in what would be Lancaster county. He was an Indian trader as well as a deputy vice-admiralty judge.

During the first half of the eighteenth century, more Jews came to Pennsylvania. There were groups in Philadelphia, Easton, Reading, Heidelberg and Lancaster. In the 1740s, there were ten Jewish families in Lancaster. The most prominent merchant was Joseph Simon. In 1727, Lancaster

County separated from Philadelphia, and three years later, the city was laid out.[60] In 1747, a deed was given by Thomas Cookson to Isaac Nunes Ricus and Joseph Senions for one-half acre of land for a cemetery for Jews. Richard Locke, in a letter to the Society for Propagating the Gospel in Foreign Parts (1747), listed ten Jewish families in Lancaster. Dr. Isaac Cohen from Hamburg, Germany, set up a medical office at an innkeeper's house. Joseph Simon came to Lancaster in 1735 and was an Indian trader, merchant and one of the largest landholders in Pennsylvania. Some of his holdings even reached the eastern bank of the Mississippi River. His growth in wealth received a setback when all of his movable resources were destroyed in an Indian attack at Bloody Run. Simon had the largest store in the center of Lancaster. He was frequently in partnership with other Jews, particularly relatives. His sons-in-law, Levi Phillips, Solomon M. Cohen, Michael Gratz and Solomon Etting, were taken into the business. In partnership with William Henry, Simon supplied the Continental army with ammunition, guns, drums, blankets, provisions and other supplies. The Henry rifle was one of the best rifles produced until that time.

Simon was an observant Jew and used one of the rooms in his house for prayer services as early as 1747. He was instrumental in forming a congregation in Lancaster in 1776.[61] The members were largely German tradesmen in the area. After the Revolution, there was a gradual loss of the Jewish population. Most migrated to Philadelphia or Baltimore. Between 1804 and 1855, no Jews were buried in Lancaster. Simon died in 1804 at the age of 92. The Jewish cemetery was turned over to new Jewish immigrants to Lancaster after 1855.

The only other community in Pennsylvania beside Philadelphia and Lancaster with a Jewish history is Easton. Myer Hart and his wife Rachel were one of 11 families that founded Easton in 1750 (or 1752).[62] There were 40 people living there when the town was surveyed. A free school was built in 1755, and Myer Hart led the list of those who supplied material (20 pounds of nails). His first listing in town was as a shopkeeper, and his county tax was 19 shillings (the largest amount). He owned three houses; several Blacks and stock for sale. In 1782, he was considered a rich man with goods valued at £439. His name appeared on the tax lists of 1762 (£50), 1767 (£60) and 1773 (£45). In 1763, he was an innkeeper. By 1780, his estate was valued at £2,095 (he was obviously not affected by the inflation of the continental currency) (or the seizure of goods by the British or Indians). His son, Michael, seems to have eclipsed his father with an estate valued at £2,261, the highest in the county. Myer Hart was naturalized on April 3, 1764. Another Jew in town, Barnard Levi, may have been a tenant of Hart's. Hart sued Levi in court in 1776.

During the Revolution, Myer Hart took charge of British prisoners in 1777. He seemed not to have gotten into trouble with the state government as did David Franks in Philadelphia. The prominent Jews in Easton all had one or two slaves they had to register when the assembly of Pennsylvania abolished slavery on March 1, 1780. Myer Hart moved to Philadelphia, was a member of Mikve Israel in 1782, and was listed in the first Philadelphia directory. He lived there from 1782 to 1795. He must have fallen on hard times and perhaps been bankrupt, because the sheriff sold his estate in 1786.

There was a Michael Hart in town, unrelated to Myer.[63] Myer was Sephardic and Michael was Ashkenazi. Born in 1738, Michael, too, was listed as a shopkeeper in Easton and was called the "stuttering Jew." Two Jewish shopkeepers in one small town led to a rift between the families. In the Revolution, Michael was a corporal in Captain Hagenbuck's company, which was part of the "Flying Camp." Afterward he returned to civilian life and took up his duties as a leading member of society. In 1807, a fire company was formed, and Michael was a guardsman. Other Jews involved were Jacob Hart (an engineer), Napthali Hart and William Barnet, the latter two were engine directors. Michael died in 1813. Jacob Hart, his son, born in 1775, became an Indian trader as well as a shopkeeper and distiller. Michael Hart bought land for a cemetery for the Hart family in 1800. It is important to note that the Jews fit in comfortably with the rest of the population in this small community.

Philadelphia, the crown of Pennsylvania and at one time the major city in America, was laid out on the banks of the Delaware River. As such, it had a good protected harbor. The area west of Philadelphia had some of the most fertile farmland in America and grew more than enough to feed its inhabitants. The excess could be shipped to the southern colonies and the West Indies, where the land was used to raise tobacco, cotton and sugar cane. The landowners there felt the land was too valuable to raise food. As Philadelphia became a large commercial center, it attracted Jews from other colonies and Europe. There were some Sephardic Jews, but the great majority were from Germany and central Europe.

Between 1706 and 1709, six Jews from New York and the Caribbean visited the area and believed it had mercantile possibilities. The first Jews to settle there permanently were Nathan and Isaac Levy from New York. In 1738, Nathan Levy's child died, and he needed a place to bury the infant.[64] Levy purchased land which became the first Jewish cemetery.[65] The anguished father received a plot of land, 30 feet by 30 feet, from John Penn on Spruce Street between Eighth and Ninth Streets. On June 27, 1752, he requested 35 feet more. Levy paid a yearly tax of five shillings on the property. In 1791, the congregation appointed Manuel Josephson, Joseph Simons, Bernard Gratz, Solomon Lyon and Samuel Hays as trustees of the cemetery.

There were two important Jewish families in Philadelphia, the Franks and the Gratzes. David and Moses Franks came from New York in 1738. In mid-century, Barnard Gratz settled there, and his brother Michael joined him some years later. In the 1760s, Philadelphia had about twenty-five Jewish families, and an informal congregation was formed for Sabbath services.[66] One of the earliest functions was to set up a fund from which Jews in financial difficulties could borrow money without interest and return it when they were able. In 1770, the city had about 100 Jews, who started services in rented quarters the following year. Some years later, Michael Gratz hired a hazzan who was also a shohet (ritual slaughterer). Among his other duties, the hazzan taught the children to read Hebrew.

The Gratz brothers came from Silesia with a little inheritance from their father, Solomon. Both studied business in the commercial establishment of their uncle, Solomon Henry, in London, who had business connections throughout the world.[67] Barnard went to America, but Michael traveled to the East Indies, perhaps as Henry's agent. He returned to London in 1759 with chinaware, seed pearls and other Oriental goods which he would sell to the newly rich in London. Michael invested some of his inheritance in this cargo. He left London on the *Britannia* bound for Philadelphia, but he sold his goods in Halifax, New York, Virginia and Georgia. He soon became active in shipping and sent beaver skins to London. In one cargo, the furs were valued at nearly £200. Michael was also active in the coastal trade from Halifax to Georgia. When the beaver trade died during the French and Indian War, the brothers turned their eyes westward to land speculation. Great Britain, strapped for money to pay for the recent victorious war, passed taxes on to the Americans to help pay the debt. In 1765, American shippers, including both Gratz brothers, signed the nonimportation resolution. To make up for the losses from Great Britain, the brothers again turned to coastal shipping, the fur trade and land speculation. During the Revolution, Michael was part owner of a privateer and helped supply George Rogers Clark's expedition in 1781 to help in the conquest of "the West." Michael was involved with a group of land speculators in planning a new colony in what would become West Virginia and northeastern Kentucky. Michael married Miriam Simon, daughter of Joseph Simon of Lancaster. One of their children, a daughter, Richea, matriculated at Franklin (and Marshall) College, the first female Jew to do so.[68]

Brother Barnard reached Philadelphia in 1754 and started to work for David Franks, as did Michael, who followed him. More involved in Jewish affairs than his brother, Barnard was appointed a member of the board of trustees to compose a series of laws by which the Jews of Philadelphia could be governed.[69] He was a member of a committee to investigate the possibility of rebuilding a house for a synagogue.[70] They decided that it would cost as much for this project as to build a new synagogue from scratch.

Barnard's name was on a petition to the council of censors of Pennsylvania in 1784.[71] Also included were "Rabbi Seixas of the Jews," Simon Nathan (president), Asher Myers, and Haym Salomon, members of the mahamid, in behalf of the Jews of Pennsylvania. (Mahamid was one or several members who governed the congregation.) The tenth section of the frame of government of the commonwealth ordered that each member of the general assembly of representatives of the freemen of Pennsylvania, before he took his seat, must make and subscribe a declaration ending in this words: "I do acknowledge the Scriptures of the Old and New Testament to be given by divine inspiration." The Jews objected to the inclusion of the New Testament because it would preclude them from being involved in the government of Pennsylvania. In 1790, a new constitution granted anyone who believed in God eligibility to hold office.

The richer Jews in Philadelphia mixed with the gentile society. Prominent Jews were members of the Philadelphia Club, the Rittenhouse Club, the Union League, and the Racquet, Rabbit and City Troupe.[72] They belonged to the Historical Society, the Philosophical Society, the Academy of Art, the Academy of Science and the Athenaeum. The elite of the Jews mixed with the gentiles more than in any other city in America. Many married gentiles and were lost to their Jewish ancestors.

Among the wealthy and "accepted" Jews was David Franks, the son of Jacob Franks, a New York merchant who died in 1769.[73] Franks had a store in Philadelphia and ran a commission business. He had ships in coastal and intercontinental trade and had an insurance company. Franks dealt in commercial paper and the fur trade and was active in land speculation. He and other traders suffered losses from the French and Indian War and the Pontiac uprising in 1763. To repay their losses, the Iroquois gave them land that would one day become West Virginia. David left the Jewish religion and later adhered to the British cause in the Revolution. He married Margaret Evans, a gentile, in 1743, and their daughter, Abigail, married Andrew Hamilton, attorney general of Pennsylvania. Phila, a daughter of Abigail, married Oliver De Lancey, who became a general in the British army. They had seven children who married Christians when the De Lanceys returned to England after the war. David Franks was in local business and was a shipper. Appointed commissary of the British prisoners of war in American hands around Philadelphia, he was to be paid by the British for feeding the prisoners. In 1778, however, he ran out of cash and could not supply the British. When American leaders recognized his Tory instincts, he was thrown in prison on a charge of treason, but the case was thrown out of court. He was freed, only to be rearrested in 1780 for communicating with the British in New York. His punishment was exile to New York. He and his daughter, Rebecca, went to New York, where she married Sir Henry Johnson. David lost his entire estate because of his British leanings, and the British never repaid his outlay. He supported himself with loans from Michael Gratz.

During the war, the British occupied Philadelphia for a short period. General Sir William Howe, commanding general, was called back to England. In his honor, a grand party, "the meschianza," was planned. Franks's daughters, Abigail and Rebecca, were intimately involved in the planning. Rebecca was crowned queen by "the knights of the burning mountain." The party took place while the Continental army was encamped in nearby Valley Forge. The girls' activities caused great damage to David's business.

During the occupation, Whig Jews who came from New York and Charleston fled to York and Lancaster.[74] After the British left, these Jews returned. There may have been 1,000 Jews in Philadelphia, about 40 percent of the total Jewish population of the colonies. After the war, some Jews emigrated to Philadelphia from Bordeaux, France. Others came with the whites who were fleeing the slave revolts in Haiti. Unhappily, they helped bring yellow fever to Philadelphia in 1793.[75] Three Jews died in the city, and five died in outlying communities while trying to escape the epidemic.

During the Revolution, the British occupied several of the major American cities. Many Whig Jews fled to Philadelphia, and the Jewish population grew. Isaac Moses brought a group of prominent Jews together on March 17, 1782, to plan a set of laws to govern the Jews.[76] Among the prominent Jews were Isaac D'Acosta, Isaac Moses, Barnard Gratz, Hayman Levy, Jonas Phillips, Benjamin Seixas and Simon Nathan. The group purchased land from Robert Wall to build a synagogue and school, but the site was declared unsuitable because it was near a German reform church. The Jews offered to sell the site to the Germans for the price they had paid, but the Germans probably did not accept the offer.

They then purchased a more expensive lot on Cherry Street and Third Street. The cost was planned at £1,815, of which Hayman Salomon contributed £304, the largest single amount.[77] He also donated a Torah scroll imported from Europe. The cornerstones were laid in April 1782, and the building was completed on September 1, 1782. Four leaders of the congregation, Jonas Phillips, Isaac Moses, Jacob Mordecai and Barnard Gatz, laid the cornerstones. They soon discovered that they were short of funds and sent appeals to other congregations in Surinam, Rhode Island, Lancaster, Cape François, St. Thomas and St. Croix.

On September 12, 1782, the synagogue was consecrated: "The Jewish congregation of this city [pray for] the protection of the president and council to erect a place of public worship in this city."[78] The request to the secular government was read and ordered to be filed. A second request from the Jewish congregation of the city to the president, vice-president and executive council of Pennsylvania was sent.[79] "The Congregation *Mikve Israel* will consecrate a place of worship. The Jews professed selves liege subjects to the sovereignty of the United States and acted accordingly. They crave the protection of the magistrates of this state to give sanction to their design and will be honored by their presence. We pray to the God of Israel for the safety of the United States and particularly this commonwealth," Philadelphia, September 12, 1782. The congregation also prayed for the government, Commander George Washington and all "kings and potentates in alliance with North America." The building was called the Portuguese synagogue, although the majority of members were Ashkenazi. Constructed of brick, the building was next to a house for hazzan. The synagogue was almost square and one story high and seated 200. The name "Mikve Israel" (Hope of Israel) was taken from the oldest synagogue in the western hemisphere in Curaçao.[80]

When hostilities ended, many Jews, including the reader, Gershon Mendes Seixas, planned to return to their old homes. This left the synagogue heavily mortgaged on a small congregation. However, in 1786, they were able to erect a *mikveh* (ritual bath). When the debt on the synagogue reached £800 pounds, the members turned to the gentiles for help. Among the contributors were Benjamin Franklin, David Rittenhouse and William Bradford.[81] Franklin had many business dealings with Jews.[82] He had business relations with Nathan Levy for 15 years. It was Levy's ship, the *Myrtella*, that brought the Liberty Bell to America. Franklin knew Jews through the Library Company and the Pennsylvania Society Promoting the Abolition of Slavery. Franklin was a lobbyist in London for the Indiana-Vandalia (land speculation) Company, which employed several Jews. He also carried on business with Benjamin Moses. In 1790, the state permitted the congregation to run a lottery to pay off the debt. This was also the year of the first United States census. It listed 250 Jews living in all of Pennsylvania.

To end this section on Pennsylvania, a quote from Hazzan Seixas is in order.[83] "God had established us in this country where we possess every advantage that other citizens of these states enjoy." Myer Lyons added, "To us, my brethren, should particularly belong a sacred love of this our country." "America was a blessed country."

Pennsylvania was the site of an interesting group. In the Middle Ages the Jews gave up proselytizing, and certainly forceful proselytizing was prohibited. A group of German Baptists, called New Dunkers, built a *shul* (synagogue) in 1724 near Conestoga Creek.[84] They turned to Judaism and kept Saturday as the Sabbath and ate a kosher diet. Their settlement was called New Judea. The group was inspired by Jacob Philadelphia, described as the first Jew born in Philadelphia. (He was probably a self-ordained evangelist.) Jacob started with a German pietist community formed in 1694. His asceticism and sacrifices energized the Dunkers, and they circumcised their male children. Finally, Joseph Simon of Lancaster explained to them that they could not be Jews because conversion required an ecclesiastical court (a *beth din*, or house of law). This discussion took place in present-day Schafferstown.

New Jersey

Northern New Jersey was settled by the Dutch from New Amsterdam, who in 1614 built a small fort at Jersey City Point.[85] Perhaps the first Jews in New Jersey came from New Amsterdam and settled on the east bank of the Delaware River. It will be remembered that Stuyvesant allowed them to go to the South River to dispose of the trade goods they had stored, but it is doubtful that they remained. In 1664, the English took New Netherlands, and King Charles II gave the land between Connecticut and the Delaware River to his brother James, duke of York. That year, James gave New Jersey to two of his creditors, Lord Berkeley and Sir George Carteret, who granted religious freedom immediately and established a government in Newark seemingly based on the Mosaic code. Religious freedom seemed almost a necessity in New Jersey because of the liberality of the first proprietors and cosmopolitan character of the early inhabitants.[86] There were Calvinists, Puritans, Presbyterians, deists, Sabbatacians, Euthycians, independents, anabaptists and Quakers. The proprietors, to stimulate immigration, stated that no one in the province would be molested or punished for a difference of opinion in a matter of religion, as long as they did not disturb the peace of the settlement. However, there was a state religion, and the legislature could appoint ministers and support them. Other groups also had the liberty to appoint and maintain their ministers. The Quakers, who urged separation of church and state, were responsible for articles 18 and 19 of the New Jersey Constitution, written in 1776, which stated that citizens were not to be deprived of worshipping God as they saw fit. The constitution abolished the state religion.

Berkeley sold his half of New Jersey to Quakers John Fenwick and Edward Byllinge. Two years later, creditors seized Byllinge's part and divided it into 100 shares. Carteret retained East Jersey. When he died in 1679, his widow sold his share to Penn and other Quakers for £3,400. With this purchase, the Quakers of Philadelphia had hegemony over New Jersey. They guaranteed full religious freedom, but only Christians (Protestants) could hold office. In West Jersey in 1693, office holders were required to "profess faith in God the father, and Jesus Christ his eternal son, the true God, and in the Holy Spirit, one God blessed for ever more." The East Jersey bill of rights stated "That no person or persons that profess faith in God, by Jesus Christ, his only son, shall at anytime be in anyway molested, punished, disturbed or be called in question for any difference in opinion, in matters of religious concernment ... provided this shall not [be] extended to any of the Romish religion." This was a step backward because it gave religious freedom to Protestants. It is conceivable that the Jews were simply overlooked because there were so few living permanently in New Jersey.

Between 1702 and 1776, no Jews were naturalized in that colony, but Jewish names are seen in court records.[87] The early Jews probably had to be litigious to maintain their equality. In Middlesex County, Abraham De Lucena sued Thomas Bloomfield for £7 on May 21, 1718. The amount was raised to £10 and was awarded to De Lucena in 1718. Aaron and Moses Louzada were frequent litigants between 1719 and 1752. There were lawsuits against David Nunes by Nathan Simson, Abraham Isaac and Mordecai Gomez. In 1724, Rodrigo Pacheco was a plaintiff in two cases. Others were David Machudo, Isaacs Levy and Isaac Polock.

There was a "black sheep" in the tiny Jewish population. In 1760, Myers Levy of Spottswood, New Jersey, ran off with £2,300 in goods and assets he had ordered from Barnard Gratz (of Philadelphia).[88] An advertisement in the New York Mercury offered $20 for knowledge of his whereabouts. "He is a Man of Middle Stature, of a rudy Complexion, wore his own hair, is black Bearded, speaks broken English, but perfect in the Dutch." The reward was later raised to $800 and was guaranteed by Joseph Morris, David Franks, Barnard Gratz, Moses Heyman and six gentile traders of Philadelphia.

There was also a Jewish Lothario in their number. In 1769, a notice appeared in the Pennsylvania *Gazette* to the effect that John Farnsworth of Philipsburg, West Jersey, would not be responsible for his wife, Deborah's, debts in view of the fact that "She [had] absconded with Nathan Levy, a Jew shopkeeper."

The ruling that only Protestants could hold office was on the books, but it was not obeyed in practice. David Nunes was a justice of the peace in 1722. Daniel Nunez was town clerk of Piscataway and a justice of the peace for Middlesex County. Perhaps the ruling referred to colony-wide offices such as seats in the legislature. The constitution of 1844 abolished all religious tests for office.

Only one Jew was on the records as a soldier from New Jersey in the Revolution, but he carried a famous name: Asher (or Asser) Levy.[89] His grandfather of the same name created all the problems for Governor Stuyvesant in New Amsterdam. As the only Jew left when the English took New Netherland, Levy "the elder" immediately took the oath of allegiance to King Charles II. Levy was reasonably wealthy when he died. His widow, Maria, married Ansell Samuel Levy in 1685, and Asser's sister, Rachel, married Valentine Van Der Wilden. One of their children was Richea Asher, who married Moses Levy. One of their offspring was Asher Levy, born in 1756 (he was not of the direct line from Asser). Asher was an ensign in the first regiment of the New Jersey line from September 12, 1778, to June 4, 1779, when he resigned. He was jailed in Burlington, New Jersey, on the suspicion of being a Tory. Levy escaped on March 25, 1780, but he was recaptured and again escaped on August 9, 1780. He went to New York to join his family, who were Tories. There he married Margaret Mary Thomson and moved to Philadelphia, where he died in 1785.

Delaware

The early history of Delaware involves the same three Jews from New Amsterdam. Abraham de Lucena, Salvador Dandrada and Jacob Cohen requested permission to trade on the Delaware River.[90] They had already shipped trade goods to the area. Stuyvesant denied them permission, but he allowed them to send two men to dispose of the goods. They sent Isaac Israel and Isaac Cardoso (Isaac Israel was probably not Jewish). Meanwhile, the governors of the Dutch West India Company ordered Stuyvesant to open the river to all inhabitants (1656). The original two Jews probably did not remain. In 1657, a Jew, Isaac Mesa, signed a treaty with the local Indians at Fort Casimir related to prices for furs. It is unlikely that he remained in the area.

The area that became Delaware was part of the territory taken by the English from the Dutch. Sir Robert Carr, British commander of the area, declared that all inhabitants were to have liberty of conscience. All had freedom to worship, but only Protestants could vote or hold office. Delaware was given to William Penn as part of his charter for Pennsylvania. George Fox, founder of the Quaker religion, and later William Penn encouraged Jews to come to the new territory. Penn hoped they would see the error of their beliefs and accept Jesus for their salvation. He at one time suggested a Hebraic frame of government for this new colony.

The three lower counties of Pennsylvania on the Delaware River were separated to form Delaware in 1702. The major commercial ports of New York and Philadelphia overwhelmed the port of Wilmington. Occasional Jews moved in to open shops, but there were no international commercial Jews. Daniel Nunez was there in the 1730s.[91] Abraham Judah was a merchant in Wilmington in the 1750s.[92] He moved back to Philadelphia around 1761. There seems to be no further history of Jews in Delaware during the colonial era.

II

Jews in New England and Canada

The Puritans in the Massachusetts Bay Colony loved the ancient Jews but had little use for their contemporary offspring and tried to get them out of their colony. That this attitude continued through the years can be seen by the lack of a synagogue in Boston, a major seaport, until 1840.

John Cotton, in his farewell sermon to England, compared their departure from England to the deliverance of Israel from Egypt.[1] He told of God's promise to "appoint a place for my people Israel." He would provide "a place of their own" from which they "would move no more." John Winthrop warned them "to serve the Lord and worke, and worke out their salvacion." "They must do justly, love mercy and walk humbly with our God. If they did these things, they would surely find that the God of Israel is among us." The Puritans designed a biblical commonwealth whose theology, rhetoric, law and literature were full of allusions to the biblical experiences of Israel. The names they gave their towns smacked of the Old Testament (Salem, Canaan, Hebron). Their preachers talked of the New England Zion. The Plymouth legal codes were based on the five laws of ancient Israel. In New Haven, the judicial laws of God as delivered by Moses were binding. John Robinson said the people of God were leaving Babylon for Jerusalem. The Puritans were Abraham's children, a people in covenant with God. "You are God's own." Puritan governors were likened to Joshua and Nehemiah. According to Cotton Mather, "You may see an Israel in America." Thomas Thacher believed "We are the people that do succeed Israel." "We are Jacob." Samuel Wakeman stated, "Jerusalem was, New England is, they were, you are God's own, God's covenant people."

Cotton Mather understood the New England experience as a reenactment of the biblical return from Babylonian exile. He intertwined the history of New England with that of Israel so completely that it became one unified narrative.

The Puritans left an England that later urged a readmittance of the Jews—not for the love of Jews, but to convert them. Then the second coming could occur. As a covenanted people, the Puritans (like the early Israelites) were the divinely chosen instrument leading to the Messiah's coming and salvation. God was intimately involved in Israel's history, but He gave up on them when they refused to accept Jesus as savior.

The Hebrew Bible provided a structure for the American experience. The Puritans, in searching the scriptures, discovered a similarity between themselves and the ancient Israelites.[2] They felt they shared a similar experience with the ancient Israelites. They had left their homes and gone into a wilderness. The Puritans turned to Jewish law, along with English common law, as a precedent for their own institutions. They gave precedence to Mosaic law when it was workable. Puritan preachers called Boston the Jerusalem of this land. New England was New England Canaan. Finally, the Puritan commonwealth was founded on "the same ethical impulse which animates the pages of the Hebrew poets and prophets."[3] They credited a theocratic state like that of the ancient Jews, and the Old Testament was a vital part of their liturgy.

Part of this theocratic ideal was the need to learn Hebrew. Hebrew was the holy tongue in which the law of God was written and in which God and the angels spoke to the old patriarchs.[4] University students were taught that when they died and went to heaven, the first sound they would hear would be the psalms sung in Hebrew. The first Hebraists came over on the *Mayflower*.[5] Governor Bradford said "the Hebrew (tongue) [was] the most of all studied, because he said he would see with his own eyes the ancient oracles of God in their native beauty." In his *History of Plymouth Plantation* there are eight pages of Hebrew roots with English explanations and quotations from the Hebrew Old Testament. Bradford wanted to see "something of that most ancient language and holy tongue, in which the law and Oracles of God were writ; and in which God and Angels spake to the holy patriarchs of old time." William Brewster was a major Hebraist and probably started as a student at Peterhouse College in Cambridge.

There were 77 ministers who fled the intolerance of the Stuarts and came to Puritan New England. They introduced Hebraic studies, which gradually declined over the years, only to see a partial rebirth with the entrance into Boston of Judah Monis. John Cotton fled England because of the "urging" of the Anglican leader Laud. Arriving in New England in 1633, Cotton could read, translate and speak Hebrew. In 1640, the Cambridge Press issued the *Bay Psalm Book*, which was the third book printed in English America. The psalms were translated into Hebrew and contained some Hebrew characters which had to be carved from blocks of wood for the press.

Henry Dunster, the first president of Harvard, made Hebrew learning a part of the curriculum. To receive a degree from Harvard, students had to read the Old and New testaments in Latin and translate them into Hebrew. They had to read Hebrew and translate it into Greek in the Old Testament and English into Greek in the New Testament. The resident fellows tutored students in Hebrew. In 1642, the first commencement after four years of students, the orations at graduation were in Latin, Greek and Hebrew. Dunster was considered the best Hebraist of his time. Charles Chauncey followed Dunster as president of Harvard. He had an M.A. from Cambridge, England, where he was a professor of Hebrew at Trinity College. Jews, who were not permitted in England until Cromwell, taught Hebrew at several universities in England. Usually, they were nominally converted into the Church of England. Trimellius, a converted Italian Jew, taught Hebrew at Cambridge, and Philip Ferdinand, a converted Polish Jew, taught Hebrew at Oxford and Cambridge. According to Cotton Mather, a Jew, de Verona, lived in Chauncey's house in London for one year and taught him Hebrew.

Increase Mather became president of Harvard 13 years after Chauncey's death. Increase was the first American-born president of Harvard. After Chauncey's death, no one was considered qualified to become president until Increase Mather was appointed. On commencement day, Increase gave an oration in Hebrew, which was a custom at European universities. When his son, Nathanael, entered Harvard at the age of 12, he knew the Old Testament in Hebrew and the New Testament in Greek, and like his father, he gave orations in Hebrew. In conversation, Increase denied the malicious rumor that Jews had poisoned wells to cause the epidemics of the plague. However, he believed they blasphemed Jesus in their synagogues and called the gospel "a volume of lies." He felt that a divine mystery would bring salvation to the Jews. Cotton Mather learned Hebrew as a child. At 14, he composed Hebrew exercises, and at 16, he received a B.A. from Harvard.

Most of the reasonably educated Puritans studied Hebrew, "that most ancient language and Holy tongue in which the Law and Oracles were writ." Many of the ten schools founded before the Revolution included Hebrew in their curriculum. At Harvard, the first teacher of Hebrew was Michael Wigglesworth.[6] His students approached him in the hope they could give up the study of Hebrew. Wigglesworth was followed by Judah Monis, a convert to Puritanism.[7] Monis was born on February 4, 1683, either in Italy or the Barbary states. He was trained at the Jewish academies of Leghorn and Amsterdam and served as a rabbi in Jamaica and New York. (He was not actually a rabbi and probably acted as a reader for the congregation.) He was made a freeman of New York City on February 28, 1716, where he was described as a merchant. He next popped up in Boston, where the luminaries of the Puritan church like Increase Mather and Mister Coleman as well as lay leaders like Leverett took an interest in him. "To crown all his knowledge of the Holy Scriptures, both the Old and the New Testament, is very happy and extraordinary, which he adorns with laudable conversation." In 1720, Monis received an M.A. from Harvard, the first Jew to receive a college degree in the colonies.[8] He was baptized by Benjamin Coleman in College Hall and then baptized in public by a Mr. Appleton. Following his conversion, he presented a speech about the nine principal arguments used by modern rabbis to explain why the Messiah had not yet come. He answered all the arguments to prove Jesus Christ was the Messiah who came. Not everyone was sure of his acceptance of Christ, however. Bishop White Kennett of London, in a letter to the Reverend Benjamin Coleman, who sponsored Monis's conversion, wrote that "The case of Mr. Monis will be a credit to our religion if he continue firm in our faith ... but I am so doubtful of the Sincerity of Converts ... [and] I shall not be surprized if we are at last deceived by him."[9]

On April 30, Harvard voted Monis instructor of the Hebrew Language, and the college treasury was to pay him £50 for each of two years. All upperclassmen except those excused by the president and tutors were to attend his classes four days a week. Those who planned to join the ministry had to attend his classes. Every student was to have a Hebrew Bible, a psalter, and a Hebrew dictionary. The lessons included writing Hebrew, copying grammar and reading, reciting, construing, parsing, translating, composing and reading with points. Monis's method of teaching was tedious, and the tutors and others were to look for ways to encourage Hebrew study. The students were not interested in Hebrew, however, and Monis was told by the president and tutors to keep a list of delinquents. These students were fined one shilling for absence, six pence for tardiness, one shilling for negligence and five shillings for "contemptuous carriage." After one year, Monis's salary was raised to £80, and the leaders told him they were "greatly satisfied" with him. On January 18, 1724, he married Abigail Marret in First church, Cambridge, and they settled near her family in Cambridge. His appointment was renewed yearly, and by

1748, his salary was £254, 16 shillings, no pence, plus extras. This was almost as much as the head tutor earned. (There were four at the time.)

After 12 years of teaching, Monis asked Harvard to publish his Hebrew grammar. Thomas Holts sent out a set of Hebrew type from England to Boston. The public of Massachusetts was urged to subscribe so they could read the oracles of the Old Testament in the original, ancient language. The cost would be eight shillings, but if six copies were purchased, the seventh was free. The college gave Monis a loan with interest to print 1,000 copies. Four men were appointed to assist Monis and put his grammar into proper shape (President Wadsworth, Henry Flynt, Reverend Edward Wigglesworth and Nathaniel Appleton). In 1735, the book was completed. It was dedicated to the governor, honorables and governors of Harvard as well as the president of Harvard and the Reverend Benjamin Wadsworth. The 1,000 copies cost nearly £220. One hundred were taken by Harvard for tutors, overseers and members of the corporation. Monis was permitted to sell the rest for 12 shillings, seven pence. Every freshman and sophomore had to buy one. For every book sold, Monis paid the treasurer nearly five shillings with interest (on his loan). He was given 50 copies to sell for himself plus £35 for his work. Monis then composed a Hebrew vocabulary called "the Nomenclatur" for the use of pupils and others desiring to know the Hebrew tongue.[10] By 1755, Hebrew instruction was down to one afternoon per week. Monis's income dropped accordingly, and he claimed he was earning only about £18 per year. He supplemented this meager income by opening a store, where he sold nails, hinges, pipes and tobacco largely to Harvard. When the store was unsuccessful, he eked out a modest sum as a Spanish interpreter for the colony. Finally, he was forced to apply to Governor Shirley and the legislature for a grant. He was given £20 for his "faithful discharge of the Trust." There may have been other grants as well, but there is no official listing. His wife died in 1760, and he resigned from Harvard at age 77. In 1763, he received a seal of honor in his brother-in-law's church. He died on April 25, 1764, and left his estate to five ministers as a fund for the widows of ministers. His epitaph describes him as "Rabbi Judah Monis, born a jew, but embraced the Christian faith." One wonders how strongly he embraced the church. He was considered as the "converted Jew," and he kept Saturday as the sabbath.[11]

Aside from being able to read the ancient tongue, another reason for knowing Hebrew (and Arabic) was to be able to convert Jews and Muslims by speaking to them in their own tongue. (However, Ezra Stiles, president of Yale, told the story in 1771 about a Jew who received a letter from Hebron, Palestine. He brought it to Stiles to translate.[12]) As early as 1645, there was the development of a feeling of toleration toward all.[13] In a letter to Governor Winthrop, Winslow described a heated debate in the legislature about universal tolerance, which idea the writer abhorred. He wrote that a particular document claimed "to allow and maintain full and free toleracon of religion to all men that would preserve civill peace and submit unto government and there was no limitacon or excepcon against Turke, Jew, Papist or any other." The governor would not allow the measure to come to a vote because "it would eate out the power of Godliness.... The Lord in mercy looke upon us, and allay this spirit of division that is creeping in among us." This was followed in 1652 by a manifesto that stated that the denial of the New Testament could lead to exile or execution.[14] No Jew was executed, but four Quakers were put to death between 1659 and 1661 for nonconformity.

The Puritans were ambivalent about having Jews in their midst. Although they felt a need to convert the Jews to bring about the second coming, they felt a need to keep their society uniform. Jews sensed the distrust of the Puritans and tended to come and go for business purposes only. In 1648, Isaac Abrahams was a witness to a bill of sale of his ship, *Bride of Enatuson*, sold to Robert Scott and John Cooke.[15] There was no record of his remaining in Boston after the sale. The following year, Solomon Franco, an agent of Immanuel Perada, came to Boston with a cargo for General J.E. Gibbons. Following the transaction he was stranded in Massachusetts. The general court granted him six shillings per week for ten weeks for subsistence until he could get passage back to Holland. In 1668, Solomon "Ye Malata Jew" was prosecuted in Essex County for traveling through Wenham on the Lord's day.[16]

There were probably no Jews allowed to settle before 1649. There was a mention of a Joseph Isaack and his sister Rebecca Isaack in 1634 and 1636.[17] Even though they had Jewish names, they were probably not Jewish. They may have converted in Europe or had Jewish ancestors. Toward the end of the seventeenth century, with the Restoration in England and the growth of mercantilism, the Puritan Charter was revoked by Charles II. Then James II, his brother, granted freedom of conscience. In 1674, on the Boston tax list there was listed Rowland Gideon, "Ye Jew," rated at 18 shillings.[18] Gideon's name later appeared in a court case where he collected £100 from a debtor over a tobacco transaction. (Rowland Gideon was hardly a Jewish name and is an example of Anglicizing, perhaps to enable one to fit in. His original name was Rehiel Abudiente.) Rowland was a representative for his family's business, first in the West Indies and then in Boston.[19] In 1677, he received letters of denization and could settle anywhere in the British colonies. His name was listed repeatedly in court. He and Daniel Barrow accused Joseph Tebo of stealing money and rings. Tebo was found guilty and was whipped in public. They later appeared against Nicholas Mouleter, a Quaker. In 1679, a suit in Boston was listed against Sarah Franks (probably Franco, from Spain or Portugal). In 1680, one Samuel Isaac was mentioned. In 1695, records in Boston listed Samuel the Jew and Raphaell Abandana. Later, Isaac De Coster and sons Isaac and Joseph settled there. In 1702, Simon the Jew was converted and became Simon Barns. The true sign of permanent settlement occurred in 1733, when Michael Asher and Isaac Solomon were permitted to set aside land for a Jewish cemetery.[20]

The name Cotton Mather "was writ large" in the early history of Massachusetts. He was a preacher, a writer, a teacher and a "doctor" without training. Most important, he had an overwhelming desire to convert Jews. In 1714, he completed a six-volume *Biblia Americana* on the history of the Jewish people from the beginning of the Christian era.[21] There were two Jewish brothers, Joseph and Samuel Frazor (or Frazier), who became merchants in Boston.[22] Cotton Mather was on the verge of converting one brother with some written material when the documents were shown to be a forgery by Judge Sewell, and Mather confessed. The potential Puritan left Mather and refused any further association with him or religion in general.

There was a very slow increase in the Jewish-sounding names on the tax rolls.[23] Barbara Hart, Isaac Lopez, and Abraham Gotatus came early in the eighteenth century. Lopez was elected a constable in Boston. This was a lowly job, so he declined the honor, but he paid a fine for his refusal. However, he received permission to put up a timber house on land he purchased—another sign of stability and permanence.

Solomon and Asher, who had bought the cemetery land, built a shop near the cemetery. To become an inhabitant of the town, one had to show the ability to support oneself. Once accepted by the town, the individual could expect to be supported by the town if he fell on hard times. Strangers without means were "warned out." John Foster put up a £40-pound security that Joseph Bueno would not be "chargeable to Boston." Poor Jews continued to be "warned out." As late as 1756, Philip Samuel, a New York Jew, was told to leave. This was repeated five months later. Isaac Moses was told to leave Boston in 14 days unless he provided a security.

During the Revolution, after the British had left Boston, there was an influx of Jews who came from areas previously occupied by the British. As the eighteenth century drew to a close, a constitution for Massachusetts was written (1780).[24] It stated that all men worship God in their own way as long as others and the public peace are not disturbed. All towns were to have public worship, and all Protestant ministers would be supported by the town. All persons were to attend services. The money a citizen paid could be directed to a particular preacher. All Christian denominations were protected by law. To take a major office, an individual was to take an oath as a Christian. Although the Jews were left out and had to support a Protestant preacher, they were allowed to practice their religion if they kept it. The constitution was an improvement over the Chapter of Massachusetts Bay (1691): "There shall be a liberty of conscience, allowed in the worship of God to all Christians except Papists inhabiting or which shall inhabit or be resident within our said province or territory."[25] Many Jews converted or married gentiles, and their children were raised in their mother's church. The Campanells, a Sephardic name, settled in Ipswich.[26] They intermarried and became Campbells.

Perhaps the most important Jew in Boston in the colonial period was Moses Michael Hayes.[27] Born in Lisbon in 1739, he settled in New York with his father Judah and became a freeman of New York in 1769. Moses tried his luck in Jamaica and then came to Newport. He married Regina Touro and went to Boston when the British occupied Newport. He brought his wife, five daughters and a son, Judah, his widowed sister, Regina Touro, and her two sons.[28] Hayes started as a merchant and then a marine insurance underwriter. One of his contributions to Boston was his election as grand m aster of the Masonic lodge of Massachusetts. He or his son Judah helped found the first bank in Boston as well as the Boston Athanaeum. Hayes started his nephews in business. The younger, Abraham, stayed in Boston and became wealthy. The older, Judah, went to New Orleans and became the wealthiest man in that city. Among many benefits in his will was money to maintain the Touro synagogue in Newport. After Hayes and his wife died, their daughters left for Virginia. Over the next few years the Jewish community dwindled and practically died. It had a rebirth in 1840 with a large immigration of Jews from Germany.

Before we leave Massachusetts let us discuss the belief that was held by many Puritans, as well as many learned men, that the Indians were derived from the ten lost tribes of Israel. In 1644, Aaron Levi stated in a deposition that the Peruvian Indians recited the Shema and observed many Jewish customs.[29] Cotton Mather stated that John Eliot, the "apostle of the Indians," strongly believed that the Native Americans were descended from Jews became they used parables in discourse, anointed their heads, told time by nights and months, gave dowries for wives and did not eat swine. Others testified to their similar looks, the similar sounds of their words, traditions and religious customs. The final proof came in 1815, when Captain Joseph Merrick, while plowing on Indian Hill in

Pittsfield, turned up a phylactery in an area where there were no Jews. It was given to the American Antiquarian Society in Worcester, but was later misplaced and never found.

In a time when relapsed "new Christians" in Spain and Portugal and their colonies in the New World were burned to death (or if they were lucky or rich, they were garroted first), when a few Jewish financiers and doctors lived surreptitiously in England but were not permitted in France or its colonies, when Jews were tolerated in Holland as long as they did not practice their religion openly, and when Chmielnicki was rousing the peasants of Ukraine and Poland to massacre the Jews, Roger Williams was like a beacon of righteousness. This Calvinist preacher, who had troubles with the Church of England while in England and with his own church in Massachusetts, was invited to leave the rigid confines of that colony. He went south and founded the colony of Providence Plantations.[30] As early as 1636, he demanded freedom of religion for all groups—Jews, Papists and Mohammedans. In 1643, Williams returned to London to receive a charter for his new colony.[31] He was particularly receptive to the Jews, "for whose hard measure, I fear, the nations and England hath yet a score to pay."[32] In 1652, the legislature of Rhode Island enacted "that all men of whatever nation soever they may be, that shall be received inhabitants of any of the towns, shall have the same privileges as Englishmen any law to the contrary notwithstanding."[33]

Williams preceded William Penn by half a century. Both men bought the land from the natives rather than taking it. Aquidneck Island, on whose southern tip Newport was planted, was purchased for 40 fathoms of white beads, ten coats and 20 hoes. With his charter in hand and the land he had purchased, Williams, with the help of John Clarke, drew of a code of laws. "And otherwise than thus what is herein forbidden, all men may walk as their consciences persuade them, everyone in the name of his God. And let the saints of the Most High walk in this colony without molestation in the name of the Eternal their God, forever and ever."

Williams's life spanned much of the seventeenth century, but his writings could easily have found a home at the end of the twentieth century. "I humbly conceive it to be the duty of the civil magistrate to break down that superstitious wall of separation between the Gentiles and the Jews, and freely, without their asking, to make way for their free and peaceable habitations among us."[34] No person should be "any wise molested, punished, disquieted or called in question, for any differences in opinions in matters of religion."[35] "I desire not the liberty to myself which I would not freely and impartially weigh out to all the consciences of the world beside."[36] "Suppose in some of the cities of Poland, Holland or Turkey that Jews, Pagans, Anti-Christians and Christians and Turks were mixed together in civil living and commerce. Why would a Turk who converted one of John Cotton's people to Mohammedanism be more punished for that crime than for turning a Jew, Pagan or Papist to his belief and worship?"[37] "Jesus and his servants professed a spiritual way against the doctrine worship and government of Jews, Turks, Pagans, and Anti-Christian religions. These fight His religion as well. This war could be so managed were men but humane civil and peaceable that no civil injury may be committed on either side."[38]

There was one defect in Williams's armor: He could not tolerate Quakers. He wanted to debate George Fox on his new religion. "A debate would present the positions of Catholic, Protestant, Quaker and Jewish positions. He said Quakers were like Jews in that they were zealous, Traditious, Superstitious, Inventious which they preferred before the Commands of god."[39]

In 1684, the Rhode Island legislature followed Williams's lead in a resolution. Jews "might expect as good protection as any stranger being not of our nation, residing amongst us in this his Majesty's Colony, ought to have, being obedient as his Majesty's laws."[40] As one might expect, the strict Puritans abhorred what was happening in the colony to the south. Cotton Mather called Newport "the common receptacle of the convicts of Jerusalem and the outcasts of the land."[41]

News of this open society spread throughout the Western Hemisphere and Europe. Different sources described different times and different locations from where Jews emigrated to Newport. There were individual Jews residing in Newport in the early part of the 1650s. Some early Jews may have come from New Amsterdam when Governor Stuyvesant ordered them out.[42] (This was later countermanded in Amsterdam.) Fifteen Jewish families arrived in Newport probably from Barbados in 1658.[43] Other sources list the 15 families as coming from Holland with earlier numbers from Curaçao.[44] In 1678, land was purchased for a cemetery by Mordecai Campanall and Moses Pachecoe.[45] There were enough Jewish men to hold services in Campanall's home. The navigation acts of the 1660s put a damper on Jewish immigration to Rhode Island because they were considered aliens or strangers and therefore could not compete legally in trade.

Several families left the island, and by 1685, the community began to break up. This happened despite a ruling by the assembly on June 24, 1684, that gave them protection under the law as resident strangers.[46] There was some influx in the early 1680s, but this was temporary, and there was further emigration. A group of 90 came from Curaçao to escape an epidemic. After 1730, there was an influx of Jews from Curaçao. Instead of the original Sephardic names, the names of these new families were Isaacs, Moses, Judahs, Benjamins and Solomons. They settled in as tailors, dry goods dealers and manufacturers of soap and brass. After 1740, more Sephardic Jews joined the community (Touro, Lucena, Lopez, Rivera and Seixas). The French and Indian War resulted in increased trade and 15 Jewish families added to the population.[47] From the French and Indian War to the Revolution, the Jewish population grew in numbers and wealth. Jews represented 1 percent of the population of Newport (6,000). In 1768, Newport had 9,000 citizens with 25 Jewish families. This last growth came from New York.

The greatest wealth in the mid–eighteenth century rested in the hands of Aaron Lopez and his father-in-law, Jacob Rodrigues Rivera.[48] Aaron's brother, Moses (his Christian name was José), preceded him to America. He married his cousin Rebecca Rivera, daughter of Abraham Rodrigues Rivera. When both men were naturalized in New York, in 1741, they were permitted to trade in all British possessions. In 1748, the family moved to Newport, which had an excellent protected harbor. It was a center for privateers to discharge their gains, and it had a hidden trade with Dutch and Caribbean buccaneers. Merchant shippers also traded in the West Indies, Surinam and other coastal areas. Newport was equally important in the slave trade.

In 1752, Duarte Lopez, his wife, daughter and brother Gabriel escaped from Portugal. He joined his brother in Newport and changed his name to Aaron. After their arrival, all of the men were circumcised. Aaron's wife Anna became Abigail. His daughter Catherine became Sarah, and Gabriel became David. Aaron received credit from the Jews in town and started trading along with Moses Gomez. Aaron took advantage of the French and Indian War and started to make his fortune. Two years after his arrival,, he was selling soap and candles outside of Rhode Island. By 1756, he was active in trade with Boston and New York. The following year, Lopez had an active trade with London, to which he shipped a multitude of products, and he smuggled in Dutch tea. Aaron became involved in the manufacture of candles from spermaceti. He also imported machinery from London to be used in rum distillation. He dealt in pewter, indigo, sugar, tea, silk, soap, "head matter from the sperm whale," coffee, chocolate and molasses. Aaron was involved in business with Jacob Rodriguez Rivera, Moses's brother-in-law.

In 1761, Aaron and Isaac Elizir petitioned the Court of Rhode Island for naturalization. When they were denied this privilege, they turned to the superior court. In 1762, that court also denied their petitions, claiming that the purpose of the Naturalization Act of 1740 was to increase the inhabitants of the colony. There were already too many in Rhode Island, so some English colonists moved to Nova Scotia and other places. The purpose of the colony was the spread of Christianity. A law of 1663 stated that only Christians could be admitted to the colony.[49] The true reason for the denial, however, was strife between Chief Justice Ward and Governor Hopkins. It meant two fewer voters in Newport as compared to Providence.[50] Elizir went to New York and was naturalized in 1763. Aaron was advised to go to Massachusetts for a short period before taking the oath. He received affidavits from citizens of Newport that he had lived in Rhode Island for seven years. Aaron moved to Swansea on the Rhode Island border. He took the oath in Taunton, Massachusetts. Lopez was the first Jew naturalized in that colony. Ezra Stiles, a Puritan minister, on hearing of their rejection in Rhode Island, said, "I remark that Providence seems to make everything work, for Mortification of the Jews, and to prevent their incorporation into any nation; that thus they continue a distinct people.... [It] forbodes that the Jews will never become incorporated with the people of America anymore than in Europe, Asia and Africa."

Lopez returned to Newport and again became active in manufacturing and shipping. Rhode Island became the center of spermaceti candle manufacture. Of the 12 factories, most were in Rhode Island, which was more than could be handled economically. Nine firms signed a trust agreement. Of the 26 signatories, six were Jewish, including Aaron Lopez and his father-in-law. The agreement ended after 17 months, and a new trust was written in April 1763. Four of the eight signatories were Jewish, including Lopez and Rivera. Between 1750 and 1770, there were 17 factories providing spermaceti candles, 22 distilleries, four sugar refineries, five rope-walks and several furniture factories.

Whale head matter was the basic ingredient of a candle. Rivera invented the sperm oil lamp, which gave a more brilliant and a steadier light than a tallow candle. Lopez had a ship built for 100 Spanish dollars for a whaling expedition to the Grand Banks off Newfoundland. By 1760, Lopez and Rivera owned the 80-ton brigantine *Greyhound*, and they later bought several sloops in partnership. Business declined after Great Britain decided the colonies would pay one-third of the cost of the French and Indian War. There was vigorous enforcement of the trade laws and collections of port fees. In 1764, 46 merchants in Rhode Island, including Lopez, petitioned the general assembly against "imperial control" of the ports and collection of fees.

In addition to the coastal trade as far south as Charleston, Lopez became active in the transatlantic trade. He, his brother Moses and Myer Pollock were in the molasses trade with the West Indies. The molasses was taken to Newport and converted to rum, which was then carried to Africa to pay for slaves which were sold in the West Indies. However, it was the coastal trade which was the mainstay of Lopez's fortune. Later, he started trade with Bristol, England, with Henry Cruger as his partner. Lopez built ships for this enterprise, and Cruger would try to sell the ships and cargo in England. In 1765, Lopez sent the *Charlotte, Friendship*, and the *Newport Packet* to England. Bristol was in a depression, and Lopez ended owing Cruger £11,000. As the Bristol trade fell off, Lopez turned again to the West Indies. Abraham Perrera Mendes in Jamaica married Lopez's daughter Sally, and his son-in-law became his representative in Jamaica. Abraham did poorly for Lopez, however.

Lopez still had family in Portugal, and he started a covert trade with that country. He was able to rescue his half-brother, Miguel, Miguel's wife and their three sons. When the men arrived in Newport, they were circumcised, which was a serious operation for adults. Benjamin Gomez wrote in a letter to Aaron Lopez: "I congratulate you on the safe arrival of your brothers whome I understand intend to undergo the operation. Pray take care to have a good surgeon present, as it will require some judgement to stop the blood and cure the wound. My compliments to them, also to Mr. Rivera and family."

In 1767, Lopez had built up a large trade with Jamaica including the sale of kosher food. However, Jamaica was still depressed, so the planters were debt ridden. In 1768, he replaced his son-in-law with Benjamin Wright, but business returns remained poor. In the 1770s, Lopez became very important in shipping. He sent material from Newport to Jamaica and reloaded with material for England. When this was sold, he picked up more cargo for Newport. By 1773, he had paid off his debt to Cruger. In 1775, Lopez was the largest taxpayer in Newport at nearly £33. His father-in-law Rivera paid only nine pounds.

Not only did Lopez ship, but he also got into the manufacturing end of the material shipped. He contracted with various craftsmen to sell their products and then bought and shipped them to a market that needed them. He also furnished the raw material his craftsmen used. In 1770, he employed 30 people, mostly women, making cloth and clothes. Lopez owned 12 distilleries that produced 12,000 gallons of rum, for which his ships brought the molasses from the West Indies. He developed a cooperage to make his barrels.

Lopez had ships built which were sent to England for sale. He imported the raw materials needed to build ships, and these were sold to the ship builders in New England. Lopez had ships built specifically for the slave trade. He supervised the building of ships for other owners, and his yard could also repair ships. Additionally, Lopez became a house builder. His yard made prefabricated frames which were shipped out. Lopez built carriages, made bottles, raised sheep to supply mutton for ship's food as well as for export, supplied pork, and also shipped kosher products to the West Indies. He had many partners, Jewish and non–Jewish. Lopez outfitted ships for whaling in the South Atlantic. It is surprising that Lopez had time for all this activity. He had seven children with Abigail, who died at the age of 36. He then married Sarah, the daughter of Jacob Rodrigues Rivera, and she bore him an additional ten children.

Lopez was not a strong supporter of independence from Britain. However, when the British took Newport in December 1776, Lopez left with his family and 2,000 patriots. His family went first to Boston and then to Leicester, Massachusetts, in the interior. His family, Rivera's family, and the slaves brought the number of exiles to 70. Lopez built a large house with a store and bought real estate. He dealt properly with the citizens and was held in high esteem. The decline of his fortune started when his ship, *Hope*, traveling from Jamaica was picked up by American privateers and taken to Connecticut. The ship was declared a proper prize, but Lopez went to congress in Philadelphia to argue his case. They found in his favor, but Connecticut would not let the ship proceed, and the case was eventually settled in 1783, one year after his death. His debtors never tried to pay him. His ships from Europe were picked up by the British blockade and were lost to him.

His death came in a very unusual way. Learning that his father-in-law was sick in Providence, he arranged a trip to that city. In Smithfield, Rhode Island, something frightened the horse pulling his sulky, and he was pulled into Scott's Pond and drowned. Lopez was buried in the Newport Cemetery. His tombstone read[51]:

> He was a merchant of eminence
> of polite and amiable manners.
> Hospitality, Liberality and Benevolence
> were his true characteristics.
> An ornament and valuable Pillar to
> the Jewish Society of which he was a
> member. His knowledge in commerce
> was unbounded and his integrity irreproachable;
> Thus he lived and died, much regrett'd,
> esteemed and loved by all.

Abraham Mendes, Joseph Lopez and Moses Lopez were the administrators of his estate. They paid off most of his debts including their cost of administration (about £646). The total value of his estate after administration costs was about £199. (His estate was destroyed by the American Revolution.) His largest creditor was Patrick Jeffreys, who was owed nearly £20,510. His son, Joseph, made the last payment to Jeffreys in 1804.

In addition to Lopez and Rivera, there were other entrepreneurs in the Jewish community. Moses Lopez received a ten-year monopoly on the manufacture of potash by a special method. Jacob Isaacs sent a note to congress in 1791.[52] He claimed he could convert sea water to fresh water. A year earlier, when President Washington visited Newport, Isaacs gave him a bottle of fresh water converted from ocean water. Washington claimed "he was highly satisfied herewith." When Isaacs found no takers in a land with fresh water lakes, rivers and ponds, he tried his hand at shipbuilding, which was equally unsuccessful. Isaacs opened an insurance agency which failed. He died in 1798.

When a Jewish community settles in and has the appearance of permanence, the first thing required is the purchase of land for a Jewish cemetery.[53] In 1678, Mordecai Campanal and Moses Pacheco acquired land for this purpose. Seventy years later the Jews formed a congregation, Nefutsi Yisrael, the "scattered of Israel." On June 13, 1759, Jacob Rodrigues Rivera, Moses Levy and Isaac Hart purchased from Ebenezer Allen of Sandwich, Massachusetts, a parcel of land for a synagogue for £1,500, Rhode Island currency. When the community could not raise the money for the building, they appealed to Jewish communities in New York, Curaçao, Jamaica and London. New York was the most generous and sent £150. Other areas gave less, and the community appealed to New York a second time. The synagogue cost £2,000 sterling, and the mortgage was 8 percent. The congregation could not meet the cost of interest and principal, so they appealed to Surinam. The Sephardic community raised 600 guilders, and the Ashkenazis raised a similar amount. The congregation then hired Peter Harrison as architect.[54] He was a pupil and associate of Sir Christopher Wren. The cornerstone was laid in 1759, and the temple was consecrated in 1763 to celebrate Chanukkah.

The synagogue was built in the Sephardic style,[55] with the reader's desk in the middle of the floor and the Ark at the east end. There were straight wooden armchairs on the main floor. The pews in the women's gallery were painted white, and the cushions on the wooden seats were of red velvet. The ceiling was painted a celestial blue. Brass chandeliers hung from the ceiling. Near the reader's stand was a small staircase that led to the basement. This may have been a throwback to the days in Spain and Portugal when the reader could move into the cellar if Inquisitors were in the neighborhood.

In 1759, Isaac de Abraham Touro came to Newport from Holland via the West Indies.[56] He was the hazzan at Yeshuat Israel ("Salvation of Israel"). He married Reyna Hays, the sister of Moses Michael Hayes, in 1773. Their union produced three children, Abraham, Judah and Rebecca. With the outbreak of the Revolution, Isaac's sympathies were with Great Britain.[57] After the Revolution, he moved to Kingston, Jamaica, where he died in 1783. His family returned to the United States as part of the Hays family in Boston. In 1802, Judah went to New Orleans on the advice of his uncle's friends. (This was still a French possession.) Judah joined the defense of New Orleans in the War of 1812. He was injured in a British cannon barrage and left for dead but was picked up and cared for by Rezin D. Shepherd. Judah started a business in soap, candles, codfish and other exports from New England. With his profits, he invested in real estate and ships. He purchased a building for $20,000 and allowed a Christian congregation to use it rent free. He distributed money to many charities in New Orleans including the Touro Infirmary. Touro gave $10,000 to complete the Bunker Hill Monument and donated $10,000 to restore the "Old Stone Mill" supposedly built by Norsemen. He built a synagogue in New Orleans at a cost of $40,000. When he died in 1834, he was still unmarried. His estate was valued at $500,000, of which two-thirds was left for non–Jewish charities. He was buried in Newport. To maintain the Touro synagogue in Newport, he left $10,000. He was a convert to Episcopalianism in New Orleans during his stay.

The Revolution was destructive to Newport. It was said there may have been 1,100 Jews in Newport among the 200 families at the start of the Revolution. I find this number untenable. In the hysteria of the fighting, the legislature passed a test oath in June 1776.[58] The committee of safety rounded up 77 people suspected of disloyalty, including four Jews: Isaac Touro (cantor of the synagogue), Isaac Hart, Myer Polock and Moses Michael Hays.[59] Isaac Touro did not sign the oath because he was a Dutch citizen. Hart and Polock said the oath was against their religion. They were all three Tories.[60]

Hays, however, was a patriot.[61] His reasons for not signing the oath were these: (1) He was never a danger to his country, and he challenged his accusers to prove he was; (2) As a Jew, he could not vote with other citizens of Rhode Island, although it was called for in the original charter; (3) The test was not general and was subject to many irregularities; and (4) Neither the Continental Congress nor any of the legislatures of any colony took any notice of the Jews in the war. He further stated that when the Congress or the general assembly made any rule or direction, he would adhere to it.[62] When all the inhabitants of Rhode Island had to take the oath, ordered by the general assembly, then he would take the oath. Hays became an open patriot, and supported the war with money. He did not sign the oath, but Hart and Polock did.[63] Hays left Rhode Island for Boston.

After the incident of the loyalty oath, the British invaded Newport in 1776. Most Jews left, as did most merchants. Shipping came to a standstill, the synagogue was closed, and most merchants left. Over the years, the Jewish merchants left for New York, Philadelphia, Charleston and Savannah.[64] The synagogue was used as a town meeting hall in 1781. Services ended in 1789, and it was closed. The Torah, given by Lopez, was shipped to New York. (The synagogue was later reopened and remained so until 1850.) The Jewish population decreased as the economy decreased. By 1789, there were ten Jewish families with 75 members. By 1820, there were only two Jewish families, and the last Jew left for New York in 1822.[65]

In 1790, the "rump" of the Jewish community sent a congratulatory message to President Washington: "[W]ith a deep sense of gratitude [we] ... behold a government erected by the majesty of the people, a government which to bigotry gives no sanction, to persecution no assistance, but generously affording to all liberty of conscience and immunities of citizenship. Deeming everyone of whatever nation, tongue, or language, equal parts of the great governmental machine."[66] Washington replied, "given to mankind examples of an enlarged and Biblical policy—a policy worthy of all imitation, all possess alike liberty of conscience and immunities of citizenship.

"It is not no more than toleration is spoken of as it were the indulgence of one class of people that another enjoyed the exercise of their inherent natural rights.... The government of the United States gives to bigotry no sanction, to persecution no assistance....

"May the children of the stock of Abraham who dwell in this land continue to merit and enjoy the good will of the other inhabitants."[67]

Ezra Stiles, a Puritan minister in Newport and Portsmouth until chosen to become president of Yale, was a friend of the Jews in Newport as well as to visiting rabbis.[68] He was born to the Reverend Isaac and Keziah Stiles in Connecticut in 1727. His mother's father was also a minister. Stiles entered Yale in 1742 and stayed until 1750. Because of his work among the Indians, he felt they were descendants of the ten lost tribes. He left mission work and became an attorney for two years (1753–1755). Stiles had difficulty accepting the Calvinist concept of predestination and was therefore slow in entering the ministry. Finally, he took the position of minister to the Second Congregational Church in

Newport in 1755, where he stayed for 22 years. He was not ashamed of explaining why he entered the ministry: "partly my Friends and especially my Father's Inclinations and Advice, partly an agreeable town and the Redwood Library, partly the Voice of Providence in the Unanimity of the people, partly my love of Preaching and the prospect of Leisure and Books for pursuing study more than I could expect in the Law."[69]

His interests were Catholic, and he studied astronomy, ecclesiastical history, technology, politics, demography, meteorology, and alchemy and also grew silkworms. His preoccupation with Hebrew started in 1767. Stiles hoped that mastering Hebrew would help him learn from the ancient sources the answers to religious questions that bothered him from his earlier years of theological study. (As a student at Yale, he did not study Hebrew because he had no intention of joining the ministry.) Stiles was able to study the "Montanus Bible," a sort of Rosetta Stone that contained Latin words with Hebrew over them. The words were then used in different texts. He also turned to "Poly Synopsis," completely in Hebrew with comments and criticisms by famous Hebrew scholars. As a result of Ben Franklin's urging, he received a sacred theology doctorate from the University of Edinburgh. Upon receiving this degree, he recognized his lack of knowledge of Hebrew, "[the] easiest of the three learned languages to be acquired." Stiles then turned to Isaac Touro, hazzan of the Newport congregation, for instruction in Hebrew. Within months, he was able to read the Hebrew Psalter, then the Psalms and then Genesis. He also acquired Hebrew grammar texts and then translated Exodus.

He hoped to live long enough to study Mishna, Gemara and the Cabala. He believed the Cabala contained truths revealed to the ancients and might show "glorious lights." By 1768, Stiles had completed the Pentateuch in Hebrew, and two years later he completed the entire Hebrew bible. As an honorary librarian at the Redwood Library, he had access to their collections and could recommend acquisitions. Stiles was anxious to obtain Biblia polyglottis—the Bible in Hebrew, Samaritan, Chaldaic, Syriac, Arabic, Armenian, Coptic, Ortheopic and Greek. (It cost $30 in Boston.) In 1774, the library obtained "Montanus Biblia Sacra Polyglottis" for about $21. Twelve citizens of Newport, including three Jews, contributed to the purchase. Stiles personally acquired the six-volume "Rabbinic Bible," a book completely in Hebrew with comments and criticisms by famous Hebrew scholars. Ben Franklin sent him a copy of the *Introduction to the Rabbinical Literature*. In 1772, he acquired the *Zohar* (a book on Hebrew mysticism).

Because Newport was a wealthy Jewish community, several rabbis came, usually for donations to maintain a Jewish community in Palestine.[70] Stiles used them to continue his studies. He met Moses Ben David, a mystic, who lent Stiles books on the study of the *Zohar*. When Rabbi Raphael Haim Isaac Caregal arrived in 1773, he and Stiles developed a close friendship, and they corresponded until Caregal died. Caregal became a rabbi at 17. He gave sermons at the Newport synagogue which Stiles attended religiously, and Caregal visited Stiles's church. Stiles placed a picture of Caregal in the Yale library. When Rabbi Tobiah Bar Jehudah followed Caregal, Stiles studied Jewish mysticism with him. Rabbi Aaron Bosquila followed Jehudah, but Stiles felt he was a disappointment. Rabbi Samuel Cohen was the last. Stiles had little time with him because of the outbreak of the Revolution.

Throughout his adult life, Stiles was interested in tracing the ten lost tribes, and he believed the Pequots were descendants of the Hebrews. In a letter to J.Z. Holwell in 1767, he discussed the Jews on the Malabar coast, Cochin, Patrea, and the Ganges. The Jews along the Ganges claimed to be of the tribe of Manasseh. Stiles felt Astrakhan had descendants of the lost tribes. He also felt there were Jews of ancient heritage in Samaria and Afghanistan.

Stiles retained a friendship with the Jews and commented in his diaries about the problems forced upon them by the gentiles. He was particularly disturbed when Jews were refused naturalization in Rhode Island. He wrote that Providence made everything work for the mortification of the Jews and to prevent their incorporating into any nation. They would therefore continue as a distinct people because the anger against naturalization of the Jews by the English "forbodes that the Jews will never become incorporated with the people of America anymore than in Europe, Asia and Africa."

Connecticut

Connecticut was very similar to Massachusetts, only it was more English (no Germans, Dutch, French and a few Scotch or Scotch Irish).[71] In the 1790 census, people of English descent made up about 96 percent of the population, and the Scotch represented 3 percent. It was more Puritan (it was illegal to give food or lodging to Catholics, Quakers and heretics—Jews were not mentioned as such[72]). All newcomers had to be accepted by a major part of the community. Looking for fertile land, the Puritans left Massachusetts under the leadership of Thomas Hooker and moved south to settle Hartford, Wethersfield and Windsor in 1636. Connecticut received a charter in 1662, which separated it from Massachusetts. It then absorbed New Haven. The charter called for the maintenance of the Christian faith only. This remained the law until 1818.[73] The preferred form of Christianity was Puritanism. In 1708, Quakers, Anglicans and Baptists were granted qualified tolerance. The Anglicans received full acceptance in 1727. The laws did not permit Jews to organize congregationally until 1843.[74] They were denied religious freedom and political equality. they could not build houses, worship, or own property for a cemetery. This last was particularly onerous because a sanctified burial ground was the first land owned communally.[75] The Jews reacted in two ways to this cold atmosphere. They either came, did business and left, or they converted or married Protestants and raised their children as Christians. (I myself lived in Connecticut, and I remember Grossmans, Schwartzes and Isaacs belonging to the "Congo" church).

Early in Connecticut's history, Jews from New York went up the Connecticut River to peddle goods to the river communities. The earliest mention of a Jew in Hartford was in 1659, when David the Jew was fined 20 shillings for illegal trading. David was from New Amsterdam. In 1660, Hartford town records listed John Allyns, who held ten shillings for the Jews (the reason was not listed). In September 1661, the Jews who lived in John Marsh's house could remain for seven moths only.[76] In 1670, Jacob Lucena of New York was arrested because he was "notorious in his lascivious dalience and wanton carriage and profers to severall women."[77] The court of assistance fined him £20 or a flogging if he could not pay. Two days later, the general court cut the fine to £10, because he was a Jew, with lower moral standards than the Puritans, it was believed. Lucena appealed to Asser Levy of New York, who used his influence to get the reduced fine cut in half.[78]

The next obstacle to the Jews was William Dyre, surveyor general of customs who enforced the navigation acts particularly where Jews were involved. In March 1685, John Carsen took a ship with cargo to New London, but the goods were seized because they weren't English made, and the owner was an alien, a Dutch Jew, who could not trade with English colonies. Carsen claimed he was English by birth and did not mention the Jewish part. The outcome is unknown. This same Dyre was involved in the seizure of goods from Jews in Newport.

By the turn of the century, there were more Jews in Connecticut, and perhaps they felt more secure in their status. Several were litigants in court: Moses Levy and Isaac de Medina (Hartford) in 1723; Jacob Franks, Abraham Pinto and Asser Levy (son) (Stratford) in 1724; Isaac Jacobs in 1725 (Branford); and Jacob Franks again in 1750. Judah Hays of New York was a disputant in Fairfield in 1747 and 1749. Isaac Solomons of Middletown petitioned the court related to a duty on goods imported from London.[79] Samuel De Lucena lived in Norwalk when he petitioned the general assembly for special privileges in the manufacture of castile soap. There is no record of whether he actually went into production.[80]

Toward the middle of the eighteenth century, Jews trickled into Connecticut. Michael Judah had lived in Norwalk since 1746. He married a Christian woman, and his son, David, served in Captain Gregory's company of the Connecticut line.[81] While brought up as a Jew, he practiced Christianity in later life. An Abraham Pinto lived in Stratford and was probably related to the Pintos of New Haven. An Abraham Pinto from New Haven was in the Tenth Company, Seventh Regiment of the Connecticut line starting in 1775. His brother, William Pinto, was a volunteer in 1779 and 1781. Abraham and Solomon Pinto were wounded when the British attacked New Haven on July 6 and 7, 1779. Solomon was an ensign (an army officer below lieutenant) in Captain Baldwin's company of the Second Regiment. He was one of the founders of the Society of the Cincinnati in Connecticut.[82] The Pinto brothers renounced their Judaism and all formal religion. The Pintos who settled in New Haven in the 1750s were sons of Jacob and grandsons of Abraham of Stratford. In 1772, a family of Jews settled in New Haven. They had traveled from Venice to St. Eustatius in the West Indies and then to New Haven. there were three brothers, an old mother, a widow and her children—perhaps eight to ten Jews and six or eight slaves.[83] The American Revolution caused a large influx of Jews, temporarily, to Connecticut. The occupation of New York and Long Island resulted in several Jewish patriotic families moving to Fairfield county. Isaac Seixas and Gershon Mendes Seixas (son) (hazzan) moved to Stratford.[84] Other families settled in Stamford, Norwalk, Wilton and Danbury. When Newport was occupied by the British, several Jewish families moved to the northern shore of Long Island Sound east of the Connecticut River.

Tory Governor Tryon, ousted from Connecticut, became General Tryon in the British army. He and Benedict Arnold raided towns along the sound, bringing devastation in July 1779. Samson Mears, Moses Isaacs, Michael Judah, Samuel Israel, Solomon Simson and the Myers brothers were financially crippled by the raids, and some moved into the interior of Connecticut.[85] When hostilities ended, most Jews returned to New York and Newport. It would be 60 years before any Jewish community life existed in Connecticut. Those Jews who remained were integrated into the larger community and disappeared as Jews. After the Revolution, none of Connecticut's "acts of toleration" gave religious or political equality to the Jews. Finally in 1818, the First Constitutional Convention met in Hartford and disestablished the Congregational Church. Religious freedom was granted to all Protestants. Later, this freedom was granted to all Christians. It took several decades before there were enough Jews to petition for religious equality.[86]

Northern New England

Of the three states that make up northern New England, only New Hampshire was one of the original 13 colonies at the outbreak of the Revolution. The attitude of the people toward the Jews was quite cold. Discriminatory wording against the Jews remained in the New Hampshire constitution until 1876.

Canada

Canada was not one of the 13 colonies. However, the Puritans of new England looked north longingly. They saw the vast wilderness as a source of furs under the control of Catholics, who had to be chased out or destroyed. Shortly after the outbreak of the Revolution, an attempt by New Englanders was made to make this region the fourteenth state, but it was severely defeated with a large loss of life. (See *Medicine and the American Revolution* by Oscar Reiss.)

The British took Canada as its prize for fighting and winning the French and Indian War, and parts of Canada were taken by the English even before the Seven Years War. The Hudson Bay area was ceded to England in the Treaty of Utrecht in 1713.[87] The Hudson Bay Company had one Jewish employee, Fernande Jacobs, but he converted. The British occupied Halifax, Nova Scotia, in 1749. It grew rapidly, and businessmen came from England and the colonies. Among them were Israel Abrahams, Nathan Nathans, Naphthali Hart, Jr., and a Levy. A Jewish cemetery was established in 1750.[88] The Halifax Jewish community shrank and disappeared by 1760.

The real influx of Jews came with and after the Seven Years War. No Jews were permitted in French Canada, France, or France's West Indian colonies by the monarch's decree. However, in Bordeau, David Gradis and family carried on an active trade with New France. His family was Portuguese, but they had lived in France for a century. Overtly, they were Catholics, but they were secret Jews. Jewish purveyors came with the British armies from New York, Albany, Philadelphia, and London. Among the earliest Jews to settle were Commissary Aaron Hart of London, and Lazarus David Hart was among the officers of General Amherst's invading army[89] He was attached to General Haldimand's infantry and was stationed at Three Rivers. At the war's end, Aaron remained in Canada, bought large tracts of land, and became seigneur of Becancour. David settled in Montreal, where, in the decade after the fall of Quebec, several Jewish merchants also settled.

Early records describe Andrew Hays, David Salisbury Franks, Jacob de Maurera, Elias Seixas, Levi Solomons, Uriah Judah, Fernandez de Fonseca and others. Jewish merchants in Montreal made up 10 percent of all businessmen in that city. They must have brought families, because they formed the Shearith Israel Congregation in 1768. Seven years later, Lazarus David bought land for a cemetery. In 1777, a synagogue was built on the cemetery land.[90] It was the third Jewish temple built in North America. The synagogue was supported by 25 Jewish families, who were merchants and fur traders. The synagogue was not able to acquire a hazzan, mohel or shohet after Hazzan de Lara left in 1810.[91]

The first occupant of the cemetery was Lazarus David. His son, David David, was one of the founders of the Bank of Montreal. Ezekiel Hart, son of Aaron, was elected to the legislature from Three Rivers in 1807. (Aaron was the richest Jew in Canada.) He took the oath of office with his head covered. The house objected and declared his seat vacant, and his election was nullified. He was again elected over three other candidates. Hart was not permitted to take his seat, and a bill was passed to disqualify Jews from the assembly. The Governor General, Sir James H. Craig, dissolved the house and castigated its members. It was not until 1831 that all such prohibitions ended.

Henry Joseph, born in England, was advised by his uncle, Aaron Hart, to come to Canada. He settled in Berthier, a distributing point opposite Fort William Henry at the mouth of the Richehieu River. Joseph extended his business east and west and was the first resident to charter Canadian ships for trade with England. He was lucky to find a Jewish wife, Rachel Solomons, from an early Montreal family. Joseph fought in the English ranks in the War of 1812.

At the outbreak of the American Revolution, Canada had a population of perhaps 110,000. Of these, 50 were Jews. Between the Revolution and the War of 1812 (called the Second War of Independence) 40,000 more people came to Canada. These included disbanded British troops, refugees, Loyalists and German Mennonites. There were few Jews in this group.

III

Jews in the South

Charles I, the "headless king," granted to Cecelius Calvert, Lord Baltimore, a charter for land in America for persecuted Catholics in 1632. Calvert had recently converted to Roman Catholicism.[1] Calvert's charter listed levels of citizenship. Any British subject who transported himself to Maryland became a free man. If he acquired land he was a freeholder. A non–Englishman was an alien, and by English common law he could not hold land, seek public office or exercise civil rights. His status could be improved by naturalization via a special act of the provincial assembly or by denization by the lord proprietor. A Jew who lived in Maryland and who did not come from Britain was an alien. To be naturalized, one had to take the sacrament. Therefore, no Jews were naturalized. One could receive denization and thereby get the privileges of domicile, freedom of importation and protection against arbitrary taxation. If a Jew was born in England or lived there a long time before coming to Maryland, he had some civil rights, but they could be revoked by the king of the lord proprietor.

Calvert invested a good portion of his fortune in the enterprise expecting a great influx of Catholics, who, however, were reticent about leaving England. The king they had was better than one they might get. The proprietor was losing money and opened the colony to Protestants. Before long, the Protestants were present in greater numbers than Catholics. By the end of the century, Catholics represented one tenth of the population, and the Protestant majority could pass laws against Catholics. In 1637, provincial legislation, which failed to pass, stated that all inhabitants who were Christian would enjoy all the rights of an English citizen. Two years later, this ruling was enacted. Part of the new legislation divested Jews of civil rights unless conferred by a specific grant. All inhabitants 18 years or older had to take an oath of allegiance upon their faith as a Christian. Noncompliance with this order led to jail and a second offense meant banishment. Later, the "faith of a Christian" stipulation was removed.

Maryland

From its beginnings until well into the nineteenth century, Maryland's laws were not receptive to Jews. However, early in the state's history, Matheas Sousa, probably a Jew, flourished. In 1641, he joined a group who planned to trade with the Susquehannock Indians, and he may have been a member of the provincial assembly. In 1648, the proprietor directed the lieutenant governor not to trouble anyone professing a belief in Jesus. This was codified as the Toleration Act of 1649. The law was passed to protect the Catholics, who were already a minority, and not to antagonize the Protestants.[2] In addition to the protection of all Christians, it imposed the death sentence on anyone who denied the divinity of Jesus.[3] This last ruling was never carried out, however.

At this point, Jacob Lumbrozo entered the story. Jacob was a Marrano from Portugal who lived in Holland. He migrated to Maryland, where he became a landowner, merchant, physician and surgeon. On February 23, 1658, Lumbrozo "uttered words of blasphemy against our Blessed Saviour Jesus Christ." The Maryland provincial court records described "Jacob Lumbrozo, late of Lisbone, Portugal, known as ye Jew doctor, committed for blasphemy."[4] In the trial, the doctor was quoted as saying "that His disciples stole him away" (after Jesus' death and burial), "that noe man ever did such miracles as he ... such works may be done by necromancy, or sorcery.... And this deponent replied to the said Lumbrozo that ... he tooke Christ to be a necromancer.... Lumbrozo didn't answer, he just smiled."[5] The prisoner was sentenced to death, but he was freed on March 3, 1658. This may have been a result of a general amnesty from London upon the accession of Cromwell, or perhaps he converted, or his services were needed in the infant colony as a physician and surgeon (of note, an antiblasphemy law remained in Maryland's code books until the 1920s).

Lumbrozo received letters of denization in 1663, and in 1665 he received a commission to trade with the Indians. With his letters of denization, he demanded land for himself and his fiancée, Elizabeth, who arrived in the colony in 1662. There is no hard evidence that she was Jewish. She came from England, and they were married in Maryland.

In August 1664, Lumbrozo acquired 200 acres of land: 150 acres secured by transfer and 50 more for bringing Jeremy Taylor to Maryland, probably as an indentured servant. Lumbrozo died on May 3, 1666. His wife was his heir; there were no children. His will ordered her to send 4,000 pounds of good tobacco plus casks to his sister Rebecca, living in Holland, two years after his death. Another 2,000 pounds were to be sent to her two years after the first. His land along Nangemy Creek went to his friend, Edward Richardson. If Elizabeth refused to administer his will, the plantation was to be sold. Elizabeth would receive her legal one-third. The rest would go to his sister, Rebecca.

In the anti–Catholic period that followed the Glorious Revolution of 1689, Lord Baltimore lost his proprietorship, and Catholics were deprived of many political rights. The fourth Lord Baltimore was Anglican, and the proprietorship was returned to him. Catholics lost the vote. Under his proprietorship, Jews had no civil rights; they were denied freedom of residence, and they could be put to death for openly confessing their Jewish religion. In 1715, a law stated that anyone who denied Jesus Christ or the trinity was fined on the first offense, and the person's tongue was burned. The second offense led to a fine, and the person's hand was burned. The third offense led to burning at the stake. An act of 1723 further enforced the act of 1715. These laws remained unchanged until 1819. Obviously, Maryland laws were unfriendly to Jews, and for the most part they avoided the colony. A Jew came, traded, and then left. However, between 1660 and 1692, then the proprietor was overthrown, some Jewish-sounding names appeared on records, but there is no proof they were actually Jews. In 1692, Maryland became a Crown Colony with an established church (Anglican) supported by general taxation. As the population grew, cities grew also, and less discriminatory laws were passed. Annapolis in 1708 gave suffrage to anyone with a freehold or an estate worth £20 sterling.

With the American Revolution, Maryland became a state rather than a Crown Colony. A new constitution was written in 1776, and the Anglican church was disestablished. The new constitution gave all Christians, except Quakers, equal protection under the law (Article 33).[6] The Bill of Rights (Article 35)[7] stated that one had to be Christian to hold office. Article 36 allowed Quakers, Mennonites and Dunkards to refrain from taking an oath. Under the constitution, the legislature could pass a tax to support Christian churches. An oath of office could be administered only after an applicant declared his belief in the Christian religion. Office holders could impose penalties on those expressing disbelief in the trinity. There were penalties for working on Sunday. Jews could not be jurors or witnesses. The marriage of Jews by their religious leaders was not clearly licensed.

The new constitution called for equality of representation from each county. The house of delegates received four members from each county and two each from Baltimore and Annapolis. The senate was elected by the electoral college and was made up of two members from each county and one each from Baltimore and Annapolis. The governor and executive council were elected by both houses. The constitution was thus unfair to the cities. Baltimore's population grew until it was equal to that of eight agricultural counties, but the number of delegates remained the same. All the while, Jews remained disenfranchised.

In 1791, Solomon Etting, a Jew, came to Baltimore from York, Pennsylvania.[8] He petitioned the legislature in 1797, claiming he was deprived of citizenship. Etting wanted Jews to be able to hold office without having to declare their belief in the Christian religion. Nothing was done, however, and he sent a repeat petition five years later, in which his brother, Reuben, joined him. In 1798, when war with France seemed imminent, Reuben joined the Independent Baltimore Blues and was elected captain. Reuben Etting was appointed U.S. marshal for Maryland by President Jefferson, but he could not hold a state office or vote. In 1802, and again in 1804, a franchise bill for Jews was entered and defeated.

A bill initially written by William Pinkney was championed by Thomas Kennedy of Washington County and was introduced in 1818.[9] The author stated that the "Constitution of the United States has guaranteed to every American Citizen the right of worshipping God in the manner he deems most acceptable to him, and this right is violated whenever the citizen is made to feel the consequences of his opinion, either by direct bodily inflictions or by disqualifications." Kennedy originally came from Scotland to Washington County. It is likely that he had never met a Jew, and there were no Jews in his county. However, he believed in the justice of the bill. In 1819, after a speech by Kennedy, the punishment for blasphemy (passed in 1715 and again in 1723) was stricken from the code of Maryland.[10] The penalties had called for branding the forehead, boring a hole in the tongue, and hanging. His support of the bill for Jewish enfranchisement probably led to his defeat for re-election. However, after one year, he was re-elected. The "Jew bill" was introduced and defeated several times until it was passed after two readings in 1825 and 1826. It enfranchised the Jews and gave them the rights enjoyed by others in the state. It further stated that anyone who was elected to office or was a witness or juror in a court case had to believe in God and a future state after death where he would receive his reward or punishment for his previous life. It passed 26 to 25, with 80 abstentions. The number of abstentions suggests that the law was still a very "hot potato." After the "Jew bill" was passed, Jacob I. Cohen and Solomon Etting were elected members of the Baltimore city council.

The Jewish population of Maryland, along with the general population, began to grow. Baltimore was laid out in 1729 and was a port city between Philadelphia and Charleston. (Richmond was still very small.) Baltimore had a population of 5,934 by 1775. This number equaled the population of Lancaster, Pennsylvania, from where seven Jewish members of the congregation migrated. The Revolution stimulated the growth of Baltimore, because the British failed to blockade the port, and Jews and Gentiles moved down from Philadelphia. In the 1770s, five Jewish families (Levy, Mordecai, Lyons, Hart and Pollock) moved to Baltimore.

Benjamin Levy opened a store in Baltimore after his arrival from Philadelphia. He was an Indian trader who had lost his caravan of trade goods to plunder by Indians. After this loss, he moved to Baltimore for a new start. His son, Nathan, fought under Lafayette in Virginia. Elias Pollock enlisted in 1778 and was wounded and taken prisoner at the battle of Camden, South Carolina. The Solomons were brothers of Mrs. Etting. They moved to Baltimore after the Revolution.

Isaac Abrahams, from Philadelphia, was considered the religious head of the small group of Jews in Baltimore. The Jewish community in Baltimore was not stable because Jews moved in and out of the city. Some returned to Philadelphia, and others moved south and to the West Indies. Jews married cousins because choices were limited, and a fair number converted. In the 1790 census, there were six Jewish families in a population of 13,502. In 1800, there were 13. In Baltimore, Jews were boardinghouse keepers, merchants, black-ball makers (a black ball was used by shoemakers to blacken the leather), ironmongers, distillers, grocers, tobacco workers, brokers and tobacconists.[11] Jacob Cohen started a bank, which soon gained a national reputation.[12]

A Simon Levy from Maryland was in the first graduating class at West Point.[13] One of two cadets in the class, he was commissioned in 1802. Levy had an army record prior to his appointment, having served between 1793 and 1801. He was a sergeant in the battle of Maumee Rapids (1794). The problem with Simon Levy was that his lineage was unknown. The family of Benjamin Levy had no mention of a son named Simon. A Levy Andrew Levy was listed in the Baltimore directory between 1800 and 1801. The family lived in Hagerstown before Baltimore and before that in Lancaster. This Levy had a son, Simeon, who was circumcised in 1774 in Lancaster. Certainly of more significance in Jewish history in Maryland was Uriah Philips Levy, the first commodore in the United States Navy.[14] His father, Michael, sold watches and clocks in Baltimore. He married Rachel Phillips from Philadelphia. That marriage produced the commodore.

Virginia

Virginia, the first English colony on the eastern seaboard, was not as hostile to Jews as Maryland. It had an established church which was supported by taxes on all residents, and citizens had to attend services. Civil rights were largely restricted to Anglicans. The problem for Jews was the absence of large cities, a middle class and a merchant group. The state was largely a plantation society built by a cavalier class.[15] The planters were often second sons of the noble or rich families who had been sent away to make their fortunes. There were two divisions in Virginia—the planters and those who worked for them. The planters dealt directly with merchants in England,[16] and they did not need middlemen in Virginia. The earliest Jew in the colony was Elias Legardo, 38, who arrived on the *Abigail* in 1621.[17] In 1634, Joseph Mosse, 34, and Rebecca Isache (36) arrived on the *Elizabeth*. (There is no proof that the latter two were Jews.) How they made a living is unknown. In 1648, John Levy received 200 acres of land. (This represented four adults. Perhaps Levy brought in indentured servants.) In mid-century, Alberno Lupo from Portugal and Amaso de Tores, a Spanish Jew, were listed in records. Selvedo and Manuel Rodriguez were inhabitants of Lancaster County (Virginia) in 1652. At a court in Yorke County on June 24, 1658, Mrs. Elizabeth Jones sued "Seign'r" Moses Nehemiah.[18] Moses brought £16 in gold and "good pieces of eight" which were due the plaintiff. The court decided that this was good pay and that he was discharged from his debt. The defendant had to pay court costs, because he had earlier refused to pay Mrs. Jones.

Although Nehemiah was an inhabitant and was protected by law, he could not be naturalized, because the oath called for a belief in Jesus, the son of God.[19] For the same reason, Jews could not testify in court. If a Jew denied the trinity within earshot of others, his rights could be removed, and he could be sent to prison. Virginia was so inhospitable to Jews that no Jew[20] sought denization or naturalization before the Revolution.

In the eighteenth century, Virginia's society was more heterogeneous, and towns developed and grew. Jews began to trickle in despite the persistence on the code books of laws against Jews and Protestant dissenters. Enoch Lyon,[21] a Jew, was an agent of Lopez of Newport, Rhode Island. The Simon-Bush-Gratz group developed large business interests in the colony. Simon bought furs from the Shenandoah Indians. He also acted as an agent for Governor Dunsmore in Dunsmore's War in 1774. Simon was also purveyor to British prisoners of war kept in Virginia during the Revolution. Gratz supplied privateers and had a share in several of the ships he supplied. Moses Myers was the financial agent of the French and Batavian (Dutch) republics in Norfolk, Virginia.[22] He also represented Thomas Jefferson as well as the Nicholas and other Virginia families. He was a major in the militia and president of the common council (city council).

The group represented by Myers outfitted an expedition to be led by George Rogers Clark to go to the Detroit area during the Revolution, but the expedition was aborted. The cost was eventually paid back in Virginia tobacco. Jacob Cohen and Isaiah Isaacs, with Jacob Mordecai as a junior partner, bought land in the Dismal Swamp. They also purchased the "Bird in the Hand," a tavern. Cohen and Isaacs's company received slaves in payment for debts. They also owned the "Jew store" in Richmond, which was very lucrative.

The group also hired Daniel Boone to scout and buy land for them in the Kentucky county of Virginia. They owned a lead mine valued at £32,000. Isaacs owned land in several Virginia counties. He was elected to the Richmond city council and helped purchase the first Jewish cemetery in Richmond. At the time of his death, he owned four slave families, who were freed in his will. The slaves that the company received in payment for debts were similarly freed.

Richmond had one[23] Jewish family before the Revolution. By the mid–1780s there were six, and in 1789 there were about 30 families, enough to form a congregation: Beth Shalome (House of Peace).[24] Membership was permitted only to free men. To join, a free man had to be over 21 and a resident for more than three months. Richmond at this time had 420 free, white, taxable families. There were ten Jewish households, nine of which had slaves.

Apparently the ability to make a living was not good, because many Jews were transients. They stayed in Richmond or other towns for a while and then moved on to Charleston, Baltimore, Philadelphia or New York. The Jews had to compete with a plantation economy. Slaves were taught skills to satisfy most of the needs of the inhabitants. Jews could serve as watchmakers, doctors, surgeons, bankers, importers and exporters. One Jewish family in Petersburg left for Charleston because they wanted their children to be brought up in a Jewish atmosphere.[25] In a letter, the wife said there were ten or twelve Jews in town. The shohet bought nonkosher meat. The community lacked a Torah as well as prayer shawls and "fringes," and Jewish shops were open on the Sabbath.

The Revolution brought a new constitution to the state. Thomas Jefferson backed an immigration and naturalization bill, particularly to bring in Jews in 1776.[26] The bill was never allowed to come to a vote, however. The fight for religious freedom was presented by Madison, who spoke for Jefferson, who was in Europe at the time.[27] Madison called for liberty of worship: "All men are equally entitled to the free exercise of religion according to the dictates of his conscience." In 1779, Virginia stopped the taxation that supported the Episcopal church. The fight between Patrick Henry to tax the residents to support all Christian churches and Madison to separate the church from the state is more completely covered in Chapter V, on anti–Semitism. In 1786, Madison,[28] Jefferson and George Mason were able to remove all religious discrimination from the state constitution.

After the middle of the eighteenth century, and particularly after the Revolution, there was a thin stream of Jews into Virginia. Enoch Lyon[29] came to Virginia as an agent for Lopez of Newport. Simon, Bush and Gratz of Philadelphia joined gentiles in Richmond in business, for whom the Jews handled credits. Simon and Campbell advanced money to repair Fort Pitt and build Fort Fincastle. They were active in land speculation in the West. While Richmond[30] contained the largest number of Jews, others were living in Amherst City, Cumberland County and Warwick County. Some Jews settled near the Ohio River. The Gratz family, in conjunction with several Virginians, speculated on 321,000 acres in Fayette and Montgomery counties. Despite their distribution, there were about 24 Jews in all of Virginia in the 1780s (outside of Richmond).

The Jews in Richmond became wealthy and subscribed to charitable institutions. The firm of Cohen and Isaacs helped found the Academy of Arts and Sciences. Joseph Darmstadt, Samuel Myers, Joseph Marx, S. Jacobs and B. Brand were early contributors to the Amicable Society to help strangers in their midst. Darmstadt[31] had an interesting history. He was drafted into the Hessian army that served with Great Britain in the Revolution. At war's end he decided to remain in Richmond. Most farmers around Richmond were German. He could converse with them and soon became a middleman between the farmers and the city dwellers. He spread his business beyond Richmond and became fairly wealthy.

In 1790 or 1791,[32] 29 organizers formed congregation Beth Shalome in Richmond. (The exact date is questionable, because the congregation joined other Jewish groups in saluting Washington, the new president, in 1790. This suggests the presence of a congregation before 1791.) Most organizers were Ashkenazi, but worship was according to Sephardic rituals. The congregation rented the first floor or a three-story building for their synagogue. They next occupied a small brick building. Finally, land was purchased and a synagogue was built. Isaiah Isaacs donated land for a cemetery in 1791. This was enclosed by a granite wall ad was used until 1816. The congregation's numbers decreased over time due to deaths and movement away from Richmond. Well into the nineteenth century, the synagogue was finally sold to a congregation named after Sir Moses Montefiore of England, a wealthy Jewish philanthropist.

North Carolina

The earliest history of North Carolina[33] started with the Ralph Lane colony in 1585 at the north end of Roanoke Island. Lane's group consisted of 107 men including English, Irish, Welsh, German, Dutch and one Jew from Prague. They remained on the island for one year busily fighting Indians. Sir Francis Drake, who attacked Spanish galleons in the Caribbean for their wealth, stopped at Roanoke Island on the way home to England. He picked up the 97 survivors and brought them back to Great Britain.

The real history of North Carolina started as a part of South Carolina. Charles II[34] granted to eight courtiers in 1663 land south of Virginia. Among the recipients were Berkeley, Carteret and Lord Ashley Cooper, Earl of Shaftesbury. They expected great wealth if they could induce people to settle there. In the "Declaration and Proposealls," August 25, 1665, they offered freedom of conscience in all religious and spiritual things. John Locke was hired to write a constitution. According to the document, any seven or more persons agreeing in any religion would constitute a church or profession. Sir John Yeamans was appointed governor in 1665. He brought immigrants from Barbados to settle the new colony. Barbados had a large Jewish population, and perhaps some Jews came with other Barbadans. In 1671, Yeamans brought more settlers from other West Indian islands.

While Jews had freedom of conscience, they could not vote or hold office. The proprietors' instructions to the governor[35] granted liberty of conscience so long as people behaved "peaceably and quietly and not using this Liberty to Lycentiousness to the Civill Injury or outward disturbance of others." The fundamental constitution proclaimed freedom of worship. The leaders wanted "Civil pease [peace] to be maintained amidst the diversity of opinions," and "heathens, Jews and other dissenters from the purity of Christian Religion may not be scared and kept at a distance." It was their hope that by showing these people the benefits of true Christianity they would "be won over to embrace and unfeignedly receive the truth." Any group forming a church would give it a name to distinguish it from others. Members of this church would not be disturbed in orderly worship services. In their church they were not to speak "irreverently or seditiously of the government, governors or State Matters."

Carolina became a royal province in 1729 and was divided into North and South. North Carolina was not important commercially and was not liberal politically. In the 1790 census[36] there were many Jewish names and Biblical first names in North Carolina. One comes across Goodman, Hays, Hendricks, Philips, Jacobs and Simpson. First names like Sarah, Lazarus and Solomon were included. There was an Elias Coen in Guilford County, Simon Cohon in Edgecombe County, Levi Cone in Martin County and Isaac Cowen in Rowan County. Despite these names and numbers, there was only one definite Jew in North Carolina in 1790. Perhaps some of the others had a Jewish heritage with conversion in the past. There was also one Jew[37] in pre–Revolutionary North Carolina. He may have been the same one.

There may have been more Jews[38] in North Carolina on the Cape Fear River between 1664 and 1667. Here there were Barbadans with some Jews among them. There may also have been Jews in 1703, because a formal protest was made about Jews, strangers, sailors, servants, Negroes and others who were not qualified to vote but had been allowed to cast ballots. In 1740, in Perquemans County, a will was witnessed by Aaron Moses, perhaps a Jew. In 1759, a Mr. Lavey was described as a Jew. He was called to testify in court in 1784.[39] A storekeeper named Haryon accused a Mr. Clay, a member of the legislature, of stealing money from his counter. Lavey testified that Mr. Haryon was a rogue who would not tell the truth. The outcome of the case is unknown.

Jacob Mordecai[40] was the son of Moses Mordecai and Elizabeth Whitlock (she was probably a gentile). Jacob married Judith Myers of New York and chose Judaism as his religion. (However, according to Jewish tradition, religion was passed on through the maternal side because in periods of pogroms, massacres and rape, one could be assured only of his mother.) He opened the Female Academy in Warrenton, North Carolina, at the turn of the century. It became a successful finishing school chosen by Christian families in Warrenton and beyond.

North Carolina established the Anglican church[41] early in its history. In the constitution of the state written in 1776, the Church of England was the established church, and only its members could hold public office. However, freedom of religion was granted to all: "[A]ll men have a natural and inalienable right to worship Almighty God according to the dictates of their own conscience." The constitution prevented all but Protestants from holding office in the state (section 32). Despite this prohibition, Jacob Henry[42] of Carteret County served a term in the house of commons. In 1808, he was reelected, but his seat was challenged, because he could not accept the New Testament. Henry gave an impassioned speech in the house, however, and he was permitted to hold his seat. The Roman Catholics[43] in the house came to his defense. They believed that if Henry were unseated, they would be next. The house stretched the law for Henry. The constitution stated that non–Protestants could not hold "an office in a civil department." The house members decided this was a legislative office not covered by the prohibition. This judgment was later stretched to include the Roman Catholics. The restrictions against the Jews lasted beyond the Civil War.[44] Finally, in 1868 North Carolina, under the control of African Americans and Republicans from the north, wrote a new constitution, which no longer said that "persons denying Christ" were ineligible for public office.

South Carolina

The charter for the Carolinas to the eight courtiers and John Locke's constitution were discussed earlier. John Locke's constitution of 1669 was of great importance to the freedom of the Jews. Equally important to Americans were his beliefs, which had considerable influence on Thomas Jefferson. Before they called on Locke, the proprietors[45] issued a declaration on August 25, 1665. Article 5 stated, "We will grante in as ample manr as ye Undertakers shall desire freedomes and libertye of contience in all religious or sperrituall things to be kept inviolable with them, we having power in or [our] Charter soe to doe." Locke[46] was called upon to write a constitution in 1669. In Article 97, he stated, "But since the natives of that place who will be concerned in our plantation are utterly strangers to Christianity, whose idolatry, ignorance and mistake gives us no right to expel or use them ill and those who remove from other parts to plant there will unavoidably be of a different opinion concerning matters of religion, the liberty of which they will expect to have allowed them—and also that Jews, heathens and other dissenters from the purity of Christian religion may not be feared and kept at a distance from it ... but, by having an opportunity of acquainting themselves with the truth and reasonableness of its doctrines ... be won over to embrace and unfeignedly receive the truth."[47]

"No person whatever shall disturb, molest or persecute another for his speculative opinions in religion, or his way of worship." Locke[48] write 16 articles about religion. The Church of England was the established church and was to be supported by general taxes. The constitution required a man to have a religion but not a specific religion. At age 17, a man had to associate himself with a religion. Abusive language against any religion was forbidden, because this prevented conversion to Christianity. The fundamentals[49] of the constitution further state that "no one could live here who doesn't believe in God." Parliament (of the colony) was to be involved in the building of churches, and ministers of the Church of England would be supported by parliament. Any seven men professing a religion and acknowledging god would be considered a church. "God is to be worshipped publicly. [It must be remembered that at this time, Jews could only pray privately.] Any man called to bear witness will tell the truth. Every church will show how they witness the truth; i.e. laying hands on or kissing the Bible; holding up the hand; or any other sensible way. No one is to revile another's religion. This will hinder their conversion to the right truth. No one was to molest another for his speculations in religion or on his way to worship."

It should be remembered that Locke was not simply hired to write a constitution and was paid for it. Rather, Locke was made chief secretary of the company of the Lords Proprietors through his friendship with Ashley, the Earl of Shaftesbury.[50] He was probably an officer of the group and would get a percent of the income derived from the charter. It is hard to believe that someone living in England at the time could be so liberal. England at this time had restored the monarchy after Cromwell's death. It was during Cromwell's reign that Jews were permitted to return to England. Many in high places wanted Charles II to deport the Jews. Those Jews who were admitted congregated mostly in London, and they controlled a large part of national and international trade to the detriment of many Anglican traders. It is believed that fear of deportation may have caused some Jews from Barbados to join the group that Governor Yeamans transported from Barbados to Carolina.

The Lords Proprietors were willing to accept all comers, except papists. They were amenable to wild schemes that would bring settlers. Sir Robert Montgomery,[51] a Scottish lord, dreamed of an empire south of the Carolinas (land that would later become Georgia). In 1717, he published *A Discourse Concerning the Design'd Establishment of a New Colony to the South of Carolina In the Most Delightful Country of the Universe.* This country he called Azilia. The proprietors were happy to have Scottish settlers as buffers against the Spanish in Florida and the French in Louisiana, so they gave Montgomery permission to settle Azilia. Montgomery, to attract immigrants, described odoriferous plants that were always green: orange, lemon, apple, pear, plum, peaches and apricot trees. Trees would bear fruit three years after planting the stone. Of course, nothing came of Montgomery's scheme. Another Scot, Sir Alexander Cumming, planned to settle 300,000 Jews on Cherokee tribal lands in South Carolina, but one wonders where he hoped to find so many Jews.

Instead Jews wandered into South Carolina slowly.[52] The first Jew arrived in 1695, 15 years after the founding of Charleston. He was an interpreter for the governor in questioning four Indians captured from Florida. They and he spoke Spanish, so he must have been Sephardic. Simon Valentine[53] was the first Jew who owned land in South Carolina. He came to Charleston in 1696. In 1697, a law was passed giving all P rotestants[54] freedom of conscience, and it made aliens free men of the province with rights equal to Englishmen if they took the oath: "Know ye that Simon Valentine, merchant: an alien of ye Jewish Nation borne out of the Crown of England hath taken his oath of allegiance to our Sovereign Lord William ye Third ... and is full ... Qualified and Capacitated to have, use and Enjoy all the rights, Privileges, Powers and Immunityes Given ... any Alien then Inhabitant of South Carolina May 26, 1697."

At the time of passage of the law, four Jews resided in the province: Valentine, Jacob Mendes, an Avila (no first name) and a fourth whose name was not listed. They were required to apply to the governor within three months of the law's passage. When naturalized, they swore allegiance to the king. There were 64 men in the first group that sought naturalization. (Obviously not all were Jews. It should be remembered that South Carolina became a haven for French Protestants.) After naturalization, the Jews felt they had the right to vote, and they voted in the assembly election in 1703. This created an uproar against Jews, strangers, sailors, servants, Negroes and almost every Frenchman whose votes were counted. In 1704, new rules for voting and naturalization were declared. Each candidate for naturalization swore an oath of allegiance to Queen Anne on the holy evangelists or otherwise according to his profession. The loophole of "otherwise" gave an exception to Jews. Naturalized subjects could not be elected to the assembly. To vote, a man had to be 21,, own 50 acres of land or £10 sterling and to have lived in the precinct for three months. A law in 1721 stated that every free white man who professed the Christian religion could vote after one year's residence and could seek public office. By law, the Jews were disenfranchised, but they continued to vote. A second law passed in 1759[55] repeated the conditions of the law of 1721 and made disenfranchisement more effective.

Jews slowly came to Charleston from Barbados, New York, London and France. In 1715, Mordecai Nathan and Simon Valentine[56] were shipping kosher beef out of Charleston. Between 1715 and 1730, the small group of Jews became even smaller as several left for greener pastures. In the 1730s, Jews started to return to Charleston. There were ten Jewish families at that time, among about 7,000 people in Charleston. Several ships with Jews, sponsored by rich Jews in London, came to Charleston.[57] In 1741, most of the Jews of Georgia migrated to South Carolina because of Georgia's illiberal policies. Moses Lindo arrived in 1756 to work with indigo. He became so adept that he was appointed inspector general of indigo drugs and dyes. Indigo was one of the chief products of the colony and was used to make blue dye. Lindo was able to donate some money to the Rhode Island College (later Brown University). As a result, Jews would be admitted. They could practice their religion and were not forced to attend Christian services.

In 1750, the Jews started a congregation called Kaal Kodesh Beth Elohim[58] (Holy Congregation, the House of the Lord). Initially they occupied a small wooden building on Union Street.[59] Isaac Da Costa was the "minister." Rites were Sephardic although the greater number were Ashkenazi. In 1764, land was purchased from Da Costa for a cemetery. The first synagogue was erected between 1792 and 1794 at a cost of $20,000 and supported by 300 Jews. By the turn of the century, Charleston had the largest number of Jews of any city in the United States. They represented 5 percent of the white population of the city. In 1820,[60] there were 700 Jews in Charleston. New York City had 550 Jews, or one-half of 1 percent of the population. The rich Jews[61] were accepted by Charleston society and were members of country clubs and yacht clubs. Jews participated actively in the economic life of the colony. Some Sephardic Jews[62] intermarried with the larger gentile community and were lost to the Jews. In 1802, the Jews organized an orphanage. Instead of the children living in one building, they were sent to private families to be raised and cared for. In 1824, Charleston's Jews developed Reformed Judaism.

At the time of the Revolution, Charleston was a polyglot city with nine ethnic European[63] groups. There were Englishmen, French, Scots, Irish, Germans, Welsh and Jews. Second to the English, the French were the largest group. These were Huguenots (Protestants) who fled France's anti–Protestant laws (revocation of the Edict of Nantes). They were joined by French-speaking Swiss and Acadians. Into this mix came Francis Salvador,[64] whose family came from Iberia to Holland to England. Their original name was Jessurum Rodriguez. Francis Salvador was the grandfather of the Francis who came to South Carolina. He was involved in sending poor Jews to Georgia. His son Joseph was a wealthy merchant in England. Joseph was president of the Portuguese synagogue in London and the first Jewish director of the East India Company. The house of Joseph and Jacob Salvador (brothers) bought 100,000 acres of land in

South Carolina, which would be the site of the town of "'96." They lost large sums of money as a result of the Lisbon earthquake and the problems in the Dutch East India Company. Their only source of wealth was their land in South Carolina, so Francis, the son of Jacob, went to the New world to recoup the family fortune.

Francis inherited £60,000 sterling when he came of age. When he married his first cousin, he received £13,000 sterling as a dowry. Francis left his wife and four children in 1773 and planned to bring them to America later. In 1774, he purchased more land and grew indigo in 6,000 acres. Then storm clouds of war spread over America. Salvador chose the colonial side perhaps due to the growing anti–Semitism in England related to the Naturalization Act of 1753. (This act would have made Jews in England citizens.) In 1774, he was elected to the general assembly—the first Jew elected to office. Later, a provincial congress was organized with delegates elected by the people. Salvador was again elected, and was appointed to the committee to carry out the provisions of the Articles of Association.

After Lexington and Concord, hostilities broke out in the Carolinas. The second provincial congress met in Charleston in November 1775. Salvador was reelected and again served on important committees. At this time, the British were successful in winning the Cherokees to their side. They planned a two-sided attack. Indians and Tories would attack from the west to pull soldiers away from the coast, where the English navy would attack from the east. Cherokees poured over the frontier. Salvador and Major Williamson led an army of 600 patriots against the combined Tories and Indians. Near Esseneba on August 1, 1776, Salvador was shot and then scalped by the Indians. He survived for 45 minutes. Williamson reached him and described his last words. "He asked whether I had beaten the enemy. I told him, "Yes." He said he was glad of it, shook me by the hand and bade me farewell and said he would die in a few minutes." Henry Laurens, president of the council of safety, said to his son, John (who would later die in the Revolution), "Frances Salvador, a gentleman whose death is universally regretted, was killed in the battle."

Salvador's marker in Charleston was engraved with these words[65]:

> Born an aristocrat, he became a democrat;
> An Englishman, he cast his lot with America
> True to his ancient faith, he gave his life
> For new hopes of human liberty and understanding

Salvador was the first Jew to hold public office and the first one to die in the American Revolution.

Many Jews,[66] who were for the most part patriots, left Charleston when the British occupied South Carolina. A group of German and Polish Jews came in with the British army. Some were sutlers and commissaries with the Hessians. Many of them remained when the war ended and went into business. There were enough of them to form a German Jewish congregation, which was slowly swallowed up by the old Sephardic group to form one congregation.

After the Revolution, Jews returned to Charleston, and the city soon threw off the effects of war and occupation. The Jews prospered. A letter written by a rich Jewish merchant, Philip Cohen,[67] in 1811, describes the scene well:

> The first immigration of Jews occurred long before the American Revolution. Since then the number has increased by marriage and by immigrants from Europe. The Jewish population is about 1,000—600 or 700 are in Charleston. They are of German, English and Portuguese descent. The Jews of Charleston observe the religious ceremonies, customs and festivals. Divine services are well attended, and the synagogue is packed. The Reverend Carvalho, previously professor of Hebrew at New York College, is minister to the congregation. Jews have the same educational advantages as other citizens. Jewish children receive a splendid education. Rabbi Carvalho teaches at the high school (Hebrew and Spanish). In dress and manner, Jews are like other citizens. Jews, like other Carolinians, are open-hearted and hospitable. Jews have great business ability and work hard. Several have official positions. There was a Jewish governor[68] of South Carolina who performed his duties well. There are Jewish benevolent groups—society to aid strangers, care for sick and needy and a free burial society. Also an orphan's home—children receive instruction in the duties of citizenship. The Jewish population of Virginia is not over 100— 30 families live in Richmond. A few Jewish families are in Savannah, but they have no synagogue or congregation. There has never been persecution of Jews in the United States. Except for Massachusetts, Jews are eligible for all offices and in southern states Jews occupy official positions. Many Jews are very prominent in American commerce.

Georgia

The founding of Georgia served many purposes for the English. Most of western Europe was in the throes of the mercantilist system. The mother country plus her colonies would produce all of its needs plus some extra, for which they would supposedly be repaid in gold. The English drank wine from Madeira.[69] They imported potash, hemp and flax from

Russia and silk from the Far East. Perhaps those could be produced in Georgia, which was on the same latitude as Portugal. London in the late 1720s had great wealth from the Industrial Revolution, shipping and the slave trade. It also had severe poverty, and its debtor prisons were packed.[70] The powers in society hoped to clean out this nonproductive group and give them a new start. It would be a place to resettle persecuted Protestants from Europe. Georgia would act as a buffer between South Carolina and Catholic Spanish Florida to the south and Catholic French lands to the west.

At this time there were 6,000 Jews in London, many of them destitute. Some fled Germany and others the Inquisition in Portugal. Many left their possessions behind in order to escape with their lives. These people plus the Protestant poor represented a serious "powder keg" for society for which a safety valve was needed. On June 9, 1732, George II[71] issued a charter for the land south of the Savannah River and north of Florida. H.E. Oglethorpe and Lord Egmont petitioned the king to create a colony where the poor of London could be sent.

Trustees were appointed who would raise the necessary funds to send the first load of emigrants. The Bank of England[72] contributed £252, Joseph Jekyl £500, Lady Jekyl £100 and the Earl of Abercorn £100. The trustees among themselves raised £900. Various roots, seeds and plants were donated along with powder, bayonets, swords and flasks plus thousands of books. The trustees gave out commissions to those who wanted to raise money for this charitable venture. Three Jews from the Sephardic Bevis Marks congregation were among these given commissions: Moses da Costa, Joseph Rodrigues Sequiera and Jacob Israel Suasso. Sequiera dropped out and was replaced by Francis Salvador (grandfather of the Francis Salvador killed in the Revolution). These three Jews were very rich. Salvador had lent money to the English government. Suasso was one of the wealthiest men of his time, and da Costa was a director of the Bank of England.

The Jewish commissioners applied to the trustees to send poor Jews to the colony at no expense to the trustees. The trustees were against the idea. They did not want the new colony to be thought of as the "Jew colony of Georgia" because they believed poor Protestants would then not go, and rich Protestants would also not supply the needed funds. "[T]he sending of Jews may be of ill consequence to the Colony." "[T]hey cannot conceive but the settling of Jews in Georgia will be prejudicial to the colony." The Jewish commissioners were supposed to turn the money they raised over to the trustees or start an account in the Bank of England in the trustees' name. Instead, they paid a ship's captain[73] for 41 places on his ship (32 Sephardim and 9 Ashkenazi Jews constituted the first group, including 15 females). They were young, under 30, able bodied and industrious.

They left London in January 1733,[74] but they had to turn back for repairs. The ship eventually docked in Savannah on July 11, 1733. Not all the Jews were destitute. Dr. Samuel Nunes Ribiero was wealthy. He brought his mother, two sons, one daughter and an indentured servant. Dr. Nunes[75] had been a court physician in Portugal. He was a Marrano who kept his Jewish religion secret. However, his religion was discovered, and he was brought to trial. He would have been burned for his heresy except for his skills as a physician. The doctor was returned home, but two Inquisitors were placed in his house to watch for signs of further heresy.

Quietly, Nunes converted as much of his wealth into gold, which could be carried. He had a party at his home one night to which he invited an English captain of a brigantine riding in the river near his home. At the proper time, he, his family, the captain and all the possessions they could carry made their way to the ship and reached London. Dr. Nunes paid the captain 1,000 mordoras, about $3,270.[76] His house, furniture and silver were seized by the Inquisitors. The following year, he and his family were in Savannah.

When the first boatload of Jews arrived on the *William and Sarah*, they found Savannah in the throes of an epidemic. The colony's doctor, Cox,[77] died on April 6. There was no one else able to treat the victims of the "bloody flux" (dysentery). Their minister, Dr. Herbert, boarded a ship for England but died en route. Of the original settlers who had arrived on the *Ann*, 20 were dead. Oglethorpe believed it was due to the consumption of rum punch. The settlers, however, believed it was due to the climate and impure water. They obtained water from the river or shallow wells. Dr. Nunes ordered a deep well to be dug in the center of town with a pump to raise the water.[78] After this, there were no new cases. Nunes cared for the 60 settlers with the disease, and none died after he started treatment. He refused to accept a fee for his care. The community was left with 275 of the original settlers.

Oglethorpe did not know what to do with the Jews, so he turned to the legal authorities in Charleston. The charter for admission exempted only "papists," so he welcomed the Jews. When the trustees in London heard of the good work performed by the Jewish doctor, they ordered Oglethorpe to pay him in specie for his service. They also urged him not to give the Jews any land,[79] but he turned a deaf ear to their request and started to disburse land grants to the heads of the Jewish families. Oglethorpe advised the trustees that the Jews would not be a detriment to the colony. He also praised the work Dr. Nunes had done to stop the epidemic.

The trustees' plan called for each man to receive 50 acres—5 in town and 45 out of town. Families with servants could receive up to, but no more than, 500 acres. (They did not wish Georgia to develop a plantation colony with slaves. They preferred small farms owned by white men who could pick up a musket in the event of invasion.) The new owners had to clear ten acres within ten years and plant 100 mulberry trees. The land was a freehold on loan from the crown and would be inherited by the son. If there was no son in the family, the land reverted to the crown. There must have been some wealthier Jews in the first group, because they had larger pieces of property, which they purchased from the poorer, mostly Portuguese, settlers. In November, a second group of Ashkenazi families came. Between the two loads, a total of 70 Jewish men, women and children had arrived in Savannah. They were predominantly Sephardic plus a few Ashkenazi and Italian Jews. The Ashkenazis Minis and Sheftalls would be important in Georgia's future. The third, Jacob Yowell, was lost to history.

Abraham de Lyon[80] had been a *vigneron* (vine grower for wine) in Portugal. Other Jews wanted to plant vines, but they received swampy land which would not sustain the grape vines. They asked to exchange swamp land for dry. De Lyon asked for a £200 loan, interest free, for three years. He promised to produce 40,000 vines, which he would sell to other settlers. Trustees agreed to the loan, but Oglethorpe disbursed it in small amounts. On December 6, 1787, an observer described De Lyon's vineyard. "They produced grapes as big as a man's thumb, almost pellucid with big bunches. He has apparently found some proper manure to improve the sandy soil." De Lyons denied the use of manure. He claimed his good results came from proper planting and pruning.

Other Jews became moderately successful. Abraham Minis became a trader with New York and soon had a vessel to trade with the new town of Frederika. Isaac Nunes Henriques went into the New York and London trade. The Sheftall[81] family was acquiring land. Benjamin Sheftall was a Prussian Jew who arrived in Savannah in July 1733, and was naturalized in 1750. He had two sons, Mordecai and Levi, from two wives.

In 1755, when Mordecai was 20, he petitioned for land. The father and two sons acquired black slaves and asked for more land, and they purchased land as well. They owned acreage in Savannah, Harwicke, St. Andrews parish, on the Little Ogechee River, and in St. George's parish and Christ Church parish. More land was obtained to build a sawmill, a wharf and a cowpens (cattle ranch). With each acquisition of land, they purchased more blacks, for whom they received more land. The original settler, Benjamin, died in 1765, but his widow, Hannah, continued land acquisition. Mordecai ran the sawmill and the ranch, and Levi ran a tanyard and butcher business. Hannah died in 1772. The boys married, and Mordecai and his wife, Frances, had five children.

With the 50-acre limit per man, how did the Sheftalls gather this immense acreage? Many of the rules laid down by the trustees had to be effaced because the colony was in severe recession. They could not compete with South Carolina because they had no slaves. Limited acreage meant limited production. The trustees also prohibited hard liquor production and transport. By the middle of the century, all of the constricting resolutions were dropped.

When the second boatload of Jews arrived in November 1773, they joined with the earlier Jews to form a congregation—Mikve Israel (Hope of Israel),[82] and in April 1738, a mikveh (ritual bath) was completed. After the second group of Jews came, a "legitimate" group of Protestants came from Salzburg.[83] (Georgia was to be a refuge for persecuted Protestants.) The group was led by the Reverend Bolzius, whose diary gives us insight into the relationship of the various groups. The Ashkenazi Jews could speak German, but the Sephardic Jews and the English could not converse with the Salzburgers. The Ashkenazi Jews were friendly and helped the Germans when they could. Bolzius described the Jews as being kind to his flock. They "showed great love," and Bolzius hoped he might convert them. "They are born in Germany and speak good German."

In a letter in 1739, Bolzius spoke of the complete separation of the two groups of Jews. The minister wrote that the Portuguese were not particularly interested in or concerned about dietary laws and other "Jewish ceremonies." The Germans felt "entitled to build a synagogue and would allow Spanish Jews to use it." The main reason for allowing Jews to remain was to produce silk and wine. The Portuguese Jews excelled in both of these products. In a paragraph in his diary, Bolzius described Sephardic Jews going into the Anglican Church. The Ashkenazi were strict Jews.[84] All the Jews "behaved themselves and are industrious in their businesses."

The Sheftall family was German and helped Salzburgers settle in. The Salzburgers misinterpreted this friendliness and tried to convert them. The Reverend Bolzius, in a letter to his supporters in Halle, described an evangelizing book he gave them which was ridiculed by the Jews. The attitude of the Jews toward the Salzburgers deteriorated after the obvious attempt at proselytizing. Bolzius's attitude toward the Jews worsened as well. "They are malicious and there is hate and persecution among them. The Sephardics persecuted the Ashkenazis severely—more than a Christian to another Christian. They want to build a synagogue, but the two groups could not come to terms. The Ashkenazi would rather starve than eat meat they did not slaughter.... The Jews drill with rifles like the English. They are farmers or in small trades. They hold services in a miserable hut with the women separated from the men. A boy is their reader, and he gets paid for his services.... The Ashkenazi have done small favors for the Salzburgers but will not change their religion.... They are treated as equals by the English. They desecrate Sunday with the English.... Five Jews left Savannah for Hampstead...." In another note in his diary[85] (apparently early in their relationship), he wrote, "They are so very willing to serve us and the Salzburgers that it surprises us, and are so honest and faithful that the like is hardly to be found." "These Jews show a great love for us, and have promised to see us at our settlement."

In the early years of the settlement, Jews and the English worked to advance and improve their status. Jews and others trickled in from New York, Philadelphia, Charleston and the West Indies. By 1742,[86] there were 21 births among the Jews, and nine adult Jews died by 1738. (The first white male born in the colony was Philip Minis in 1734.) The hopes for vineyards and silk slowly disappeared. Because the colony as a whole was in recession, Jews and the English started to leave. The Jews moved to New York, Jamaica and Charlestown, and some lived with the Salzburgers.

In addition to the recession, the English were engaged in another war with the Spanish (the War of Jenkins' Ear).[87] They feared an invasion from Spanish Florida to Georgia. Several Jews were Marranos who reverted to Judaism when they reached England. They feared being turned over to the Inquisition. Where the Jews had represented about one-third of the white population of Savannah, only the Minis, Sheftall and De Lyon families now remained. A member of the De Lyon family died, and the family donated a plot of land for a Jewish cemetery, which was known as the "De Lyon Cemetery." Mordecai Sheftall set aside a five-acre tract for a Jewish cemetery and a synagogue.

Because the mulberry trees were untended, the silkworms died. The grape vines similarly deteriorated. The congregation themselves folded like the vines. By 1741, there were only 42 families in Savannah, four of whom were Jewish. Mordecai Sheftall[88] tried to keep the Jewish presence in Savannah intact despite the great emigration. He set aside a room in his house for prayer.

In the mid–1740s, Jews and English people started to dribble back into Georgia. In 1752, Joseph Solomon Ottolenghe, an Italian[89] Jew who had converted to the Anglican church, came to rebuild the silk industry. It is said he increased silk production to 10,000 pounds of silk per year. Slaves were allowed in Georgia at this time. Ottolenghe hoped to teach them how to produce silk and also convert them to Christianity. Ottolenghe worked at this plan until 1759, when the Society for the Propagation of the Faith stopped his subsidies. He turned to politics in 1755 (George House of Representatives, then a judge). He retired in 1769.

Other Jews came to the colony, but not as farmers. They were small merchants, tavern keepers, Indian traders, slave traders, butchers and agents for Newport and New York firms. In mid-century, Jews were permitted to vote,[90] and in 1765, two Jews were port officials in Savannah. Moses Nunez[91] was a "searcher" for the port of Savannah. A Mr. Lucena was a justice of the peace, and Moses Nunez was an Indian interpreter. Others were involved in the collection of taxes for court expenses and for the militia.

Events in Massachusetts in 1775 had a ripple effect in the southernmost colony. Many, including the Jews, took sides. James Lucena,[92] who may have converted to Christianity in Rhode Island, and his son, John Charles, were Loyalists. James Lucena returned to Portugal and his son to England, where he was appointed consul general to Portugal. Philip Minis[93] and Mordecai Sheftall were in the parochial committee to enforce the decisions of the patriots to prevent the unloading of British ships in Savannah. The governor forbade any Jews from coming to Georgia, because "they were violent rebels and persecutors of the King's loyal subjects." In October 1775, the patriots led a group that stormed the custom house and rescued the *Charlotte* from Loyalist hands. In 1777, Mordecai[94] was appointed commissary general of purchases and issues for the Georgia militia. In 1778, his son, Sheftall Sheftall, age 16, was appointed assistant to John B. Geradieu, the deputy commissioner general of issues of the continental troops in Georgia. Mordecai succeeded Geradieu.

When Savannah fell, the two Sheftalls became prisoners of war. In an attempt to avoid capture, they came to Musgrove Creek. The younger Sheftall could not swim, and his father refused to leave him, so they were taken prisoner. In January 1779, both were kept on the prison-ship *Nancy*. In April 1779, Mordecai was paroled to Sunberry. His son joined him in June 1779. They were next shipped to Antigua. In April 1780, they were paroled to New York, where they were exchanged and left for Philadelphia (which was in patriot hands).

Sheftall Sheftall was made flag master on the *Carolina Packet*, a mercy ship, and Sheftall Sheftall reached Charleston. Mordecai was appointed

Georgia's agent to purchase clothes. He was also involved in privateering. After the war, Mordecai and his family returned to Savannah. In February 1783, he was back at work as a merchant and shipper. He continued to accumulate land, much of it confiscated from Tories.

His brother Levi's[95] politics were different. Levi was appointed a guide for Count D'Estaing in 1779. The count was to recapture Savannah from the British, but the expedition failed, and Levi was accused of taking the patriot army on the wrong path. He was declared a Tory (at most, he was an "in-between") and forced out of Georgia, and his citizenship was revoked. After the war, his brother worked to allow Levi back into Georgia. He succeeded, and Levi was declared a citizen, but he could not vote for 14 years. In 1787, the legislature gave him full rights.

Major Benjamin Nunez,[96] a Jew, emigrated from France to Georgia in 1777. He joined the patriot army and participated in all the battles in South Carolina. On occasion, he acted as adjutant to Washington and Lafayette. Israel Joseph[97] of Charleston was also a German Jew who came from England to New York and then to Charleston in 1775. He mobilized his resources to defend the back country of Georgia and South Carolina. When the British took Savannah and were marching up river to capture Augusta, Israel Joseph was called upon to gather the back-country inhabitants and cooperate with General Williamson to oppose the British move on Augusta. David Sarzedas[98] was a lieutenant in the Georgia continental line. The Jews of Georgia supplied six soldiers to the patriot service.

After the war ended, there was a trickling back of Jews to Georgia. Mordecai Sheftall helped to resurrect the congregation. In 1786, they rented a building for a synagogue in Savannah. There were about 12 families in 1790, when they received a charter to incorporate from the state.[99] In 1820, they built and dedicated a synagogue for 20 families containing 94 Jews. Some Jews moved from Savannah to the back country. Frederika, Hampstead and Augusta had some Jews by the end of the century. Moses Sheftall,[100] son of Mordecai, went to Philadelphia to study medicine under Dr. Rush. His brother, Nathan, was killed on a privateer in 1794. Mordecai represented Chatham County in the legislature in 1796 but died of a stroke the following year.

IV

Jews and Slavery

Unhappily, the Jews in the New World, with a history of slavery in their own past, were involved in that unsavory practice. One might think that 3,000 years would dim the memory. However, we Jews celebrate our freedom from Egyptian slavery every year at Passover.

Like their Christian neighbors, the Jews, if they thought of it at all, considered the blacks as not quite human. At best they were a subspecies of *Homo sapiens*. Thomas Jefferson, a thinker who was years ahead of others, thought of Africans as occupying a space between European whites and the "oran-utan." He believed the American Indian could be assimilated into the greater population of whites in three or four generations of inbreeding. Not so the Africans. His hope to create a unified society required the removal of blacks to an area beyond our boundaries, Sally Hemings notwithstanding. The eighteenth century was a period of classification, and the cultures of the world did not escape classification. At the top of the ladder were the European whites. Below them were the American Indians, Laplanders, Malaysians, and Chinese, and on the very bottom rung were the Africans.

Few men in the colonies could finance a slaving voyage. A slaver, built to accommodate its terrible cargo, had to be owned or leased for a year. The slaver traveled from Newport, Boston or New York to Africa and stopped at several forts along the Guinea coast. Sometimes American captains traveled down the west coast of Africa, around the cape to the east coast of Africa to fill his ship, then back to the West Indies or Charleston to sell off his cargo. He might then pick up barrels of crystallized sugar to carry to Rhode Island or Massachusetts, the largest distillers of rum. He might also carry back tobacco for smoking or snuff.

The owners needed insurance against a loss at sea or the ship's seizure by a privateer during the two centuries of almost constant warfare. The ship's captain and crew had to be paid for a year. Provisions for the captain and crew were needed as well as enough calories to keep the cargo alive and presentable at the time of sale. Trade goods for the African king were stored on board for the trip east. These were predominantly casks of rum as well as firearms. The African leader used guns to go into the interior, where the tribes were unfamiliar with firearms. The power of a musket could easily bring him as many slaves as he wished.

The ship also carried trinkets, mirrors, shackles and other manufactured goods. Jews, like their Christian neighbors, bought shares in a slaving expedition. If the trip was successful, the return on an investment might be 100 percent. To the best of my knowledge, Jews were neither captains nor crew members on this nefarious journey. A captain might throw overboard a violent or sick slave without losing any sleep except over the loss of profit.

The Jews of antiquity had slaves, but it was a patriarchal type of slavery. The slave worked alongside his master, ate at his table and slept in his house. After seven years the slave was freed, and in the jubilee year (50) all slaves were freed. Jewish law and ethics demanded humane treatment of slaves.[1] There was no recognition of the moral wrong of keeping slaves. Maimonides' Code of Laws states that it was forbidden to give a document of manumission to slaves of Canaanite descent. The Bible states, "Forever you shall keep them as slaves, but if he is manumitted, he is free." It was permitted to manumit for religious purposes so that he could form the tenth at a *minyan*. In the case of a female slave, it was best to keep her to prevent her from falling into vice. Talmudic[2] law accepted Jewish involvement in slavery, but the owner was to treat them humanely. He was not to be involved in their punishment.

In the Middle Ages Jews were involved in a minimal slave trade. Jews served a purpose in all trade at this time. Since they were neither Christians nor Muslims, they could be intermediaries between the two major religions. There was a limited need for slaves because most plots of land were small, and the owner or serf and his family could manage them. The New World had enormous acreage, so slaves were required. Originally, the Spaniards used Indians, but they died off too quickly. Las Casas, the Roman Catholic clergyman, proposed black slavery to save the Indians.

In the early history of the English colonies, the slave trade was a royal monopoly. The king gave charters to companies for this commerce. Later, the monopoly was lifted, and any individual with enough resources could be involved. The government in London ordered royal governors to veto any bills passed against the slave trade. In some areas, the government offered bounties to settlers proportional to the number of slaves they possessed. Jews were involved, as were their Christian neighbors.

Jews in Brazil, Surinam and most islands in the West Indies had slaves. Seven years after the arrival of Jews in New Amsterdam, several Jews were wealthy enough to own blacks. Surinam[3] moved back and forth between the English and the Dutch. In the treaty of Breda, 1667, Surinam was restored to the Dutch. In the Treaty of Westminster (1674), the English were permitted to leave and sell their estates, and the British sent three ships to remove their subjects. On the list of those going to Jamaica there were ten Hebrew names. They had 322 slaves among them.

When one thinks of Jews in the slave trade, the names of Aaron Lopez and Jacob R. Rivera come to mind.[4] They joined the slave trade in 1762. In the 1760s the Rhode Island merchant marine had 184 large vessels and 342 small coasters. Newport was the major trade center, and half of its vessels were in the slave trade. As an aside, Newport had more than 20 rum distilleries to predominantly supply the trade. In January 1763, Lopez and Rivera sent the brigantine *Greyhound* to Guinea, where they picked up 134 slaves, who were sold in Charleston. In 1764, the sloop *Spry* was sent out. In 1765, Lopez[5] and Rivera sent the *Betsey* and the *Africa* to Guinea. *Betsey* carried 1,300 gallons of rum as well as razors and penknives.

Provisions for the crew came to £206 and wages were £2,400. An additional expense was insurance. They could receive £1,050 in coverage for £82.2.3 in London. A male slave in Africa cost about 180 gallons of rum. The *Ann* carried 95 live slaves on its first trip (six had died). The slaves suffered from "swelling." When the swelling reached the stomach, they died (perhaps the malady was scurvy or hypoproteinemia). The remaining 95 slaves were sold in the West Indies for £3,620 with expenses of £1,399. This represented a profit of £1,259 (90 percent).

Before the Revolution, Lopez owned outright or was in partnership in 30 ships in the slave trade. Between 1764 and 1775,[6] Rivera and Lopez had at least one ship constantly active in the trade. In 1772 and 1773, Lopez sent out four slavers to Africa. In the 1770s, Aaron Lopez[7] was importing 250 to 300 slaves each year, who were sold in the West Indies and Charleston.

Aaron Lopez was busy in contracting for the building of new ships which he used or sold in Europe or the West Indies.[8] The ships had gratings and handcuffs and were therefore slave ships. In a letter he described a ship as being a double-decked brigantine of 113 tons—furnished for the "African trade." It was rigged and equipped with the same number of sails as the brigantine *Hannah*. The ship was sheathed with one-inch pine boards or one-half-inch cedar. It had one anchor cable of 80 fathoms and nine and one-half inches. A second cable was 90 fathoms and eight and one-half inches. The hawser measured 120 fathoms and six inches. Its anchors were "in proportion." The ship carried a yawl of 18 feet and was to have gratings and air ports like a Guineaman (a slave ship) and was painted in a plain manner. The awning, a second boat, caboose, colors, small arms, chains and handcuffs with every other small utensil was to be provided by Captain Clarke. The cost of the ship to Clarke was £690 sterling.

The ship owner received information which he had to get to his captain, usually through another captain. Thus, Rivera and Lopez advised Captain Nathaniel Briggs to stay away from the French island of St. Lucia. The French were confiscating ships that entered the harbor without authorization. In a postscript to the letter they stated there were seven ships in Newport Harbor ready to take off for the Guinea coast. One belonged to Jews. Isaac Elizer and Samuel Moses[9] of Newport, who were second to Rivera and Lopez in the trading of slaves, sent a ship to Africa on October 29, 1763. They were able to get a letter to Captain John Peck. "With your cargo head for Africa. In Africa dispose of the cargo for the best price.... Invest the proceeds into as many good merchantable young slaves as you can.... Then sail to New Providence in the Bahamas—dispose of your slaves for cash. If the market is poor, come back to Newport and declare the cargo ... for your commission, four slaves upon the purchase of 104, and the privilege of bringing home three slaves, and your mate, one." The captain was advised to be careful of his vessel and slaves and "as frugal as possible in every expense relating to the voyage. If you sell the slave in Providence use every money for any commodity of the island." From this note, we can see that the captain was a part owner of the cargo.

There were other Jews in the slave trade, but none could compete with Lopez and Rivera. Simon the Jew[10] (his last name may have been Bonane) sent a slave ship to Guinea. Nathan Simon[11] and his New York and London associates owned the *Crown* and the *New York Postillon*, slavers that brought in 217 Africans. Franks, Pacheco, Gomez and Levy imported slaves from the West Indies. Because blacks from Africa were too wild for many purchasers, they were taken to the West Indies for a year or two of "seasoning." If they survived the harsh treatment in the islands, they were more easily controlled on the continent.

As written in the U.S. Constitution, the external legal trade in Africans had to end in 1807. However, within the confines of the new country, slave trading was legal until the Civil War. An auctioneer[12] (*vendue* master) who did this as a full-time occupation could accumulate a substantial estate. In Jacob Jacobs's will in 1797, he left small amounts to his synagogue, his sister, brother and sister-in-law. To a friend, Gershon

Cohen, he left gold, silver and stone buckles, His wife, Katie, received the house, furniture, horses, carriages, bonds, notes, "debts owed me" and his slaves. These were Toby, Scipio, Jack, Jenny and her three children (Peter, John and Eve), Flora and her two children, Rachel, Lucy and any other slaves not already mentioned. If Katie remarried, the slaves were to be auctioned off and the proceeds were to go to the children of Gershon Cohen. If Katie remained single, she had the use of all of his real estate, lands and tenements. His land in Charleston passed to Cohen's children. This clause about the widow remarrying was common in many wills at the time.

During the colonial period, there were few Jewish internal slave traders. More entered the business in the nineteenth century. The largest Jewish internal trader was the Davis family of Petersburg and Richmond. Manuel Jacob Monsanto in New Orleans and his brother Benjamin in Natchez were full-time traders.[13] Others, including Solomon Cohen of Atlanta and Augusta, Georgia; B. Mordecai of Charleston; J.F. Moses of Lumpkin, Georgia; and Abraham Smith made their living from the trade. In places like Virginia and Maryland, the land was "used up," so they became "incubators" for slaves shipped to the Deep South and new states along the Mississippi River. Slaves could be placed on coast-wise ships and sent to New Orleans. Some coffles of slaves could be marched over-land to the Mississippi River and sent downstream to Natchez.

There were few Jewish plantation owners in the South. In Europe, Jews could not own land, so they were unable to learn the skills of agriculture. Furthermore, Jews felt safer in urban areas. In cities, there were often enough Jews for fellowship and prayer.[14] Many were still poor merchants and peddlers and could not afford the cost of a plantation. According to their wills, about one in four Jews in the South owned slaves. Slavery was part of the fabric of southern society, and they wanted to "fit in." The Sheftall[15] family of Georgia owned a great deal of property and needed Africans to work the land. They were probably reasonably good to their chattels if one accepts the story of a slave in St. Augustine, Florida. He claimed he was taken from Sheftall's cowpens. He and his family belonged to Sheftall, and he wanted to return.

Rich Jewish merchants and professionals in the South owned slaves, but they preferred white indentured servants who were less rebellious because they could see an end to their time of servitude. In the first U.S. census in 1790[16] in South Carolina, there were 73 Jewish households. Of these, 34 owned one or more slaves for a total of 151. The largest owners were Jacob Jacobs of Charleston (11), Abraham and Solomon Cohen (30) and Esther Myers of Georgetown (11). Before leaving the South, there is one small footnote. In 1806, two Jews, Marcus Levi and Reuben Cantor, were prosecuted for keeping their stores open on Sunday.[17] They did so, however, because this was the only day slaves could shop in town. In addition to the shopkeepers' legal sales to slaves who could earn some money on the plantation, the slaves stole whatever items they could and brought them in to town to sell on Sunday. The slaves did not consider this as stealing, but rather their due.

In the North as in the South, Jews preferred indentured servants to slaves. This was brought home to them by the slave revolt in New York City in 1741.[18] The city had a population of 12,000 people, of whom 2,000 were slaves. The slaves hatched a plot to kill all the whites and burn the city down. Several slaves belonging to Jews were involved. Cuffee, who belonged to Lewis Gomez, was burned to death for punishment. Cajve Africa, owned by Mordecai Gomez, was shipped to Madeira. Others included Windsor and Hereford, slaves of Sam Myers Cohen, and Jack, who belonged to Judah Hays. They, too, were sent away. In the North as in the South there was no animosity toward Jews who had or dealt in slaves. Abraham Mendes Seixas was a brother of Cantor Gershon Mendes Seixas, leader of the Jewish congregation in New York during the Revolution. An auctioneer, he was respected in his community.

The concept of manumitting slaves was not very common in colonial America.[19] The preaching of the Pennsylvania Society for Promoting the Abolition of Slavery (Quakers) moved many to free their bondsmen. Manumission was relatively easy in the colonial period. Later, southern states passed laws against this act. In many cases the free blacks had to leave the state or risk being reenslaved. Samuel Myers[20] of Petersburg, Virginia, purchased "Mulatto Alice" in 1796 and freed her one year later. Joseph Tobias of Charleston bought Jenny for $300 in 1798 and promptly freed her. Solomon Raphael of Richmond freed Sylvia and her child in 1798, and six years later he freed Priscilla. Many Jews followed George Washington's lead and freed their slaves in their wills.[21] In the last testament of Philip Hart of Charleston, he freed Flora. Jacob Cohen freed Tom. Samuel Jones freed Jenny and her son Emanuel. Jones left her a bed, sheets, bedstead, blanket, tables, pots, plates, chairs and a looking glass. Jones gave the income from his property to Jenny and her son. She shared this income with six slaves who were not freed. Jenny and her son could stay in his house until they found a place to live. Isaiah Isaacs of Charlottesville, Virginia, freed his slaves in 1806. He testified that all men are by nature equally free.

Like their gentile neighbors, some Jews were violent toward their property.[22] Joseph Cohen of Lynchburg, Virginia, murdered a slave in

1819. He was tried and convicted, but his penalty was minimal. The Jews who resided in towns lived with and accepted the cruel punishment given to blacks. In 1798, Polly, a mulatto, was tried for taking two dollars' worth of white sugar from Benjamin Solomon's home. She received five lashes and her left hand was branded. Joseph Darmstadt in 1800 had 50 shillings' worth of beeswax stolen by David Clayton, a freed black, who received 39 lashes to his bare back. Some Jews were public officials who tried blacks. In 1792, Mordecai Sheftall of Georgia issued warrants for runaway slaves in his district.

In several cases Jews cohabited with blacks.[23] The will of Moses Nunes of Savannah in 1797 acknowledged "Mulatta Rose" as his concubine and her children, Robert, James, Alexander and Francis as his. He bequeathed 13 slaves to her and her children. Barnet A. Cohen from Bristol, England, moved to South Carolina and fathered Barnet Owens Cohen and Benjamin Philip Owens Cohen by a free black, Catherine Owens. After the turn of the century,[24] fornicating with a black woman was illegal, and several Jews were brought to court for this offense.

Many Jews were unhappy with or even frightened by their slaves and tried to sell them off. The Pennsylvania *Journal* of January 4, 1786,[25] ran this ad: "For Sale: A young likely Negro-Wench About eight years old, has twenty years to serve. Enquire of Isaac Franks." (The meaning of "20 years to serve" relates to Pennsylvania's abolition of slavery by law. Not all slaves were freed at once. It was gradual, and children were slowly manumitted and trained for freedom.) Meyer Josephson,[26] an immigrant from Germany to Pennsylvania, described a problem with a slave wench whom he wished to sell to a free black who wished to marry her. She had a bastard child, and the price for the two was £110. "She is drunk whenever she gets liquor. She is mean and his wife is afraid of her." Barnard Gratz[27] in 1772 tried to sell a rebellious slave. The black refused to be sold at public auction and threatened to kill the person who bought him. He refused to work when sent to jail. He was in chains and handcuffs and almost nude because of his threats. Finally, to end this sad chapter in Jewish history, some offspring of Jewish and black cohabitation chose the Jewish religion, but they were not permitted into synagogues.

V

Anti-Semitism

It is natural to assume that "anti–Jewishism" developed from the crucifixion of Christ; the rejection of Jesus as the Messiah; and the writings in the New Testament. However, there was anti–Jewish feeling centuries before the Christian era. In a period of small city-states and tribes, each group had its own gods to which the populace prayed, as well as many house gods. With the subjugation of an enemy, its gods were joined to and incorporated into the victor's gods. Not so the Jews. They had one god who was superior to the gods of their neighbors. This resulted in a feeling of hatred toward this stiff-necked people.

When the Babylonians conquered Judea, some Jews escaped back to Egypt and were accepted as mercenaries in Egyptian outposts.[1] One such fortress was Jeb, on the northeast border of Egypt. The Persians later invaded and occupied Egypt. Jewish soldiers in Jeb and other posts supported Persia. The Egyptians rebelled against their overlords in 485 and 464 B.C., while the Jews remained loyal to Persia. However, in 405 B.C. the Egyptians threw off the Persian yoke and turned their hatred on the "fifth column" in their midst. Egypt was next conquered by Alexander the Great and his Greek (Macedonian) army. The Greeks had a positive attitude toward the Jews and invited them to settle in occupied lands. After Alexander's death and the division of his empire, his successors, the Ptolemies and the Seleucids, favored the Jews. Many Jews moved to Alexandria, where they were welcomed. There was a large migration of Greeks to Egypt, and they found that most trades and high positions were occupied by Jews. This led to an anti–Jewish feeling which was intensified as Jews gained influence in the royal house and their position on the economic ladder was elevated. The Greeks discovered that they competed in political, social, economic, religious and intellectual spheres.

Rome was the next invader, and the Jews sided with the new conquerors. The Egyptians and Greeks united in a pogrom in Alexandria in

A.D. 38. They expressed their hatred by cutting off their victims' limbs, trampling on them, and then hitting them with clubs in nonfatal places so it would take longer to die. They also desecrated the dead bodies (Philo).

The earliest piece of anti–Jewish literature appeared in Egypt. In 270 B.C., Manetho, an Egyptian priest, published *A History of Egypt* in Greek. He described the Jews' ancestors as a band of foreign conquerors who joined Egyptian lepers in their cruelty and hatred of the natives. The monograph led to anti–Jewish agitation and further poisoning of the Greek minds against the Jews. The Greeks recognized major differences between themselves and the Jews.[2] For example, their concept of the "oneness" of humanity was not accepted by Jews. Greeks felt circumcision was barbaric. Jews kept themselves isolated from others, and their dietary laws prevented them from joining others at feasts. Also, Jews refused intermarriage. After the Roman invasion, Jews refused to worship their emperors as gods. Greek intellectuals were able to poison Roman minds against the Jews, and they became the civil servants and tax gatherers under their Roman overlords.

The spotlight of history moved to Palestine. The Hasmoneans signed an agreement with Rome, and the Jews later became subjects under Roman rule. Jerusalem was the site of religious and political turmoil. Jesus was born, preached his religious ideas and was crucified. Early in its history, Christianity was a sect of Judaism, and its followers were Jews who accepted Christ's teachings. The sect would surely have become a footnote in history were it not for the one Jew, Saul of Tarsus, later called Paul. Paul took the new religion to the gentiles, and advised his listeners that they did not have to accept the stringent rules of the Jews to become followers of Jesus, who was born, lived and died a Jew. The new sect split completely from their Jewish predecessors. The Romans felt this new group was a political and disruptive thorn in their side, so they tried to destroy them. Their actions only produced saints in the new religions.

The martyrdom of Christians came to an end when the Emperor Constantine accepted Christianity as a religion of Rome in A.D. 313. He converted and moved his seat of government to Byzantium (Constantinople). Following the acceptance of Christianity as separate from Judaism, the Christian Greeks turned on the old religion, and laws were passed against the Jews. They were not allowed to hold Christian slaves or hire Christians to work for them. Christians could purchase Jews' slaves at a price the buyer set. Jews were not permitted in the army and could not practice law. In Antioch, the Jews were forcibly converted or executed. More importantly, mobs could attack them with impunity. This led to the burning of synagogues and the homes of wealthy Jews along with killing and stealing. The Greek Orthodox church, which separated from the Latin church, accepted the hatred of the Jews, so much so that it almost became a part of their religion.

Early in the seventh century, this anti–Jewish feeling spread westward. The Roman west had suffered repeated incursions of Germanic tribes who cut out pieces of Roman territory to create separate entities like Spain and Gaul. The Jewish condition under German hegemony was reasonably good because both were outsiders. This changed when the Germans accepted Catholicism. The Franks became Catholic in 496, and in 629, King Dagobert ordered the Jews to convert or leave the country. In Spain, the Visigoth kings wanted their subjects to intermarry with the Hispano-Romans to form a unified nation. King Recorred converted to Catholicism, and in 616 the Jews in Spain were forced to convert or leave. Perhaps half of the Jews in the Iberian peninsula converted.

The millennium between the rapid growth of Christianity and the seventeenth century was a period where Christendom could develop new concepts to attack this foreign group in their midst. The Crusades, a war to regain Jerusalem from the Mohammedans, resulted in the almost complete destruction of Jewish communities in the Rhineland. When the German knights decided to join the fray, they and their peasant followers decided they could start by annihilating the heretics in their midst. The number of Jews killed there far exceeded those killed in the Holy Land. It is said that the capture of Jerusalem by the Crusaders led to a bloodbath of immense proportions. This was true anti–Semitism, because Jews and their Semitic cousins, the Moslems, were equally butchered. The fall of Jerusalem, it was believed, was proof that God hated the Jews.

In the late thirteenth or early fourteenth century, an English boy was last seen going into a Jewish house. He disappeared, and the concept of making matzoh from gentile blood developed. This belief was picked up by Spain and became another reason for killing Jews in the area.

The Black Death was caused by Jews poisoning the town's wells, or so the Jews said after torture. That the Jews of the community suffered a mortality almost like their Christian neighbors was of no consequence. Jewish mortality was lower than that of society at large because their rules of diet and cleanliness may have helped. The attack on the Jews was most intense in France, Spain, Germany and Austria.

The most extreme isolation of the Jews occurred in Venice. In 1515 and 1516, the Venetian state confined its entire Jewish community to an abandoned cannon factory, called the ghetto nuovo, on an island farthest from the Piazza San Marcos. The Jews were forced by the state to take out a lease on the island at an exorbitant price. In addition, they had to pay ten Christian watchmen and boatmen to keep them contained. The ghetto nuovo ("new ghetto") was restricted to Italian Jews of German origin, while the ghetto vecchio ("old ghetto") was developed for Jews from the Levant. A ghetto novissimo contained Jews from Western Europe. By 1632, there were 2,412 Jews in the ghettos out of a population of 98,244 Venetians. Although the inhabitants were forced to pay high taxes for their isolation, they felt the guards gave them a sense of security against the wanton hate of the mobs. Several of the popes had a benign attitude toward the Jews because of their business abilities and the revenue they brought to the papal states and Italy in general. However, Paul IV changed this attitude and attacked the Jews. He established a ghetto in Rome and ghettos in all of the papal states as well as the other states in Italy.

The Reformation at the beginning of the sixteenth century was initially "good for the Jews" because there was another group of nonconformists. Luther initially looked kindly at the Jews, because he felt he could explain the Scriptures to them and prove Christ was the Messiah. He believed he could bring about a mass conversion of the Jews. When this failed to happen, he turned violently against them. His pamphlet *On the Jews and Their Sins* was violently anti–Semitic. He urged the burning of their synagogues and the destruction of their prayer books. Rabbis were not permitted to preach, their homes were destroyed, and they were forced to live in stables. Jews were banned from the markets and their property was seized. They were forced to perform hard labor and were finally forced out of German cities (in the 1540s). Luther attacked Jewish money lenders because he claimed they were thieves and murderers. The Reformation's attempt[3] to convert the Jews was strongest in Germany and Holland. The Dutch University of Halle trained and sent out missionaries to proselytize the Jews. Charles V was against the Jews in his Iberian possessions, but he supported them in his German domains. He felt the Catholic bishops of Germany could use them against the advances of Protestantism.

Of the states of Western Europe, Spanish anti–Semitism was very early and most notorious. At the Council of Elvira (306), Jews were to be separated from the rest of the inhabitants. The condition of the Jews improved following the Visigothic invasions. This lasted until the Visigoths accepted Catholicism under King Recorred, and in the following centuries the condition of the Jews deteriorated. The Visigoths joined the Hispano-Romans to create a unified nation—except for the Jews. In 616, the Jews were forced to convert or leave (the first of many such decrees). Those who stayed would be executed. King Sisebut demanded a unified nation under Catholicism and forced Jews, pagans and Arians to convert.

About one-half of Spain's Jews converted, but many migrated north to Gaul. The kings after Sisebut varied in their attitude toward the Jews, and many Jews returned to Spain. King Erwig demanded conversion, and this time Jews fled to North Africa.

The invasion of the Moors in 711 ended these attacks on the Jews. The Hebrews welcomed the Moslems. They manned the forts in southern Spain so that Moorish soldiers could fight their way north, and Jews supplied them with the provisions of war. By the tenth century, the Jews occupied high administrative positions in Moslem states. Between the eighth and eleventh centuries, the Jews enjoyed a "golden age" as writers, doctors, traders and advisers to the Moslem kings.

The Catholic kings of the north regained their strength and started to push the invaders south. These kings invited Jews to return to their newly acquired realms. In Castile, from 1075 to about 1375, the Jews rose to high positions as advisers to the kings. They became tax farmers, which angered the Catholics (the tax farmer paid an agreed amount to the king or noble and forced as much as he could from the people). There were violent uprisings against the Jews in Toledo and Seville. The Jewish situation deteriorated under King Pedro of Castile, because his unjust acts were blamed on the Jews around him. He was followed by Enrique, who showed the Spaniards that the Jews could be butchered without retribution, robbed, and sold into slavery.

Ferrán Martinez, a virulently anti–Semitic priest, demanded that Jewish rights, received over the centuries, be removed. He started converting Moorish slaves to Catholicism, and they then had to be freed. The priest told the poor they could please the king by killing Jews. The King (Juan I) was helpless against him, and the archbishop threatened him with excommunication, but Martinez had the masses in his camp. A violent attack against the Jews in Seville spread to all of Castile and to Aragón in 1391 and destroyed most of the Jews in Seville. Thousands of men were killed, and women and children were sold into slavery. Seventy thousand Jews were killed in the pogrom, and 100,000 converted.

The pogrom spread to Majorca, Barcelona, Madrid and Valencia. People like Paul of Burgos, a chief rabbi, converted in 1391 and turned on the Jews. He was made Pope Benedict's representative to Castile. Pope Paul forced King Enrique III to enforce the laws against Jews including the demand that they wear a special badge. In 1412, the Jews and Moors were forced into ghettos. They were fined if they tried to carry on a business in the town square. If they tried to leave the country, they were sold into slavery. They could not work; they could not leave the country; the only outlet was conversion. More Jews converted at this time than in the pogrom of 1391. These New Christians, with their Jewish abilities and training, soon reached places of honor in the church, the administration and trade. Their children were sent to Catholic schools, and many lost their Jewish roots. The Old Christians and particularly the poor developed a hatred for the conversos (those who had converted) and their ascendancy to power. An outbreak in Toledo in 1449 was directed against conversos. Spanish hatred of the Jews took a major step forward because it was racial, not religious. In the past, Jews who converted were accepted. Toledans anteceded Hitler by 500 years. Alfonso VII joined his subjects and decreed that no convert or his offspring could hold office in Toledo.

The Old Christians accused the New Christians of being Jews covertly. A commission was called, and the members proclaimed that there were secret Jews among the conversos. A tribunal was established to judge Judaizers, and the people were called to come forward and identify them. The pope and archbishop were against this grasp of power from their hands. Pogroms now turned their attention to conversos. The king and the conversos turned to the pope for help, and Cardinal Torquemada was directed to help the New Christians. A petition from Toledo against conversos eventually led to the Inquisition. In Toledo, it was decided that five generations of being Catholic could clear the blood of Jewish pollution.

Cardinal Juan Torquemada, uncle of the Inquisitor General, supported the conversos. (It was believed his grandparents were Jews who converted.) The Toledans advanced the racial theory. The conversos were of a race predisposed to crime and evil. In 1451, the pope issued a bull to establish a formal inquisition in Castile and all the domains of Juan II. The bull reiterated the church's position that New Christians were equal to Old Christians, but those under suspicion, no matter what their position, would be tried as heretics. After Juan II died, and Enrique III became king, the bull was suppressed. In 1468, the Jews of Sepulveda were accused of blood torment and found guilty of ritual murder. In 1471, eight were sentenced to death.

In 1461, Enrique IV's emissary to Rome requested of Pius II an inquisition for Castile. There were anti-converso riots in Carmona in 1462 despite many conversos who truly accepted Catholicism. The riots were based on socioeconomic factors. The commoners were envious of the conversos' achievements in the administration of royal, clerical and judicial affairs. They were also urban tax gatherers. Conversos were the major merchants in the cities. More significantly, they were intermarrying with the Old Christians, which was opposed on racial grounds. There was also an early element of nationalism. They were not really Spaniards, despite the fact that many conversos could trace their family roots in Spain back for centuries.

Ferdinand established the Inquisition to appease the anti–Marrano group in hopes they would stop the riots. He believed the conversos would be exonerated by the church and could then go about their business of increasing the wealth of his kingdom. The purpose of the Inquisition was to discover lapsed Christians. Jews who had remained Jews during the mass, forced conversions could not be touched, because they had not lapsed. They could be tried if they helped Christians relapse. In Andalusia, 1483, the bishops involved in the Inquisition forced the king to expel the Jews. There were said to be more than 600,000 conversos in Spain in the 1490s, and many New Christians could show conversion in their families as early as 1109.

The Inquisition started in 1480 in Spain, despite the objection of the pope. Earlier, the popes opposed the Inquisition because they believed it was a royal and national institution not under their immediate control. They also felt "heretics" should receive more leniency. In 1483, the entire operation was placed in the hands of Tomas de Torquemada, who considered himself a converso. In fewer than 12 years, the Inquisition condemned 13,000 conversos for practicing Judaism. During its existence, the Inquisition would claim 341,000 victims. Of these, 32,000 were burned, 17,659 were burned in effigy and 291,000 received lesser punishments.

In 1474, Isabella ascended the throne of Castile, and in 1479 Castile and Aragón (Ferdinand) were united by marriage. Isabella felt Spain should be totally free of Jews. Between the Inquisition and expulsion, massive estates could revert to the royal houses and the bishoprics. The Inquisition coincided with the war against the Moors, who were finally defeated at Granada in January 1492. On March 31, 1492, the Edict of Expulsion was proclaimed. Any Jew who did not convert had to leave Spain. At the time there were about 200,000 Jews in the kingdom. Many converted, and about 100,000 fled to Portugal. By July 1492, Spain no longer had Jews. In 1497, as a result of a royal marriage between Portugal and Spain, Jews were evicted (Isabella refused to sanction the marriage until the Jews were forced out of Portugal). About 50,000 went to North Africa or Turkey, but many Marranos and Jews remained in Portugal. It was said that young Jewish children were taken from their parents and sent to "Islas Perdidas" by order of the king of Portugal. The animosity of the king toward the Jews was said to arise from a promise of the Jews to the king of a large sum of money when they were expelled from Spain. They could not raise it, and the king sought vengeance. Many of the children died on board ship. Others reached the "Lost Islands" (St. Thomas off the coast of Africa) and were "devoured by crocodiles." The children grew up as savages and "married" their sisters (this story of questionable veracity was told by Solomon Ben Verga in *Shebat Yehudah*).

The Inquisition came to Portugal in 1531, and the Marranos fled to Holland. The Inquisition seized relapsed Catholics as well as priests who preached a concept not accepted by the church. In 1726, a newspaper in Lisbon described a trial of 39 men and 32 women. Two men and one woman were ordered burned. One rich merchant recanted (and paid), and he was pardoned. A priest, Manoel Lopes da Carvalho, was burned at 4 A.M. Despite the flames, he persisted in the opinion that Christ came, not to destroy the law of Moses, but to perfect it. He believed circumcision was as necessary as baptism. When advised to recant, he refused. The priest told the Inquisitors they were idolaters, not Christians. In the flames, he called on the God of Israel. Carvalho asked God to accept his humble sacrifice. The priest rejoiced in God's having chosen him to be a martyr to the law of Moses and Christ. He looked around at the mob like a man sitting in an easy chair. His body was not completely consumed until 9 A.M.

The Spanish and Portuguese sent the Inquisition to America.[4] Early, the Portuguese shipped their heretics to Lisbon for trial. The Spanish saved them the trip by setting up courts in several of their colonies in America. The Maranos were tried from 1574 to the beginning of the nineteenth century. There were nine autos-da-fé (acts of faith) in the colonies. In the first, there were 63 penitentials, of whom five were burned. In 1596, there were 60 victims, and in 1602, more than 100.

The expulsion of Jews from the Iberian peninsula is well known by most historians because of the magnitude of those forced out. Less well known is the expulsion of Jews from England in 1290 and from France in 1306. The numbers were small and represented a footnote in history. One should ask, where did they go? They moved east to Poland, where they were welcomed by the king. He believed an infusion of Jews would stimulate his sagging economy. Unhappily, these Jews did not learn history's lessons. The peasants (Roman Catholic) were oppressed by the nobles (often Greek Orthodox). The nobles placed the Jews between themselves and the tillers of the soil. The Jews became lessees of the land. When the nobles raised the rent, the Jews raised the taxes on the tenants. The peasants of Ukraine rose up in 1618[5] under a petty aristocrat, Bogdan Chmielnicki, who was joined by Cossacks and Tartars. They attacked the nobles, but most of their ire was directed against the Jews. Polish soldiers turned Jews over to the rebels to save their own lives. It is estimated that 100,000 Jews were massacred, and 300 of their communities were destroyed. The destruction in Eastern Europe caused the Jews to turn inward from the outside world. They prayed for the coming of the Messiah, and many "messiahs" preyed on them. Jewish history records names like David Reubens, Solomon Molcho, Shabbetai Zevi and David Frank. The latter two ended up before the Sultan of Turkey, where they converted to Islam to save their lives if not their souls. The eighteenth century saw the growth of the Hassidic movement in Poland, in which some Jews attempted to find happiness in their status along with a strict observance of the religion. In the middle of the seventeenth century, those Jews with money fled west to Germany and Holland.[6]

Holland

Holland was a haven for the Jews of Iberia and middle and eastern Europe. The Dutch did not attack and kill Jews, but religious liberty did not exist for them. The Dutch Reform Church refused to allow public worship by these outsiders, and they could not join the army. The Dutch government, interested in world trade, welcomed them to a point. That point was reached when too many poor Jews flocked to the cities. As described earlier, they turned to England as a safety valve to export some of the poor. True freedom did not come until Napoleon's[7] army occupied Holland at the end of the eighteenth century. The Jews asked for the right to vote and to join the army. The Dutch opposed their requests and advanced the following arguments: (1) Jews always lived apart from other nations and did not look upon Christians as brethren. They were forbidden to marry a person from another nation. (2) It was due to the bad faith of Jews that Nebuchadnezzar and Titus conquered Jerusalem, and Hadrian banished them from Palestine. If they converted, they hid their Judaism as they did in Spain and Portugal. (3) Despite their haughtiness, when in trouble, they became sycophants. In Holland, from 1784 to 1787, they sided with the Prince of Orange. (4) The Jewish expectation of the Messiah was incongruous with Republican principles. (5) In the event of Jewish emancipation in Holland, there would be a pouring in of German Jews. Despite these arguments the Jews could expect justice from the courts as described in the following case: Christoffel Herricks,[8] originally from Konigsberg, aged 26 and a corporal in Prince Charles's regiment, sold pewter to Jews. They believed it was gold and silver and paid him in florins according to what they believed was its true value. He admitted defrauding them, because he thought the law in Holland was the same as in Germany, where defrauding Jews was legal. The court banished him for three years, and he had to pay prison and judicial costs.

It will be remembered that Jews were forced out of England in 1290, but they were permitted to enter under the protectorate of Cromwell in the mid–seventeenth century. Earlier in the century, there was debate about the position of the Jews in society. In 1608,[9] Coke stated, "Jews are perpetual enemies" and should be shunned by Christians. After the Jews were admitted, a court case, *Rex v. Taylor* (1675), brought out the belief that "Christianity is a part of the Common Law" and that "infidels including Jews are subjects of the devil and perpetual enemies, with whom [among] Christians there is perpetual hostility and no peace." In 1667, in *Robley v. Langston*,[10] the court held unanimously that Jews were competent witnesses and could be sworn in on the old Testament. Again in 1684, the court found in favor of Jewish witnesses. The Jews were happy to be merchants and to be left alone in religious matters. Early in their history in England, Jews could not vote for members of parliament. Rodrigo Pacheco,[11] colonial agent to parliament (1731), advised the Jews to let sleeping dogs lie. He felt that if hot heads pushed hard enough, parliament might give them the vote, but this would arouse the anger of English mobs. The vote would come to them in time. When Pacheco presented himself to parliament as a Jew, nothing was said.

The trade and navigation acts between 1650 and 1663 were passed to foster mercantilism and to "cut Jews, French and other foreigners" out of trade. Jews were penalized by appropriation of their cargoes if they were found engaged in trade. The Jews and other foreigners could legally trade if they were endenized (a state between alien and citizen). In 1740, the Naturalization Act gave foreigners in the colonies the right to become citizens, but not many took advantage of the law. In 1753, a "Jew bill" was brought up in parliament that would give foreigners living in England the right to become citizens, similar to the rights given to aliens in the colonies in the Naturalization Act. When mobs rose up against the bill, it was repealed. When violence spread against the earlier Naturalization Act, it was almost revoked.

The English inhabitants of West Indian islands were more virulent toward their Jews than in the home country. Most likely, Jews represented a threat to their businesses, and the number of Jews could not be lost among the small number of whites. In 1670 and 1671, Jews started to arrive in Jamaica.[12] In 1693, an "Act for and toward the Defense of this Island" was passed (against French incursions). All inhabitants were taxed, but a special tax of £750 was levied on the Jewish community.[13] The total to be raised was £4,000 in three months. The Jews responsible for collecting the levy from their community were listed—all had Sephardic names. If they failed to raise the money by June 10, 1693, an additional levy of £250 was added. Any Jew who refused to act as assessor or collector was fined £100. Later, an additional tax of £1,000 was levied on the Jews to be paid by January 10, 1694. Again, in August 1705, the ruling group resolved to tax the nation of the Jews £1,000 to pay for the recently fought war. In 1706, officers and soldiers were to be billeted in Jewish homes. A law of 1707 grouped Jews with mulattos and Negroes. No member of these groups could vote for members of the assembly. More money was needed in 1728 to put down slave revolts, and again, Jews paid an additional tax. A measure to raise money for "exigencies" passed in 1733, and a tax of £1,000 was levied on the Jews. In 1738, the Jews sent a petition to the king asking relief from these special levies. The English in Jamaica countered this petition. They claimed Jews were exempt from certain offices because of their religion. They also claimed Jews were trading with the Spaniards and that the Jews were spreading false rumors about goods brought to the island which damaged the reputation of English traders.

The petition was signed by many Jews, probably all traders and planters. In response to the English, the richest Jews threatened to leave the island and the poorest Jews would be left to pay the levies, which they could not do. The king ordered Edward Trelawny, the new governor, to investigate the claim and stop all special levies until he reported to the king. The legislature sent further information to the governor. It was claimed that money was raised to pay the officers and men of eight companies. The Jews did not supply white men as soldiers, and therefore the tax was levied. The soldiers would act to prevent (Jewish) trade with the Spanish and French islands. The king's verdict was to allow the special levies for that year, but it was to stop thereafter, and they were to look for other ways of raising money. The chief justice of the island supported the island legislature:

> That the Jews in this island are a very wealthy body, their gains considerable, and acquired with great ease and indolence, and with little risk, and their fortunes so disposed, that the usual methods of laying taxes will not affect them; they are generally concerned in, nay have almost entirely engrossed, the whole retail trade of this island, furnish our people with materials of luxury, tempt them to live and dress above their circumstances, carry on a traffic with our slaves ... encouraging the Negroes to steal commodities from their masters, which they sell to the Jews, they lay out their money at interest.... It is against interest and policy of every country, to encourage the heaping up of such riches among them. That it is in this light the Jews are taxed separately and not on account of religion or country ... nor does the present tax exceed what they have paid 40 years

ago, when their riches were not near so great as they are at present, and their numbers have been daily increasing.... That this bill raises annually £12,000 ... a very inconsiderable part must fall upon the Jews without this separate tax.... That £10,000 of the money raised by this Bill, is applied to subsist His Majesty's troops.... They do not pay tax on importation of slaves—none of them [are] involved in this trade. Only 5 or 6 pay tax on export of Negroes.

The judge went on to question the efficiency of the law which raised £7,000 per year to bring in white servants while the cost of bringing in these servants was nearly £20,000 per year.

Jews are exempt. This duty [is] on owners of at least 30 Negroes or 150 cattle. (Jews are exempt because they don't own these things.) These imported whites are used against slave uprisings and outside enemies while Jews are safe and pursue their private concerns.... Jews import dry goods—not taxed. They do not consume liquor from which most money is raised. They are exempt from various offices, civil and military, which receive no pay." "and as to military posts in our Militia, they were very unfit for, never desirous of, nor would they accept of them. They are exempt from jury duty which saves them many pounds and time away from business. The Jews have all the benefits that other residents have. Their taxes are collected by their own people. On May 9, 1741, the legislature passed a bill to levy taxes for the upkeep of soldiers.

Jewish conditions improved on the island. In 1740, Isaac Fustado was listed as an attorney; therefore he was an officer of the court. In 1741, Moses Gutteres was listed as an owner of land slated to be condemned (this meant Jews could be landowners).

Barbados was similar to Jamaica in the makeup of its population—English, Jews and blacks—free or slave. There were Jewish thieves and rogues as in every population. In 1665, Isaac Israel de Piso[14] failed to find gold in Barbados as he had promised the authorities. He had to return the land given to him, and he and his family were banished from the island. Later, Governor Davidson complained that some Jews cheated him, so they were ordered to leave the island, but they paid no attention to his edict. In 1668, it was ordered that no Jews were to be in the retail trade. This was to be left to "the poor of our nation." It was also decreed that no Jews were to trade with Amsterdam, which was against the acts of navigation. In 1669, orders were given to seize the ships in this trade.

Things began to improve in Barbados when Governor Willoughby decreed that there would be no more oaths of allegiance and supremacy and that no man was to be molested in the peaceable exercise of his religion. In 1673, Jews were allowed to give testimony in certain cases. In 1674, Jews could take an oath on the Five Books of Moses in testimony about trade if they were men of "Credit and Commerce." In 1675, Jews could testify in all cases. Things were reversed for the Jews in 1756, when a special tax of £270 per year was levied on them. Five years later, this was repealed, and an act was passed stating that there would be no distinction between Jew and Christian when a tax was levied.

Anti-Semitism in the American Colonies

Some colonial Americans may have carried anti–Semitic attitudes from Europe. Fortunately, they did not extend these feelings to killing the outsiders, but many nevertheless wanted to keep them outside. In New Amsterdam, Governor Peter Stuyvesant and Dominie Johannes Megapolensis of the Dutch Reform church wanted to remove the Jews from the Dutch colony. A small boatload arrived in New Amsterdam in September 1654. Stuyvesant[15] sent a letter to the directors of the Dutch West India Company, wherein he stated that "the Jews who arrived would like to stay, but they were repugnant to the Inferior Magistrates (with their customary usury and deceitful trading with Christians). The Deaconry felt they would become a charge in the coming winter because of their indigence. Because our colony is new and weak, we asked them in a friendly way to leave. We prayed that this deceitful race—such hateful enemies and blasphemers of the name of Christ not be allowed to infest this colony." The Jews wrote to their coreligionists in Holland in October 1654, requesting money to pay the debts due the captain of the ship that brought them from the West Indies.

The Dutch West India Company replied to Stuyvesant's letter in 1655: "We would have liked to agree with your wishes and request that the new territories should not be further invaded by people of the Jewish race, for we foresee from such immigration the same difficulties which you fear, but after having further weighed and considered the matter, we observe that this would be somewhat unreasonable and unfair, especially because of the considerable loss sustained by this nation with others in the taking of Brazil (by the Portuguese), as also because of the large amount of capital which they still have invested in the shares of this company ... that these people may travel and trade to and in New Netherland and live and remain there provided the poor shall not become a burden to the company or to the community but be supported by their own nation. You will govern yourself accordingly."[16]

Stuyvesant was initially taken aback by the director's reprimand, but it did not last long.[17] On October 30, 1655, he wrote, "To give liberty to the Jews will be very detrimental here, because the Christians there will not be able at the same time to do business. Giving them liberty, we cannot refuse the Lutherans and Papists." On March 13, 1656, the directors sent another letter. "[W]ithout giving the said Jews a claim to the privilege of exercising their religion in a synagogue or a gathering ... your considerations and anxiety about the matter are premature." The directors of the company were also subjected to a letter from the Jews of Amsterdam. "[Y]our Honors should also please consider that many of the Jewish nation are principal shareholders in the Company.... The French consent at the present time that the Portuguese Jews may traffic and live in Martinique, Christophers and others of their territories. The English also consent at the present time that the Portuguese and Jewish nation may go from London and settle at Barbados."

More Jews arrived in 1655.[18] The Jews in Amsterdam mounted a further intercession. They pointed to the concept of mercantilism and fears of an English invasion. The governors of the company in Amsterdam insisted that the Jews have the same privileges as in the home country. Most residents in New Amsterdam accepted the Jews. Stuyvesant recognized that the Jews would stay, but he continued to harass them. He refused to permit them to trade at Fort Orange (Albany) and on the South River (Delaware River). He prohibited their purchase of real estate. A Jew, Dandrada,[19] tried to purchase a house from Teunis Cray in 1665 for 1860 guilders—about $740—because Cray was returning to Holland, but the council turned the sale down. The council paid Cray half the difference between the Dandrada bid and the next lower Christian bid. With each restriction placed upon them, the Jews petitioned the company for redress. Almost by return ship, the petitions bore fruit in overruling Stuyvesant. A letter on February 15, 1665, said this: "Jews or Portuguese people, however, shall not be employed in any public service. Nor allowed to have open retail shops ... and exercise in all quietness their religions within their houses, for which end they must without endeavor to build their houses close together in a convenient place on one or the other side of New Amsterdam—at their choice—as they have done here."

With Stuyvesant properly chastened, we now turn to Dominie John Megapolensis, who came as minister to the patroonship of Rensselaerswyck in 1642 and seven years later became minister of the church at New Amsterdam. He hated any group who was not Dutch Reform. In 1654, he prevented the Lutherans from building a church in New Amsterdam.[20] In 1659, the Lutheran preacher Johannes Ernestus Gutwasser[21] was deported because he preached to his congregation. In a letter to the *classis* (church governing body) in Amsterdam,[22] he complained (about the Jews); "These people have no other God than the unrighteous Mammon, and no other aim than to get possession of Christian property, and to win all other merchants by drawing all trade to themselves. We request your Reverences to obtain from Messirs Directors that these godless rascals, who are of no benefit to the county (be removed).... For, as we have here papists, Mennonites and Lutherans among the Dutch, also many Puritans or Independents, and many Atheists and various other servants of Baal among the English under this government ... it would create a still greater confusion if the obstinate and immovable Jews came to settle here." A letter from the classis of Amsterdam to the consistory (leaders of the congregation) in New Netherlands (May 26, 1656) replied "In fact we are informed that even the Jews have made request to the Honorable Governor and have also attempted in that country to erect a synagogue for the exercise of their blasphemous religion." The classis learned that mercantilism was more important than religion.

Once the Jews were reassured of their stability in New Amsterdam, they tried to raise their acceptance by their neighbors. Asser Levy and Jacob Barsimson went to court to be allowed to join the militia. Jews were not permitted to join, but they had to pay a tax instead of serving. They received this privilege because the Algonquin Indians threatened the weak community. The Jews slowly received their civil rights and were also given the right to purchase a cemetery, but they could not hold public services. Despite their advances civilly, they were not advancing economically, and many left for the West Indies. Asser Levy was one of the last remaining Jews. In 1664, the English annexed New Amsterdam and gave the Jews greater religious and civil rights.

The Dutch were not the only group that had to deal with Jews in their midst. The Puritans had a similar problem. As early as 1645,[23] there were thoughts of toleration of other religions in Massachusetts. In a letter from Edward Winslow to Governor Winthrop, "I utterly abhorred it ... to allow full and free toleracion of religion to all men.... [T]here was no limitacon [*sic*] or exception against Turke, Jew, Papist, Arian ... or any other sect." In 1649, Solomon Franco came to Boston with a cargo consigned to Major General John Edward Gibbons. Franco was an agent of Immanuel Perado, but he planned to settle in Boston. The Great and General Court passed a ruling giving Franco six shillings per week for ten weeks out of the treasury for subsistence until he could get passage to Holland. In 1674, Roland Gideon "the Jew" was on the Boston tax list. He had a letter of denization from Great Britain which allowed him to reside in any British colony. By 1695, there were two Jews among the inhabitants of Boston.

The towns in Massachusetts did not want strangers in their midst who might later be in need of support by the town.[24] They had to purchase land or post security. In 1680, John Foster put up £40 for security for Joseph Bueno. In 1756, Philip Samuel, a Jew, was warned to leave town. David Campanell, Jew from Rhode Island, was warned out of Boston in 1726. Isaac Moses was warned to leave Boston or put up security.

In Delaware, the Swedes barred Jewish settlement.[25] Jews were also excluded from Virginia early in its history. At the time of the Revolution, there were six Jewish families in the Old Dominion.[26] Maryland was hostile to Jews until well into the nineteenth century. Jews entered Georgia against the will of the trustees.[27] Georgia was planned as a haven for the poor of England. Commissions to obtain revenue were given to Thomas Frederick, Anthony Da Costa, Francis Salvador, Jr., and Alvaro Lopez Suasso. The last three were Jews. The trustees wanted their help to collect money and to assist the poor to reach Georgia, but they did not want their poor Jewish coreligionists to go to Georgia. The trustees asked that the Jews return their commissions to Mr. Martyn, the secretary. One trustee, in a letter to the Board of Trustees, feared Georgia would become a Jewish colony, and all good Christians would leave except those who would build housing for the Jews. This letter was included as part of an explanation titled "A brief account of the Causes that have retarded the progress of the Colony of Georgia in America." The trustees vacated the Jews' commission, but the money the Jews collected was used to send Jews to Georgia. A vessel from England with 40 Jews, partly paid for by the subscriptions, subsequently arrived in Georgia.

Although the Jews left forced conversion behind when they left Europe, in America, particularly in New England, they were faced by an intellectual form of conversion. To put the best face on it, the Puritan theologians were trying to save the souls of the Jews so they could spend eternity with God. Many Jews succumbed, but most considered it as a covert form of anti–Semitism. The Puritans[28] accepted a prophecy that as soon as the Jews were dispersed to every land on earth, there would be a calling of the Jewish nation and their conversion to Christianity. This would bring forth the millennium. To convert a Jew was a personal glory and a step toward accelerating the establishment of the kingdom of God on earth. Cotton Mather's diary describes his almost maniacal need to convert a Jew. "This day[29] from the dust where I lay prostrate before the Lord I lifted up my cries... For the conversion of the Jewish Nation and for my own happiness, at some time or other, to baptize a Jew, that should by my ministry, be brought home unto the Lord." He studied Hebrew and claimed to have mastered it perfectly. Mather also said he had an acquaintanceship with the "*Talmuds*." Every Jew with whom he came into contact was an object of his missionary zeal.

He had printed *The Faith of the Fathers*, an attempt to show the Jews the error of their ways ("Return O backsliding Israel"). If they would return to the faith of the Old Testament, they would see the error of their ways and be converted to Christianity. The work consisted of passages from the Old Testament so arranged as to prove Jesus was the Messiah of the Jews. He dedicated the book to the "Jewish Nation." He wanted the Jews to see the error of their ways and be converted to Christianity, which is only the true, complete Jewish religion developed through Jesus, he believed. Mather had a one-on-one relationship with a Jew, Frazon, but he was unsuccessful in his conversion attempts. His success rate in conversion was minimal if at all. A Jew in Carolina supposedly read the tract and converted. Mather produced a second book in 1700 on the same subject. This was equally unsuccessful because his diary failed to show any references to Jews for ten years. His father, Increase Mather, wrote the *Mystery of Israel's Salvation*, which failed to produce any results.

Ezra Stiles,[30] a minister in Newport, knew many Jews, learned Hebrew and attended Jewish services. After he heard Hazzan Seixas preach, he wrote in his diary: "How melancholy to behold an assembly of worshippers of Jehovah, open and professed enemies to a crucified Jesus."

Numbers are hard to prove, but it is said that one of seven to one of ten Jews converted in New England.[31] There were many more Jewish men than women, and most Jews were related. Men who went to Connecticut from New York and became permanent settlers married gentile girls, and their children were brought up in their mother's religion. Rich Jews who were in business with Protestants mingled socially with them, and their children often intermarried. Their grandchildren were raised as Protestants.

In the first census in 1790, there were about 1,500 Jews among three million whites. Most Americans never saw a Jew, let alone talked with one. The theater in America[32] developed during the eighteenth century, and most early plays were taken from the British stage. English theater depicted Jews as a comic element in the play, but Shakespeare's *Shylock* presented a different sort of Jew. Between 1701 and 1733, nine British plays portrayed Jews. Theophilus Cibber pantomimed Jews. In *Love à la Mode* (1759), the author described a Jewish character, and this portrayal became the stereotype of a Jew in stage productions thereafter. In *The Cozzeners* (1774), Jews were social climbers. In *Devil's Law Case*, a Christian took a Jewish disguise, and this was used thereafter in many plays. *The Heiress* (1786) portrayed the Jew as a "fence" of stolen goods. *The Young Quaker* (1783) introduced the Jewish dialect, and the play was introduced to American audiences (1794). In the production, Jews could not use the English language properly. In *Fashionable Lover*, an unsavory Jew was a broker and a money lender. One of his lines was, "War is a very coot thing; and then the plague a blessed circumstance, tank Heaven; coot seven percent." In *Trial Without Jury*, Isaac is heard offstage, "Knifes! Fine knifes! Chewels! Fine lace! Chentlemen and ladies, come puy, come puy." In *Slaves of Algiers*, the villain is a Jew who converted to "Mohammedanism" and has the accent of a stage Jew. His daughter, who wants to convert to Christianity, speaks perfect English. The father wishes to marry Rebecca. Rebecca responds, "You who worship no deity but gold, who would sacrifice friendship, nay, even the ties of nature at the shrine of your idolatry." In *Algernine Captive*, published in New Hampshire (1797), Royall Tyler describes "the artful Jew," and "the wily Israelite." Bad Jews were deceitful, venal, grasping, subordinating all values to money. In *American Captive* (1811), the Jew is introduced counting his money, "Vat smiling dogs they are! Vat comely form!" He compares women's beauty to gold; "Women fade, gold remains glittering."

In the midst of this virulent anti–Semitism, an occasional play depicted Jews in a positive light. In 1794, *The Jew* depicted a money lender, like Shylock in *The Merchant of Venice*. His soliloquy started, in perfect English, "We have no abiding place on Earth, no country, no home. Everybody rails at us, everybody points out for their way-game and then mockery. If your playwrights want a butt or buffoon, or a knave to make sport of, out comes a Jew to be buffooned through five long acts, for the amusement of all good Christians." A theater reviewer saw *Liberal Opinion* (1801) and praised it for its tendency to obviate "those unjust and illiberal prejudices which have too long been entertained in every country except this against that unfortunate race of men."

The Jewish accent was the playwright's attempt to impersonate the most recent immigrants. The Sephardic Jews were in this country for several generations and spoke like their Christian neighbors. By 1740, the Ashkenazis outnumbered the Sephardic Jews. It was this group from Germany to Poland who spoke with a German accent.

In the Revolution, most Jews were patriots and supplied more Jewish soldiers per capita than any other group, although there were some Jews loyal to the crown. It was this minority that led to anti–Semitic remarks. Jacob Franks[33] was the first of the Franks to reach America in 1711. He was a purveyor to the British troops in Britain's wars with France. In King George's war, he and his sons made large sums of money supplying the troops. They had a business that spanned the ocean. In the French and Indian War, Jacob's son Moses was the central player in a group of politically active people who supplied British armies in North America. Moses continued to service the British armies into the 1780s. His brother, David, in Philadelphia, supplied English troops at Fort Pitt and the Illinois country. Between 1740 and 1780, the Franks family had contracts worth about £1,000,000 sterling.

Despite the overwhelming support of Jews for the patriots, some attacks against them reached the newspapers. A letter in a Charleston newspaper[34] accused Jews of loyalty to the Crown and shirking military duty. Jews were said to take advantage in trade in Georgia. When Georgia was invaded, the Jews fled to Charleston. This attack was answered by "A real American and True-hearted Israelite," who pointed out that Jews took their families to Charleston to keep them out of harm's way. Then the men returned to Savannah to try to save the state from the British. The anti–Semitism at this time was a war of words. There were no organized mobs that attacked Jewish homes or workplaces, and at no time did any government support any attacks.[35] The Jewish support in the Revolution is covered more fully in another chapter.

Anti-Semitic Jews

In Philadelphia there was a split between "old Jews" and "new Jews."[36] The old Jews looked down upon the new Jews, who were Ashkenazi, as opposed to the earlier Sephardim. The more recent Jewish immigrants felt the need to "catch up" and were more interested in business and making a living than attending strictly to piety and Jewishness. The Sephardic Jews considered the later Jews as dirty, smelly peddlers who could destroy the position of the old Jews in Christian American eyes. They spoke with accents and pronounced Hebrew differently, and their Sabbath services were different. The Ashkenazi Jews spoke Yiddish (a combination of German, Hebrew and words from the country in which they lived.) The new Jews had large, hooked noses and did not have olive-colored skin. The new Jews had names with "schiene" or "schon." The Sephardic Jews referred to them as *sheeny*, which spread through Christian America. The Ashkenazi Jews believed the Sephardim were too inbred, which made them "strange."

The Sunday "blue laws"[37] meant it was *the* Sabbath in America. This denied the Jew his Sabbath and forced him to accept Sunday. Timothy Dwight, in a speech, favored the Sunday blue laws, which led to a Massachusetts law in 1792: "Irreligious or like-minded persons must be kept from violating the Sabbath. This way of acting is against their interests as Christians. It upsets those who follow Sabbath laws. It damages society by introducing a taste for dissipation and bad habits. Many consider this law an encroachment on personal rights. Our blue laws are right, founded on the laws of god and necessary for the preservation and enjoyment of that important institution. All of the states had these laws, and most Jews totally ignored them. In Pennsylvania, the Presbyterians tried to enforce these laws. They had vigilantes who arrested Sunday travelers.

A law in New York State (1788) stated that by the authority of the senate and assembly, "there would be no travelling, servile labor, working (except of necessity, or of charity), shooting, fishing, sporting, playing, horse-racing, hunting or frequenting tipling-houses or any unlawful exercises or pastimes by anyone in this state on the first day of the week, commonly called Sunday. Anyone over 14 offending the law shall pay for the poor of the community six *shillings*. No food goods were sold except small meat, milk and fish before 9 A.M. Those breaking the law shall forfeit goods placed on sale. The legal officer [mayor or alderman] tells constable of law-breaking. He seizes goods and sells. Money to overseers of the poor. Offender is placed in the stocks for two hours."[38]

In Pennsylvania,[39] court cases were held on Saturday as well as the weekdays. In the case of *Stansberry v. Marks*, tried on Saturday, the defendant had Jonas Phillips, a Jew, as his witness. When Phillips refused to be sworn in because it was his Sabbath, the court fined him £10.

In 1816, Abraham Wolff was convicted under the Sabbath act of 1794 for performing worldly employment on the Lord's day—Sunday. His defense was that he was a Jew and therefore not included within the meaning of the act. He cited the fourth commandment: work six days and rest the seventh. The court did not support his construction of the commandment, however, and affirmed the conviction.

While these blue laws interfered with the Jew's right to observe his Sabbath and work on Sundays, it only meant a fine or loss of goods. In Maryland,[40] notorious for its treatment of dissenters, a Sabbath law passed one century earlier called for no work and no travel and to stay off public streets on Sunday. For violating the law, the accused could be fined, imprisoned or put to death.

Early in their experience in America, the Jews were not involved in politics. They were happy to be overlooked by the Protestant majority. They preferred not to "make waves." Jews,[41] throughout their existence in Christian lands, recognized the need to adapt to their situation in order to survive in reasonable comfort. Jews were passive about political rights. They feared that political demands (voting, holding office, serving on a jury) might cause a backlash with removal of any rights they had achieved earlier. After several generations in America, Jews did not simply want tolerance: They wanted equality before the law.

In my eyes, the most bigoted colony during the colonial period was Maryland, which was founded shortly after Virginia as a haven for English Roman Catholics.[42] The Catholics became a minority as a result of a massive immigration of Protestants. By the time of the American Revolution, Anglicans were in the majority with large groups of Quakers, Presbyterians, Lutherans, Baptists, Methodists and Catholics. It took Maryland well into the nineteenth century to grant Jews equality under the law.

On April 21, 1649,[43] an act of the assembly was ordained by Cecilius, Lord Baltimore, proprietor of this province, with consent of the general assembly:

> Any who blaspheme God that is curse him or deny Saviour Jesus Christ to be son of God and the Trinity (father, sonne and holy Ghost) or speak reproachfully of Holy Trinity will suffer death and confiscation of lands and goods to the Proprietor and heirs. Also reproachful words against Virgin Mary, holy Apostles, Evangelists—For first offense forfeit to Proprietor £5, he is whipped then jailed at the pleasure of the Proprietor. Second offense £10 or whipped and jailed. Third offense he forfeits lands and goods and is expelled from the province. Anyone in the province who uses a term of derision toward any Christian sect—the fine is 10 *shillings*—one half to the person offended, the other half to the Lord proprietor. If he has no money, he is whipped and jailed until he asks forgiveness.... To profane the Sabbath by swearing, drunkenness or working when not necessary will bring a fine of two *shillings* six pence. The second offense is five *shillings*. The third offense is ten *shillings*. If he has no money he is jailed and declares in open court that he profaned the Sabbath. This for first and second offense. For a third offense, he is whipped.... Any person who believes in Jesus will not be troubled or molested and allowed free exercise of that religion and not be forced to accept another religion. Any who trouble those who believe in Jesus—pay treble damages and pay 20 *shillings*, one half to molested person, and one half to the Lord Proprietor. If unable to pay the fine, he is whipped and kept in prison on the pleasure of the Proprietor. The Sheriff may seize his goods and sell them to pay the fine. The remainder went to the molester.

It was under this law that Jacob Lumbrozo was tried. He was bound over for trial explaining Christ's miracles and the resurrection as magicianship and shrewd body stealing. A Quaker charged him with blasphemy against Christ, which was punishable by death. John Fossett was the first witness. He told of the accused's explanation of Christ's miracles and resurrection. Richard Preston, the second witness, concurred with Fossett's testimony. Lumbrozo, in his defense, told of Moses and the magicians in Egypt who could perform "miracles." "He did not scoff or derogate Him that Christians called the Messiah." Lumbrozo was sentenced to death, but he was freed when Cromwell became protector in England. Lumbrozo later converted, and his name appeared as a jury member without objection from the people or government of Maryland.

There were few Jews in Maryland due to the anti–Jewish atmosphere. They kept to themselves, predominantly in Baltimore and made no demands on the government. In 1775, the congress, meeting in Philadelphia, advised the colonies to draw up constitutions. Maryland's constitution[44] stated in Article XXXIII that "it is the duty of every man to worship god in such manner as he thinks most acceptable to him; all persons professing the Christian religion, are equally entitled to their religious liberty." Article XXXV stated that "no other test or qualification ought to be requested on admission to any office of trust or profit ... and a declaration of a belief in the Christian religion."

This situation was quietly accepted by the Jewish community until Solomon Etting, a Jewish merchant in Baltimore, petitioned the state government for Jewish equality and rights of citizenship in 1797, but nothing came of his request. Several more petitions after the turn of the century brought similar results. Finally, Thomas Kennedy,[45] an immigrant from Scotland, was elected to the legislature in 1817. He represented Washington County, where there were no Jewish inhabitants. In 1818, he requested that a committee be appointed to investigate the rights of Jews. The committee turned in a positive report, and William Pinkney presented a bill "that every oath to be administered to any person of the sect of people called Jews, shall be administered on the Five Books of Moses." The bill was called the "Jew bill" and Kennedy's "Jewish baby" and was defeated in 1819. A second bill was introduced in 1822, with no mention of Jews, and was passed on its first reading but defeated on its second reading. Kennedy was defeated for reelection by a federalist, Benjamin Galloway. He called himself the head of the Christian ticket and said that Kennedy was head of the Jew ticket. Galloway's handbill stated, "Preferring as I do Christianity to Judaism, Deism, Unitarianism or any other new-fangled ism I deprecate any change in our State government calculated to afford the least chance of the enemies of Christianity, of undermining it in the belief of the people of Maryland." Kennedy was reelected the following year, however. The bill was passed in 1825 with 26 yea and 25 no votes and with 80 abstentions. In 1826, the bill was confirmed 45 to 32. This bill gave the Jews the right to hold office.

The need to emancipate the Jews was pushed by newspapers in several states.[46] They printed editorials against Maryland's "bigoted constitution." The *Freeman's Journal* and *Aurora* in Philadelphia, the *Southern Patriot* in Charleston and the *National Advocate* in New York all joined the fray. Charles Carroll, a Catholic, a signer of the Declaration of Independence, and the most prominent Roman Catholic in Maryland, called for the change.

Puritan New England was not too far behind Maryland. Connecticut functioned under a royal charter and did not write a constitution for 40 years. Its legislature passed an act of toleration, but this did not apply to Jews. Religious freedom ensured there would be "no preference ... given by law to any Christian Sect or mode of worship." Christianity was the state's belief and actively put down Jews and Unitarians. In 1818, Connecticut disestablished the congregational church. Rhode Island's[47] criteria for freemanship were more than economic. From 1714 to 1783, Catholics and Jews were ineligible for this status. This action countered a law in 1665 which permitted Jews and Catholics to vote and hold office. The Massachusetts law of 1778[48] gave religious freedom only to Protestants. A non–Protestant could not hold office in that state. A second constitution in 1780 proclaimed that all Christians were protected under the law and only those who believed in Jesus could hold office. Catholics had to "swear off the pope." In the Massachusetts constitution of 1821, Jews could hold office, but only with great difficulty. Finally in 1833, Massachusetts gave protection to all sects. The constitution of New Hampshire in 1782 called for political restrictions against non–Protestants.[49] This restriction was not removed until 1876, when any citizen of New Hampshire could hold office.

The thirty-eighth article of the constitution of New York on April 20, 1777, stated that everyone within its borders was to enjoy freedom of conscience. Voters for legislators and governor need only be freeholders[50] "and by the authority of the good people of this State, ordain, determine, and declare that the free exercise and enjoyment of religious profession and worship, without discrimination or preference, shall forever hereafter be allowed, within this State to all mankind."[51] Jews could hold office at this time, but Catholics had to wait until 1806. The Jews of New York voted quietly and unobserved for much of the eighteenth century.

However, in 1737, in the election of Adolph Philipse over Cornelius Van Horn,[52] Philipse's win was declared illegal because Jews voted for him. The New York legislature decided that since Jews could not vote for parliament in England, they could not vote for the legislature in New York. This disability was slowly removed by time rather than by an act of the legislature. During that century Jews were elected to the office of constable (a less than desirable position). They served warrants, kept the peace, served as night watchmen, and controlled vice, profanation of the Sabbath, and excessive drinking.[53] In New Jersey in 1776, believers in any Protestant sect could be elected to office, but all were granted religious freedom.[54] Delaware ordered all state officers to swear to uphold trinitarianism in 1776.

Pennsylvania was a major state because of the prominence of Philadelphia. The actions of Pennsylvania were watched by the rest of the states. Jews and atheists could not take seats in the legislature. Benjamin Franklin succeeded in adding that no "further or more extended Profession of Faith shall ever be enacted." He was attacked by the Reverend Muhlenberg, who worried that Christian people would be ruled by Jews, Turks, Spinozists, deists and perverted naturalists.[55] The Pennsylvania constitution allowed free worship to all, but a belief in God was needed for civil rights, and a religious oath was required upon taking office. The oath called for a belief in one God: "it is ordered that each member of the general assembly of representatives and the freemen of Pennsylvania, before he takes his seat, shall make and subscribe a declaration which ends in these words, 'I do acknowledge the Scriptures of the Old and New Testament to be given by divine inspiration.'"[56]

The Jews were allowed freedom of conscience in the Constitution, much to the chagrin of many Protestant citizens. This would allow Jews and Turks and other enemies of Christ to achieve financial and political power to the eventual harm of Christians. Others worried that giving equal rights to all would promote the building of all types of Christian churches (including those of the Roman Catholics), such as synagogues, mosques and heathen temples. The deficiencies of the Pennsylvania constitution[57] bothered the Jewish citizens. Jonas Philips asked the constitutional convention that met in Philadelphia on September 7, 1787, to emancipate the Jews: "I ... behold with concern that among the laws in the constitution of Pennsylvania, there is a clause, section 10 to viz, 'I do believe in one God the creatur and governor of the universe and rewarder of the good and the punisher of the wicked and I do acknowledge the Scriptures of the Old and New Testament was given by divine inspiration.' To swear and believe that the New Testament was given by divine inspiration is absolutely against the religious principle of Jews.... By the above law a Jew is deprived of holding any publick office or place of government."[58] The Pennsylvania constitution in 1790 stated that a believer in God could hold office.[59]

Virginia, the first colony and birthplace of Washington, Jefferson and Madison, was where religious freedom was fought for and won by Jefferson and Madison. After the Declaration of Independence, Virginia set out to write its constitution.[60] A committee under Colonel Mason stated that all men should enjoy the fullest toleration of their religion. Madison objected to the term "toleration." Toleration meant to suffer that which you could. If you wished, you could prevent and prohibit. It was an idea of compassion that degrades men, so the concept of toleration was changed: "All men are equally entitled to the free exercise of religion, according to the dictates of conscience." After putting toleration in the grave, Jefferson, through Madison, fought against a tax to support the Episcopal church (offshoot of Anglicanism), and this was defeated in 1779.

Many in Virginia opposed the separation of church and state. Patrick Henry led the movement to pass a tax to support all Christian sects, because Christianity was the religion of the majority. He also claimed "all men are equally entitled to the free exercise of religion." The states allowed them freedom to worship as they pleased, but they had no right to participate in government. This adopted, and Henry was appointed to draft such a bill, which passed two readings. Madison prevented a third reading and passage until the bill could be circulated throughout Virginia for the citizens to see and comment upon. He wrote a diatribe against the bill, which he compared to the Inquisition. It would prevent immigration to Virginia and cause emigration from the state. The assembly abandoned the bill after extensive reaction from the people of Virginia. Jefferson's concept of total separation of church and state became the law of Virginia.

George Washington initially supported the assessment bill of 1784, but he asked that Jews and other non–Christians be exempted from taxation.[61] The statute of 1786 stated that no man should suffer because of religious beliefs. Everyone could profess their beliefs in religion without affecting their civil rights. This could not be repealed because this would be an infringement of natural rights. Madison wrote that the assessment bill (supporting Christian sects) "degrades all those whose religion does not bend to the religion of the legislative authority." He believed that state support of Christianity would remove its vitality and make it less attractive to possible converts. The Virginia bill of rights attested that religion and the manner in which we discharge our duty to our creator is directed by reason, not force. Therefore, all men are free to practice their religion in their own way according to their conscience. Furthermore, the bill of rights called for separation of church and state (pushed by Jefferson) and "no state religion or support thereof." It further stated [62] that "no religious test shall ever be required as a qualification to any office of public trust."

The concepts of the emancipation of Jews and the separation of church and state were brought to Europe by Jefferson. The French Revolution started to give rights to all. Napoleon carried the concept of equal rights wherever his armies went. Lafayette, who was in America, returned to France with these beliefs. Mirabeau, in 1787, published the concept of Jewish emancipation. The French national assembly stated in 1784 "That no one shall be molested on account of his religious opinion, insofar as their outward expression does not disturb public order as established by law." In 1791, the national assembly passed a law banning all regulations imposed against Jews and making them citizens.

It took a Jefferson, behind Madison, to turn Virginia completely around. In the seventeenth century,[63] all residents of Virginia took an oath that they believed in Jesus Christ. This prevented Jewish settlement. In 1705, Jews, Negroes, Catholics and convicts could not testify in court. As late as 1755, Jews could not employ Christian servants in their homes.

As one of his many accomplishments, Jefferson listed the Virginia bill establishing religious freedom as one of his most important. It was the earliest law in history to grant full equality to all citizens regardless of religion.[64] There were other forces also at work at this time. In Virginia, there was an influx of Baptists and Presbyterians,[65] who opposed the establishment of the Episcopal church. Taken a step further, they recognized that Jews should not have to support any Christian religion: "to compel Jews by law to support the Christian religion ... is an arbitrary and impolitic usurpation which Christians ought to be ashamed of."

In addition, the Enlightenment challenged the concept of the Christian state. It questioned the church's authority in civil affairs. This in turn led to the emancipation and integration of Jews and other sects into the nation. The U.S. Declaration of Independence and the French Declarations of the Rights of Man allow Jews to be elevated and accepted as equal human beings. The Jews were not totally passive and dependent upon what the greater Protestant nation deigned to give them, however. In a quiet way, they pushed for equality.[66] They fought for the right of settlement, trade and free worship (see Stuyvesant and New Amsterdam). They fought against Christian oaths and Christian symbols in schools and public places. They worked against the Sabbath blue laws, which were forced upon them as tradesmen. The Jews recognized that they were a minute part of the nation, but they objected to being second-class citizens. This could change only when Christianity was removed from public life. The Jews felt that separation of church and state was the key to equality.

Just as Jefferson was responsible for the Declaration of Independence, so was Madison largely responsible for the Constitution. Article VI, Section 3[67] states, "no religious test shall ever be required as a qualification to any office or public trust under the United States." In 1791 the First Amendment stated there would be no established religion or prohibition against the free exercise of religion. Many Americans feared the absence of a religious oath when the president took office. A Protestant oath[68] was needed, or "a Turk, a Jew, a Roman Catholic and worst of all a Universalist might become president of the United States." A letter was written to the New York *Daily Advertiser* that expressed worry that the Constitution gave command of the militia to the president. If he was a Jew, our children might be asked to rebuild Jerusalem.

Article VI, Section 3 of the First Amendment prevents the federal government from restricting religion. However, the states felt they were separate entities under a federal union. After the Constitution was accepted, New York, Pennsylvania, North Carolina and Maryland[69] still had laws that discriminated against the Jews. When this discrepancy came to the attention of the various state legislatures, it was corrected fairly rapidly, except in Maryland. The federal government received its first "colony" when several of the states gave up their rights to the Northwest Territory. Congress, on July 13, 1787, passed the Northwest Ordinance. Article I declared that "no person, demeaning himself in a peaceable and orderly manner, shall ever be molested on account of his mode of worship or religious sentiments, in the said territory."[70]

At the outbreak of fighting in the Revolution, North Carolina had no Jews. Its constitution, drawn in 1776, decreed that no one who "denied God, or the truth of the Protestant religion or divine Authority of the Old and New Testament," could hold office.[71] The constitution did grant religious freedom, however, and Jews began to drift into North Carolina after the Revolution. Jacob Henry,[72] a Jew born in the state, was elected to represent his county in the house of commons. He served in 1808 without taking the Protestant oath, and he was later reelected. Hugh C. Mills of Rockingham county objected to his seating because he refused to take the oath on the New Testament. Henry supported his position with great elegance. The problem was solved by the members stating that the legislature was not a civil organization; therefore, the oath was not required. This meant Jews could serve in the legislature but not in the governor's mansion or in the judiciary. In the constitutional convention at Raleigh in 1835, the members tried but failed to remove Article 32. They changed it so that "Christian" could replace "Protestant." When North Carolina seceded from the Union, restrictions against Jews persisted. In 1868, they were abolished when the state was controlled by radical Republicans.

South Carolina's constitution was written by John Locke and Jews, like others, were given freedom of religion. In 1691,[73] a law allowed Jews to be naturalized and to cast votes. This was repealed in 1721, but the vote was rescinded. The constitution of the state, written during the Revolution, granted religious freedom,[74] but only Protestants could vote and hold office. A second constitution in 1778 tolerated all who accepted one God.[75]

Jews entered Georgia "by stealth" in July 1733. The trustees claimed they did not have permission to enter the colony and urged General Oglethorpe to get rid of them.[76] They urged him not to encourage them or give them settlement (a grant of land). "They will be of prejudice to the trade and welfare of the colony." Oglethorpe's letter to the trustees crossed theirs on the ocean. He described an outbreak of disease that had killed 20 settlers. A shipload of Jews had a doctor who stopped the epidemic. The trustees responded that Oglethorpe should pay the doctor, but he was not to give him land. The trustees further claimed that the Jews ran away from Christian creditors, and they did not want to work. The trustees tried to have the Jewish commissioners in London get them back from Georgia. All of their attempts failed, because Oglethorpe did give them land grants and was happy with their productivity and the crafts they brought to the colony. Georgia [77] permitted multiple religious establishments and received tax money for their support. The money was used to support Christian churches. Georgia granted religious freedom, but only Protestants could hold office. In 1798, Georgia[78] ended religious qualifications for office.

After the Revolution, newspapers sprouted like mushrooms after a spring rain. These gave editors and letter writers a large audience for their anti-Semitism. The 1790s saw the unified nation under Washington split into the Federalists under Hamilton and Adams and the Democratic Republicans led by Jefferson. For the most part, Jews were followers of Jefferson.

James Rivington,[79] a loyalist in the Revolution, was a Federalist after the war. He published the New York *Gazeteer*, which was "anti" many groups: French, Negroes, Democrats and Jews. Rivington republished the

Democrat, written by Henry James Pye. In a preface, Rivington described a Democratic missionary from France, which was a place of sedition and murder, who came to spread French principles. Democratic clubs in America were made up of French agents waiting for French gold to start an insurrection. Rivington claimed they could easily be recognized by their physiognomy. "They all seemed to be like their vice-president, of the Tribe of Shylock. They have that leering underlook, and malicious grin, that says 'do not approach me.'" The "itinerant gang" described by Rivington was probably the Democratic Society in New York founded in 1794. The vice-president and one of the founders was Solomon Simson, a merchant and active patriot during the Revolution. There were one or two other Jews in the society. A member of the society, Thomas Greenleaf, founded the New York *Journal and Patriotic Register* and the *Argus, or Greenleaf's Daily Advertiser*. He attacked Rivington's anti–Semitism in both papers (1795). In his "letter" he stated, "It is a good maxim not to ridicule religion, or the natural defects of the human body. The first shows the depravity of the head, the latter the malignity of the heart.... If by the word Shylock, you mean a Jew, from my knowledge of the vice-president, I dare say he would think himself honoured by the appellation, Judaism being his religious profession, as Democracy is his political creed." Greenleaf attacked Rivington for being a loyalist in the war. In a letter that Greenleaf signed "Hortenseus," he attacked the *Democrat* as one of the most impudent works that ever appeared in any age or country. "The invidious and impudent remarks that it contains, not only upon a worthy individual, but also upon a numerous class of citizens who are more sincere in their attachments to the interests of America than you, merits censure, and if repeated may involve you in consequences that may prove disagreeable, if not dangerous to yourself." He then advised Rivington "to abstain from a course of conduct that may prove injurious to you and subject you to consequences for which the writer will not be answerable." (It seems that a Henry Cruger had horsewhipped Rivington.)

In 1800, Dr. Benjamin Rush sued William Cobbett for libel about his treatment during the yellow fever epidemic. When Rush's lawyer, Moses Levi, won $5,000 for Rush, Cobbett attacked Levi. "Moses Levi had the charity to suggest that I, being a 'royalist,' might possibly have hoped, by discrediting the Doctor's practice, to increase the mortality amongst the 'Republicans.' Such a diabolical thought never could have engendered but in the mind of a Jew.... I cannot for my life, however, muster up anything like anger against a poor devil like Moses; he did not believe a word he said—he vash vorking for de monish, dat vash all."

The Democratic Society of Philadelphia held a meeting on July 30,

1800. It was covered by the *Gazette of the United States* and *Daily Advertiser* (Federalists). In the audience was Benjamin Nones, a Jewish immigrant from France who had been a major in the Revolution. The chairman of the meeting called for contributions to pay for the rental of the hall. The newspaper "quoted" Nones, "I hopsh you will consider dat de monish ish very scarch, and besides you know I'sh just come out by de Insholvent Law." Nones replied in the Philadelphia *Aurora* (Democratic) to the charges of being a Jew, a Republican, and poor.[80] He pleaded guilty to all three counts. "How then can a Jew but be a Republican?" He described his war service under General Pulaski at Savannah and stated that he had been impoverished by the war.

In the history of individual attacks on Jews, William Usselinx,[81] a native of reasonably tolerant Holland, should be mentioned. In the charter of the Dutch West India Company, he proposed the following: "No trust shall be put in the promises made there (Brazil) by the Jews, a race faithless and pusillanimous, enemies to all the world and especially to all Christians, caring not whose house burns so long as they may warm themselves at the coals, who would rather see a hundred thousand Christians perish than suffer the loss of a hundred crowns." His proposal was not accepted by the company.

The Puritans,[82] who loved the biblical Jews, could not relate to the contemporary Jews in their midst. They saw only the Jews' "stiff-necked obduracy" in accepting Jesus.

Jews were accused of deicide and hostility to Christianity.[83] They introduced superstition, bloodshed and intolerance. They had an insatiable appetite for wealth, taking advantage of others in the conduct of business. They had undue influence on government ministers, thereby corrupting society. They were disheveled peddlers, and filthy hawkers of old clothing. The Reverend David McClure of Pennsylvania described them as dishonest people more concerned with the minutiae of ritual than the greater moral values. They defrauded others when the opportunity itself presented itself. Jewish merchants were disloyal and took advantage of the misfortunes of others and of hard times.

Thomas Paine,[84] the author of *Common Sense*, one of the writings that helped bring on the Revolution, violently opposed Christianity and Judaism. Gentiles could "unlearn" Christianity, he believed, whereas Judaism was biological. Moses was an assassin and an imposter. In *Age of Reason*, he claimed the early pagans were blackened by the Jews. Jews had to be cured of their character because they were a danger to enlightened society. If they assimilated they might be acceptable.

In 1751, Nathan Levy[85] placed a notice in the Pennsylvania *Gazette*:

"People have set up targets and shot at the wall of the burying ground—destroyed fence and tombstone. He erected a brick wall and asked sportsmen not to shoot at the wall. Anyone who informs and the person is convicted, informer receives 20 *shillings*." In Philadelphia, the Jewish congregation[86] raised enough money in 1782 to build a synagogue. They bought a lot in Sterling Alley next to a Reformed German congregation. The Germans raised an uproar against the proximity of a synagogue to their church, so the Jews bought another lot in Cherry Alley.

A trader who returned to Edenton, North Carolina,[87] from New York believed he was cheated by Solomon Townsend. "I suspect the fellow is a Jew."

William Duane[88] edited the *Aurora*, a Republican newspaper. He was attacked by the Federalist press, which targeted his Irish ancestry. "Duane was once a Jew Cloathsman in London from which place and from which occupation, his integrity expelled him.... He passed in London under the name Jew Aine."

There was an attack on "Jew brokers"[89] in the Pennsylvania legislature. During a fight about the Bank of North America, one legislator said he "could discover worse than a Shylock's temper remaining in the hearts of those despisers of Christianity." Miles Fisher, a Quaker, referred to them as "usurious Jews." "Jews did not contribute to the community, were parasites, despised physical labor and refused to become loyal permanent members of society." (Fisher was a Tory who was expelled from Pennsylvania during the Revolution.)

I wish to end this chapter with several paragraphs which I call "anti-anti–Semitism." It is about people whose writings and actions were positive toward their Jewish neighbors.

Peter Zenger,[90] whose trial for freedom of the press is in all high school history books, observed a Jewish funeral in New York in 1743:

> With little thought of returning the better Friend of that Nation, which was so much ridiculed and despised by ours. But alas, to my Friend of that Nation, which was so much ridiculed and despised by ours. But alas, to my Sorrow, I've only reason to abhor and despise many who (O Impudence!) dare stile themselves Christian. Of these Rude unthinking Wretches such a rabble was got together, it was with much Difficulty the Corpse was interr'd. I must confess I k now nothing but Decency on their Part. O that I might say the like of ours. But my mouth shall speak 'Truth and Wickedness is an Abomination to my Lips.' Lost to Shame and Humanity they even insulted the Dead in such a rude manner, that to mention all would shock a human Ear. One whom by his dress I should have thought to be a Gentleman, seem'd to Head this

Mob, he when the coffin was let down, held out an image (which I fear he's so fond of) and Mutter'd in Latine, as I suppose, his Pater Noster. God preserve his Majesty and Liege Subjects, who have too often felt the heavy hand of their outrageous self principled Neighbors. This Wretch and Scandle to Mankind to Christianity in particular, that real Christians may use him as he deserves.... I think it is my duty to Publish and utter (as a Christian) my Abhorrence of this Wickedness.... I am persuaded there may be good and Virtuous Men of all Societys.... Let us therefore have a Regard to our fellow Creatures, and only expose and ridicule Vice, Punish the Criminals and them (Tim. V20) that Sin Rebuke.

Of the Jews who fled Newport during its occupation by the British and remained in Leicester, Massachusetts, Emory Washburn[91] said,

They always observed the rites and ceremonies of their law and their stores were closed from Friday to Monday morning. They were prudent, industrious, and enterprising and many of them were elegant in their address and deportment and possessed an extreme knowledge of the world. They were always respected and esteemed by the inhabitants of the town and always seemed to remember with pleasure the kindness and civility they on their part received while residents there and availed themselves ever afterwards of every opportunity that presented to express those feelings, as many who experienced their attentions when in Newport would attest.... They kept stores closed on Sundays to regard sentiments of the others in the town. They won confidence and esteem of all by their upright and honorable dealing, the kindliness and courtesy of their intercourse.

Ezra Stiles,[92] the Puritan minister who vacillated with regard to Jews, said of Mr. Lopez, who died accidentally, "a Merchant of the first Eminence; for Honor and Extent of Commerce probably surpassed by no Merchant in America."

A letter in the Pennsylvania *Packet* and *Daily Advertiser*[93] on December 23, 1784, deplored how Christians worked on Good Friday instead of observing it. He pointed to Jews who observed Passover: "The Jews set us the example ... [and] refrain from the tempting lucre of gain.... Let not us Protestants ... in shewing respect to the dying day of Jesus Christ."

I would guess that neither Washington nor Jefferson was exposed to Jews in his youth or young adulthood. However, their relationship with Jews was most cordial. Washington[94] was a leader in creating better relations among religions. In 1790, he called for amity among Roman Catholics, Quakers and Jews. He wrote to a congregation in Newport, "It is now no more than toleration is spoken of, as if it was by indulgence of one class of people that another enjoyed the exercise of inherent natural rights. For happily the government of the United States, which give bigotry no sanction, to persecution no assistance, requires only that they who live under its protection should demean themselves as good citizens.... May the children of the Stock of Abraham, who dwell in this land, continue to meet and enjoy the good will of other inhabitants." Washington received letters of thanks from all the Jewish congregations of America[95] upon being elected president. He responded: "The affection of such a people is a treasure beyond the reach of calculation." It should be remembered that Washington's formal education stopped when he as age 14.

Jefferson was a bright, well-educated (William and Mary College), thinking deist. He saw and criticized the irrationalities of Judaism and Christianity.[96] He thought about the assimilation of Jews, but he felt they were a permanent alien element in American society. He was not well informed about Judaism and felt it had not changed since Moses. Jefferson found Judaism defective: "They claimed the authority of divine revelation; fostered priestcraft; its scriptures showed a garbled probably fraudulent historical record; it proclaimed a capricious, vicious God; it fostered depraved chauvinistic morality; its worship was meaningless mummery and it ignored the existence of an afterlife.... Supernatural revelations survived due to trickery and coercion which was the work of greedy conspirators, 'priests,' mountebanks with an eye for parasitical living." He believed Judaism could produce tyrants as it had in the past if given a chance. There was religious tolerance in every sect including Judaism. He opposed facts in the bible which contradicted the laws of nature (the sun stood still for Joshua). In a letter to John Adams, he questioned the Ten Commandments, which were initially destroyed by Moses. He attacked the picture of God in scriptures: "The Jews' idea of God is degrading, and injurious, a Being of terrific character, cruel, vindictive, unjust." Jefferson opposed the injustice of punishing sins to the third and fourth generation. The principle of the Hebrews was fear. He could not accept the morals and ethics of Judaism because, he believed, they were superficial and imperfect and against the dictates of reason and morality. Ethics was not understood by Jews as seen in their Talmud, which has only one treatise on moral subjects. He could not accept any system that did not explicitly explain an afterlife. Jefferson felt Judaism's worship was idle ceremonies and mummeries which failed to result in the essence of virtue and the value of worship. Jefferson did not stop with the Jews, however; he took the Christians to task as well.

Jefferson believed Jesus came to reform the corruption of Judaism.

Jesus' teachings required careful study, which was the highest practice of morality. Jesus was the greatest reformer of the depraved religion of his country. Jefferson attacked the New Testament because the writers could not describe the true Jesus, who was a benevolent moralist. The New Testament needed correction. His followers' writings suggested him as an imposter, so we had to separate Jesus from the writings of his followers, Jefferson felt. Jesus seemed to accept the traditions and assumptions of Judaism. Perhaps he did this to survive.

Jesus set out without pretensions to divinity and ended up believing them. In Jefferson's monologue on "The Life and Morals of Jesus of Nazareth," he excluded all supernatural character or endowment and rejected miracles. He said Jesus was an unusual man, but not supernatural, who tried to reform his people's depraved religion. Jefferson could not charge the Jews with deicide, because Jesus was not God. He blamed the killing of Jesus on the chief priests, Pilate and Herod. (It should be remembered that Herod died long before Jesus' crucifixion.) Matthew described Pilate's washing his hands as a means of exonerating Rome, but Jefferson felt Rome was responsible for the crucifixion. Jesus was punished for sedition. Jefferson did not believe in inherited guilt. He thought it was impossible to accuse a race of any crime. The death of Jesus had one historical consequence: The defects of Judaism were uncorrected for 1,800 years. Jefferson felt the reformists of Judaism met his rationalist ideals.

Jefferson's attack was on the concepts and philosophy of Judaism, but not on the Jews. However, his denial of Jesus' divinity violated the whole basis of Christianity. If he believed in an afterlife, he had to believe in God, but his mind could not accept the Trinity. Jefferson had a positive feeling toward the Jews and other minorities and wanted to secure their freedom and equality as well as to eliminate discrimination. He developed this feeling after studying John Locke, who believed no Muslim, pagan or Jew should be refused his civil rights because of his religion. In 1820, he wrote to Dr. Jacob de la Motta[97] "That his country has been the first to prove to the world two truths, the most salutory to human society, that man can govern himself, and that religious freedom is the most effectual anodyne against religious dissension: the maxim of civil government being reversed in that of religion, where its true form is 'divided we stand, united we fall.' He is happy in the restoration of the Jews, particularly to their social rights, and hopes they will be seen taking their seats on the benches of science as preparatory to their doing the same at the board of government."

In a letter to Joseph Marx,[98] who had sent Jefferson the proceedings of the Sanhedrin convened by Napoleon, he wrote, "And with the regret he has ever felt at seeing a sect, the parent and basis of all those of Christendom, singled out by all of them for a persecution and oppression which prove they have profited nothing from the benevolent doctrines of him whom they profess to make the model of their principles and practice."

He also talked of Jewish youth being excluded from instruction in science by forcing them to theological reading, which their consciences did not permit. Jefferson's letters show no prejudice in the form of nicknames, code words and demeaning anecdotes. However, he did pillory Presbyterians and Jesuits.

Jefferson probably had no Jewish friends, but he did trust individual Jews and did not overlook them for high positions in civil government. On January 11, 1787, when Jefferson was an ambassador, he signed a treaty with Morocco that would help American trade because American ship owners would not have to pay high insurance rates because of seizures by Barbary pirates. He turned to David Franks, a Jew who had reached the rank of colonel, to carry the treaty back to the United States. When Jefferson[99] was president and looking for an attorney general after Lincoln resigned, he questioned Secretary of the Treasury Gallatin to see if Moses Levi of Philadelphia would make a good replacement. Gallatin advised against it because he thought Levi was second rate. Also, it was unlikely that he would give up a practice of $6,000 to $7,000 per year to become attorney general.

To close this chapter on a happy note, I quote part of a speech by Mordecai Noah[100]: "Our Country, the bright example of universal tolerance of liberality, true religion and good faith ... the sages and patriots whose collected wisdom adopted them, closed the doors upon that great evil which has shaken the Old World to its centre. They proclaimed freedom of conscience.... Here no inequality of privileges ... no invidious distinctions exist ... justice administered impartially ... this is their chosen country ... protected from tyranny and oppression."[101] Myer Moses, a Jew in Charleston in 1806, described it more succinctly. In the Passover service participants say "next year in Jerusalem." The Charlestonian rose to praise America and hoped that the United States might be the place to which the Jews should be gathered. He described the freedom, civic equality and dignity accorded Jews. It was the promised land, the New Jerusalem. Moses called on God to transport all the Jewish people to America. Their gathering place should be this "land of milk and honey."

VI

Jews and the Wars

The early Israelite tribes were probably no more or less warlike than the other tribes in the Middle East. They fought for land occupied by Edomites, Moabites, Canaanites and Philistines. Their downfall came when they took on the Romans. After the destruction of the Second Temple, they were denied their homeland and dispersed to the four winds. For approximately 16 centuries, they were at best guests and at worst strangers where they settled. They lived where they were permitted, bur they were never citizens. As such, they never took up arms for the land in which they lived. In the late seventeenth and eighteenth centuries, Great Britain allowed some to become endenized, a station above alien but below real citizen. In the colonies, Jews and other aliens could become naturalized citizens. They therefore had a stake in the land in which they lived.

The eighteenth century was a period of almost constant warfare between England and France. What started in Europe spread across the ocean to America. In America, the Indians were allies of the French and introduced the concept of total warfare, which means that there were no such things as civilians to the warriors. The fighting was predominantly on the frontiers, which early in the century might have been 30 miles west of the ocean. The Jews were city dwellers, so the violence to the west of the seaport did not cause any loss of Jewish life. Occasionally one saw a Jewish name on a soldier. This was not significant. Many in England gave their children Old Testament names (Puritans). On the other hand, many Iberians anglicized their names. Pardo became Brown; Campanal, Campbell; and Franco, Franks, and so on.

The Jews were purveyors and sutlers to the British or colonial regiments. Abraham de Lucena[1] sent grain to Europe in the War of the Spanish Succession and supplied the British troops with wheat when they invaded Canada. He was a partner of Justus Bosch,[2] a gentile, in the war. Joseph Isacks was a British soldier in the King Williams's War (1689–

1697). He enlisted in the militia in America before 1690. In these early wars, Jews invested in privateers. If successful, a privateer (a pirate with a letter of marque from a governor or legislature) could bring large returns to shareholders. In King George's war (the War of the Austrian Succession), the Jews of Newport were partners in the *Defiance* with 14 cannon and 22 swivel guns. Levy and Franks owned the *Myrtilla* with 10 guns.

In the warfare of the seventeenth[3] and eighteenth centuries, the supply service became important and remunerative. Civilians supplied food to the soldiers and prisoners of war and provided hospital facilities and transportation of baggage. When wars were fought in America, the British turned to American commissaries to save money (as compared to transportation across the ocean). Jews acted as commissariats to the various armies as well as sutlers to supply food and strong drink to the soldiers with money. In North America, Jewish merchants took to the business. Samuel Jacobs, a German Jew, was commissariat to the British in King George's war and the French and Indian War. His station was in Quebec, where he was a merchant to Canadian civilians, sutler to the British troops and commissary to troops stationed in northern New York and lower Canada. He remained loyal to the king in the Revolution and supplied British and German troops in Canada.

Jacob Franks came to America in Queen Anne's war. Between the War of Jenkins's Ear and the Revolution, members of his family were purveyors to the British in North America and in the Caribbean. In London, Naphtali Franks and Simpson Levy sent cargoes to New York to their agents, Jacob and Moses Franks. These were traded for provisions and building materials which were shipped to Jamaica for the British navy. In return, they carried sugar to England. Moses Franks returned to London and became part of the group that supplied British troops in the French and Indian War. The Franks family supplied General Oglethorpe in his attack on Spanish Florida (1740–1743), which was a complete failure. The Franks family had Jewish agents in Charleston (Samuel Levy and Moses Solomons) as well as in Savannah (Minis and Solomons).

(The war of Jenkins's Ear has an interesting name and history. The Spanish interdicted any foreign ships from sailing into Spanish waters in the Caribbean. Jenkins was captain of a cargo ship picked up by Spanish ships guarding Spanish interests. As a lesson to others, they cut off his ear. He put the severed part in a box protected against further trauma. When he returned to London, he opened the box in parliament. The members were so incensed that they declared war on Spain [1738–1740]. This war dissolved into the War of the Austrian Succession.)

The French and Indian War was a battle for a continent. The debts amassed by the English were beyond anything previous to that time. The attempt by the English parliament to pass on some of the debt to the colonies was one of the causes of the American Revolution. The stamp tax, the tea tax and taxation without representation caused anger among the colonists. They believed the losses they suffered both as civilians and soldiers and the loss of crops must have been worth what they received from the war.

In the war, the Gradis Family[4] of Bordeaux (Jews who fled from Spain and lived as Catholics so that French authorities would allow the to stay) supplied the French in America. Their business became a "quartermaster corps" for the French armies under General Montcalm in Canada. Many of their ships were lost to the British blockade. The Franks family was the chief supplier to the British, and its activities were respected in London. Moses Franks had his father appointed king's agent in New York and the northern colonies. Jacob Franks was a merchant and shipper in New York in the first half of the eighteenth century and also an army purveyor. His son, Naphtali, lived in England. In King George's war (1744–1748) the Franks family was importing cannon for privateers and sending food to Jamaica. Moses Franks was part of a large syndicate that fueled the British armies from 1760 to the Revolution. They supplied troops in Canada, the American colonies, and the Caribbean and along the Mississippi and Ohio rivers. This probably involved millions of pounds sterling. Moses' younger brother was David Franks in Philadelphia. He serviced British troops in Pennsylvania, Virginia, the trans-allegheny area and the southern colonies. In Philadelphia, David was in partnership with his uncle, Nathan Levy. The Franks family[5] was appointed official purveyors and agents for the Crown in the French and Indian War. Prior to the final conflict they were in the tea trade, and they outfitted privateers against the French and Spanish in the War of the Austrian Succession (1740–1748). (King George's war was the War of the Austrian Succession fought in America). David Franks,[6] along with a partner Joseph Simon of Lancaster, lost large sums of money early in the war.

When the Franks were appointed agents and contractors along with Colebrook and Nesbitt, they handled £750,000 in contracts during the conflict. This money[7] covered provisions for the British armies and garrisons in North America, particularly New York, Maryland, Fort Pitt, the Illinois country, Canada and the West Indies. David Franks and William Plumsted rounded up provisions and wagons for General Braddock's march to Fort Pitt (Fort Duquesne to the French). Braddock's defeat was a commercial disaster to the Franks. David Franks also served as agent to Washington's army at Fort Duquesne (1758). At the time, David was also involved in maritime insurance, soap making and candle making. Franks became a partner of Michael Moses in the candle business until Moses died (1769), and his part was taken over by Matthias Bush.

Some background explanations are needed at this point. First, partnerships were joined on only one project. When it was completed, the partnership ended. This explains the multiplicity of partnerships of the period. Second, the wealthy Jews and Christians had their fingers in many pies. A successful operation brought tremendous profits, which compensated one or several failures

Beside the Franks family and other Jewish merchants, there were smaller Jewish companies that supplied the troops. Mathias Bush[8] (the same Bush as in the candle-making business) supplied Pennsylvania militia forces during the war. Naphtali Hart[9] and Company supplied Rhode Island troops with tent duck, lead, flints and clothing. Hart's bill for clothing was £13,236.7s.11d ("old tenor"). (Old tenor was paper currency printed by Massachusetts and Rhode Island. There were old tenor, middle tenor and new tenor, depending on the time of issuance.) Aaron Hart[10] was a sutler to the British army. He came to New York in 1759 and followed the British army to Canada and settled in Three Rivers, where he became a rich merchant.

Ezekiel Solomons[11] came to Canada from Berlin with the British army as a purveyor. After the war, he stayed and went into the fur trade out of Mackinac. In June 1763, Solomons was captured by the Indians and ransomed. This was obviously paid, because he was later free to set up his headquarters in what is now Michigan: the first Jew in Michigan. Like most Canadian merchants, he was loyal to the crown in the Revolution.

Hayman Levy was purveyor to troops in northern New York and near Lake Champlain. He also commissioned privateers. Levy was joined in partnership by Samuel Marache. Joseph Simon[12] was an Indian trader, peddler and merchant. He joined the consortium of Trent, Levy and Frank, but he left at the start of the French and Indian War to join Alexander Lowery (Christian) as purveyors to the American army. They also supplied privateers. Simon was very wealthy at the end of the war, and he became one of the founders of the New York Board of Stockholders, which became the New York Stock Exchange.

Jews were also in the "lines," including Jacob Wolf and Jacob Wexler.[13] Lieutenant Joseph Levy was at the Cherokee uprising in South Carolina in 1761. Levy was in the South Carolina Regiment of Foot commanded by Colonel Middleton. Captain Elias Meyer was in the royal American

Regiment from 1761 to 1763. George Washington was sent to occupy out-posts on the Ohio River[14] and fought the French at Great Meadows. Michael Franks and Jacob Myer were in the Virginia Regiment. Michael Israel was a member of the militia of Albemarle County and a "border ranger" against Indian incursions. David Franks of Philadelphia supplied Washington with military supplies when he reorganized Virginia troops after Braddock's debacle.

Some Jews did not enlist in the army, but circumstances frequently made them into fighters.[15] Jewish traders were in Michigan along with the earliest white settlers. They were caught in Detroit due to Pontiac's siege in 1763. Nathan Chapman, along with two other Jews (not named) were captured by the Indians. In his diary Major Roberts described how Indians took captives and bargained for their release. On May 23, 1763, a message reached the English from the Huron tribe, who had taken traders named Chapman and Levy along with five Englishmen in a canoe coming from Sandusky (Ohio). There were two Jews among them. The Indians wanted to know if the commander of the English would make peace with them. If so, they would give up their captives and pay Chap-man for his loss of merchandise that fell into their hands. On July 11, the Hurons brought in the merchandise that belonged to Chapman, Levy and others. (The story of Chapman appears in volume 12 of the *Memoirs of the Historical Society of Pennsylvania*.)

At the start of Pontiac's war in 1763, a trading Jew named Chapman was going up the Detroit River with a bateau of goods he had purchased in Albany. He was taken by the Chippewa Indians and was to be put to death. However, a Frenchman with motives of humanity and friendship stole the prisoner and kept him hidden from his captors, but he was betrayed and discovered by an Indian who took him across the river to be tortured and burned. The prisoner was tied to a stake, and the fire was started. The heat of the fire made him thirsty, and he asked for water. Among these Indians, when a prisoner was put to death, they gave him his last meal. A bowl of broth was brought to him. It was hot and burned his lips. He lost his temper and threw the bowl at the man who brought it. All the Indians cried out, "He is mad, he is mad," so they untied him and let him go. Chapman later became a merchant in Detroit. There is also a story of a Mr. Jacobs, a trader, taken by the Chippewa. In a fight, Jacobs was mortally wounded, but he managed to kill one of the Indians before he died.

A Levey, first name, unknown, lost considerable wealth due to Pon-tiac's uprising. Levey and four soldiers at Presqu'isle were delivered up by the Wyandots. They were seized after Ensign Christy, leader at the

Presqu'isle fort, gave up after a three-day siege. He was promised safe conduct to Fort Pitt, but the deal was not respected by the Indians. This Levey may have been the Levy Solomons described as the "York trader" in Amherst's journals. Levey (or Levy) escaped from the Indians and reached Detroit. Another Levy, Levy A. Levy, died as a result of Indian action in Pontiac's war. (Pontiac was an Ottowa Indian chief, allied to the French in the French and Indian War. After the French were defeated, the British turned against him. He led an uprising in 1763 and 1764. The chief caused great damage to the British and American soldiers and settlers. Pontiac signed a treaty in 1766 and was killed by a Peoria Indian in 1767.)

After Fort Duquesne was taken, the victory opened Indian trade to the British without fear of French intervention. Purchases for the Indian trade were made from Joseph Simon[16] and his associates, Levy A. Levy and David Franks. Simon was in the Indian trade early and made trips to the Ohio and Illinois country before the war. Levy A. Levy was Simon's nephew and partner in their organization in Lancaster. Levy was later killed east of Detroit.

Hayman Levy was a New York merchant and purveyor to British troops and he had an important branch in Europe. (It was usually the other way around.) His organization owned many vessels in privateering. Levy furnished all necessities to the Forty-Third British Regiment. He also supplied camp equipment to the Fortieth Regiment. In supplying these regiments, he had a partner—Isaac Moses. Hayman Levy was also involved in a group of financial disasters: Pontiac's uprising, which destroyed merchandise; support of George Rogers Clark's (the ranger) aborted venture for Virginia; and other failed ventures in Montreal and Albany.

The Franks family was the major name in victualing the British forces. General Amherst's papers described the important activities of Jacob Franks and his sons, Moses and David. Jacob was in New York, Moses in London and David in Philadelphia. In London, Moses was in partnership with Colebrooke and Nesbitt. David was associated with Plumsted in Philadelphia. In Amherst's journals there were 49 references to the Franks family.

Early in the French and Indian War, Great Britain faced defeat by a French army markedly inferior in numbers. The Braddock expedition to take Fort Duquesne[17] was a major fiasco. Braddock died in the debacle, but because of this defeat, George Washington became the best-known colonial soldier. The American militia units, looked down upon by the British regulars, handled themselves well. They knew Indian tactics, but Braddock tried to fight the way European armies fought in tight formation on the plains of Europe.

The purveyors to this army, Simon Levy and the Franks family, lost thousands of pounds sterling which were never repaid by Great Britain. The destruction of the army and loss of fighting equipment left the frontier open to Indian depredation, so families pulled up and headed east for protection. The situation was turned around when Pitt became prime minister. He turned the European war over to Frederick of Prussia and the American war over to young, efficient leaders. General Wolfe would take Quebec, which ended the active fighting. General Amherst at Crown Point sent a message to Wolfe with Captain Kennedy. In Kennedy's retinue was a Mr. Abrahams. In 1760, Jacob Wolf and Joseph Wexler, German Jews, enlisted in the Second Battalion of the Royal American Regiment of Quebec.

In a war front in South Carolina, the British had to subdue the Cherokees, who initially were allied to the English, but they committed depredations that were put down by the English. During this action, a corporal deserted and was later court-martialed. Lieutenant Joseph Levey was on the court-martial board. A Captain Elias Meyer was a member of the Royal American Regiment commanded by Colonels Bousquet and Haldenand. This was basically a Pennsylvania Regiment, and there were a few German Jews in the unit. German Jews, along with other Germans, lived in Pennsylvania in considerable numbers. The first mention of Captain Meyer was in a letter by Bousquet when he was stationed at Fort Pitt (1761), stating he had received a letter from Amherst delivered by Lieutenant Levey. One month later, Bousquet sent out a detachment of the Royal Americans under Meyer to Sandusky Lake (Ohio). He was to build a blockhouse as a halting place on the way to and from Detroit. Meyer, in a letter of September 1, decried the conditions at Sandusky (mainly there was a lack of provisions for his men). At the end of the year, he completed the blockhouse. In February 1762, Meyer was back at Fort Pitt, and Bousquet and Amherst recommended him for promotion. He was a lieutenant for 13 years and spent 11 of these in the engineers.

Meyer was the oldest lieutenant in all four battalions. He was then shipped to Quebec to join the Second Battalion of the Royal American Regiment. In 1763, after the peace treaty was signed, the army was reduced in size. After 16 years of service, Meyer was discharged on a lieutenant's half-pay. Murray, the governor of Quebec, wanted Meyer attached to him where he was involved in building barracks for troops stationed in Quebec. Another Jew, Private Hyman, was a gunner in an artillery company when he was captured in 1760. After his release, he was dismissed from the company without a formal discharge. Hyman was next described in the personal service of Governor Barnard of Massachusetts, for whom he worked as a gardener. (He may have been a deserter.)

In 1759, a fleet from Britain carried 8,000 troops under General Wolfe to Nova Scotia.[18] In the ships were Jewish sutlers—Abraham Clapman, Gerson Levy, Jacob de Maurera and Ezekial and Levi Solomon. They reported to Commissary General Aaron Hart. Hart had come to America in 1745 as a lieutenant in a German legion. Other Jewish sutlers from New York joined the army—Benjamin Lyon, Manuel Gomez and Isaac Miranda. The French General de Montcalm had as his first aide Brigadier General Gastogne François de Lèvis (the Lèvis were Marranos). Wolfe's commander of the frigate *Diana* was Captain Alexander Schomberg (a convert to Christianity). Schomberg led soldiers up a 275-foot bluff to take the heights commanding Montmorency Falls, followed by Wolfe and 5,000 men. Wolfe met and defeated de Montcalm on the plains of Abraham (both Wolfe and de Montcalm were killed). After Quebec was taken, the British secured Montreal. In the action in Quebec, de Lèvis received the title of chevalier for his gallantry. Schomberg was knighted for gallantry in action at Quebec by George III. Aaron Hart opened a general store between Quebec and Montreal at Three Rivers and became one of the founders of Shearith Israel in Montreal. That congregation built a synagogue in 1777, the third on the North American continent.

Chapman Abram[19] was in Canada with British troops around 1759 or 1760. He and four partners were purveyors in the French and Indian War. After the war, they became fur traders. Abram's home base was Detroit. He was captured by Indians during Pontiac's rebellion in 1763, but he escaped. In the Revolution, he was a loyalist and fought the American invasion of Canada.

Several Jews were partners in privateers.[20] In the French and Indian War, Samson Simpson leased four ships to the Royal Navy as privateers: Hayman Levy leased two; Jacob Franks, one; and Judah Hays, one. The ships were the *Hardy, Sampson, Union, Polly, Dreadnaught, Orleans* and *Duke of Cumberland.*

The American Revolution, to me, was a civil war between Englishmen on both sides of the Atlantic. Perhaps one-third of the colonists were patriots (Whigs). Another third were loyalists (Tories), and the rest were not interested. In England, many were sympathetic to the colonials' complaints. Several generals were ready to give up their commissions rather than fight Englishmen who were fighting for the rights of all Englishmen. The average "man in the street" did not wish to volunteer to travel three thousand miles to fight Englishmen. This explained the need for parliament to pay German princelings to conscript their subjects to fight in America. Much of this sympathy for America changed after they proclaimed their Declaration of Independence, however.

The Sephardic Jews,[21] particularly the rich, were patriots. The merchant shippers felt they were adversely affected by the British policies. As long as they were citizens under the Naturalization Act of 1740, they could trade under the navigation acts, but they could not trade with foreigners. The Ashkenazi Jews were divided. Most of them came from Germany to Holland to England and to America. They remembered or were told be their forebears about pogroms in Eastern Europe. In Great Britain, however, they had complete freedom of religion (although they had to pay taxes to support the Anglican church). They had freedom to go into any trade to earn a living for their family. The only thing lacking was political equality. They could not vote or hold office, because this entailed swearing on the New Testament.

In the colonies,[22] many Jews were not yet particularly active politically or intellectually in the events swirling around them at the time. If they did not yet have complete political freedom, it would come gradually under British rule. The biggest political incident in which the Jews involved themselves was the nonimportation protest. In Philadelphia, 10 Jews among 375 merchants signed. In New York, 12 Jews signed. In New York at the start of the Revolution, 16 Jews signed an address of loyalty to the crown. These included Absolam and Moses Gomez, David and Barach Hays, George Simpson and Isaac Solomon. Dr. Rush[23] wrote, "The Jews chose for the most to be Whigs, even though they had no particular grievances against the British." Jewish services in the Revolution raised their status among other Americans, and it increased their self-assurance. They changed from passive onlookers to activists for their equality. They also changed from a submissive group happy for any favors they received to an active group demanding equality based on their service and blood shed in the war.

They did serve in the war, and they bled for America. At the outbreak of the Revolution, there were about 500 Jews of military age in America. About 100 volunteered for the continental line. Others joined the militia to protect their communities. The first to bleed for America was Francis Salvador,[24] whose story is told in Chapter 3.

The soldiers of the continental line were the "regular army," which means they were soldiers from the time of their enlistment to the time of their death or discharge. There trained every day and withstood the onslaught of the British or Hessian troops. These were the men who were wounded or killed outright. If a wounded man was treated at a local farm-house, his chances of survival were good. If he was unfortunate and taken to an army hospital, he was likely to die of tetanus, typhoid, typhus or pneumonia. If he survived the hospital, his health was frequently broken and he became a "pensioner" for life. The militia were local men who were poorly trained. The generals early in the war recognized that militias were frequently untrustworthy. When they were placed on the line, they often broke and fled at the first noise of the battle. This led to a hole in the line which the enemy were able to use to their advantage. This was not the situation in every case, however; many militiamen were wounded and died like the regulars.

Lewis Bush[25] was made a first lieutenant of the Sixth Pennsylvania Battalion on January 9, 1776. He was promoted to captain on June 24 of that year. The Jewish captain was transferred to a continental regiment and commissioned a major in March 1777. Bush was wounded at the battle of Brandywine (Pennsylvania) and died of his wounds on September 11, 1777. Solomon Bush[26] was luckier. He was enrolled as a captain and deputy in the Flying Camp of Associations of Pennsylvania (a "flying camp" was a rapidly mobile unit). Bush fought in the battle of Long Island (a serious defeat for Washington) and was promoted to major. At the battle of Brandywine, his thigh was broken. He was taken to his father's house and was made a prisoner of war when the British took Philadelphia. He was promoted to lieutenant colonel and deputy adjutant general of the Pennsylvania militia. His wounds were treated by a British surgeon in his father's home. Bush gave his parole to the British and was given freedom to move around. He continued to receive medical attention at British headquarters, where he learned of a spy in Washington's headquarters. Bush passed the news to Washington through General John Armstrong. Because it was felt he was incapacitated for further services, he was discharged. In 1781, Bush applied for the Corps of Invalids (men who could not perform active duty but were able to do something; like clerks, quartermasters or hospital orderlies). This was denied, and in 1785 he received a pension from Pennsylvania. Bush applied for several political positions including in a direct letter to General Washington. All were turned down. Solomon Bush had a brother who fought under General Nathanael Greene in the South. He was a prisoner of war when he went mad. Nothing else is known of his history.

Isaac Franks was only 17 when he enlisted in Colonel Lasher's Volunteers of New York (he was a brother-in-law of Haym Salomon). Franks was wounded and taken prisoner at the battle of Long Island. He was fortunate to be taken prisoner and sent to a British army hospital, which

were far safer that the American hospitals. After he was well, he escaped
and joined Washington's army in New Jersey, where he became a forage
master. In 1781, Franks was commissioned an ensign in the Seventh Massachusetts Regiment at West Point (ensign was one level below a lieutenant). He was discharged in 1781 with "kidney gravel." Franks returned to
Philadelphia, where he became a successful merchant and purchased a house
in Germantown. (It was the house the British General Howe occupied during the British occupation of Philadelphia.) President Washington moved
from Philadelphia, the nation's capital, to Germantown and occupied the
house for two months during the yellow fever epidemic. Not impressed that
the president occupied his house, Franks submitted a bill to the president[27]:

On November 6, 1793, Franks hired a two-horse wagon driven for six days at $2 per day to take Franks and wife to Germantown to get the house in order to accommodate the president	$12.00
Expenses of the journey	$18.00
Hire of beds and furniture to accommodate the Franks family while Washington used his house	$12.00
Franks left Bethlehem for Germantown to talk to the President about how long he would keep the house so he could act accordingly. Cost of journey back to Bethlehem	$10.00
Cash paid to clean the house and put it in the same condition it was in prior to the president's occupancy	$2.50
For damage due to a large double Japand [sic] waiter used by president	$6.00
One flat iron missing	£0.15.10 ½d
One large fork missing	2s.6d
Four platters @ 1	4s
3 ducks @ 2.6	7s.6d
4 fowls at 15.9d	7s
1 bushel of potatoes	7s
One Hundred of hay	6s
	£4.12.10 ½d—$4.40
Two months house rent @ $400 per year	$66.66
	$131.56

It is not known whether he received payment.

In 1789, Governor Mifflin of Pennsylvania appointed Franks a notary and Tabellion public (an official scribe), and he was reasonably prosperous for 25 years. In 1789, he joined Dr. Benjamin Rush in the purchase of nineteen tracts of land in Westmoreland County (in present-day Indiana). In 1794, Governor Mifflin appointed him a lieutenant colonel of the Second Regiment of the Philadelphia County brigade of militia. In 1811, his sources of income deteriorated, and he tried to get a pension from the government for war service. After many attempts he finally was awarded $20 per month in 1818.

An unsuccessful battle was fought at Beaufort, South Carolina,[28] in February 1779. Involved in the battle was Captain Richard Lushington's "Jew company." (There were 26 or 28 Jews in the company of 40 men.) The company's other name was the King Street Company, because many of the Jewish volunteers lived on King Street in Charleston. The battle of Beaufort developed when British troops under Colonel Maitland[29] arrived at Beaufort for "rest and rehabilitation." Maitland sent a flag of truce to the colonials because he did not wish to fight civilians. If the American commander still wanted a battle, he should fire a cannon, Maitland said. General Moultrie urged the Americans to fight, and there was some fighting before the British retreated. An American Lieutenant Reid was killed, as was an ensign, a known cabinet maker in Charleston. Among the Jews, Moses Rohen was killed, as was Joseph Solomon.[30] Ephraim Abrams was wounded in the engagement. The Jew company also fought under General Benjamin Lincoln in his unsuccessful attempt to retake Savannah from the British in 1779. The company was involved in the British siege of Charleston in 1780. Rachel Moses,[31] daughter of Myer Moses, was accidentally killed by an errant cannonball in the battle. When the British took Charleston they seized many soldiers, including Jews, involved in the defending force.

When the British occupied Charleston, many Jews fled to Philadelphia, while other Jews remained in the occupied city (Abraham Alexander, Levi Sheftall, Emanuel Abraham, Gershon Cohen and Jacob Jacobs). When the war ended, a committee of patriots examined those who remained. The Jews mentioned were exonerated of disloyalty, but several Jews were banished for disloyalty (Isaac de Costa and Abraham Seixas).

In South Carolina, the battle of Camden was a fiasco. General Gage, the victor over Burgoyne at Saratoga, marched American troops down to South Carolina. Many of his troops were sick from eating green corn and from malaria. The American troops were defeated, and General Gage fled early to avoid capture, but his reputation was destroyed. There were several Jews involved at Camden. Colonel Isaacs[32] of the North Carolina militia was wounded at Camden and was a prisoner of war. He was exchanged in 1780. Elias Pollock,[33] 23 enlisted under the name of Joseph Smith in May 1778 in Baltimore. He served in Philadelphia and New Jersey. Pollock was in several minor skirmishes in the successful attack on Stony Point as well as several expeditions in Staten Island. His unit was marching to Charleston when they came upon the battle of Camden. Pollock was wounded in the side, made a prisoner of war and shipped to St. Augustine in east Florida. When the war ended, he was shipped to Halifax. Nova Scotia. From there, he made his way back to Baltimore. Major Benjamin Nones[34] (a Jew from France) started as a private under Pulaski. He served with gallantry and heroism at the battle of Savannah. Nones was commissioned a major over a unit of 400 men, several of whom were Jews. He was then attached to Baron De Kalb. In the unit under De Kalb were Captain Jacob De La Motta and Captain Jacob de Leon. The unit fought at the battle of Camden. It was Jacob de Leon who helped carry the fatally wounded De Kalb off the field.

Benjamin Nones's gallantry was described by Captain Verdier, a captain of volunteers.[35] At the siege of Savannah, "his behavior under fire in all the bloody actions we fought, have been marked by the bravery and courage which a military man is expected to show for the liberties of his country and which acts of said Nones gained in his favor, the esteem of General Pulaski as well as that of the officers who witnessed his daring conduct." Nones, who later served on the staff of LaFayette and Washington, stated, "I fought in almost every action which took place in Carolina and in the disastrous affair of Savannah shared the hardships of that sanguinary day."

Many inhabitants of Georgia were loyalists. The wealthy men of that colony had close financial links to Great Britain. The Jews for the most part were Patriots. The "greatest rebel" was Mordecai Sheftall, according to Governor Wright.[36] The governor wanted to keep Jews out of Georgia because they were violent rebels and persecutors of the king's loyal subjects. (This statement was in a letter from Wright to the principal secretary of state for America.) A royal proclamation in the Georgia *Gazette* (1780) listed Sheftall as a great rebel. Among others named in the proclamation were two signers of the Declaration of Independence and two generals in the American army (Sheftall was in excellent company).

Sheftall, along with two others, initiated resistance in Georgia on August 10, 1775. He was elected chairman of the parochial committee[37] of Christ Church parish (including Savannah), which established the first American government in Georgia. They took control of the port and custom house and prevented English ships from landing. Governor Wright named Sheftall the leader. "The conduct of the people is most infamous. One Sheftall, a Jew, is chairman of the Parochial Committee as they call themselves, and this fellow issues orders to captains of vessels to depart the king's port without landing any of their cargoes." When Richard Bussell landed the ship *Clarissa* in Savannah with molasses from Jamaica, he was told to appear before the parochial committee. At the committee "he there saw sitting in the chair, one Mordecai Sheftall of Savannah, Minis of Savannah, both which persons profess the Jewish religion. The said Mordecai Sheftall told this deponent that the aforesaid molasses could not be landed ... or abide by the consequences."

In 1777, Sheftall became commissary general of purchases and issues to the Georgia militia with the rank of colonel. In 1778, he became deputy commissioner of issues to the continental troops in Georgia and South Carolina and supplied his own money for supplies. On December 29, 1778, the British[38] attacked Savannah with a force of 3,500 British and Hessian troops. Sheftall was active in its defense. When he recognized the British would be successful, he and his son Sheftall Sheftall, age 15 who was his lieutenant, tried to escape across Musgrove Creek with colonel Samuel Elbert and Major James Habersham. They were under fire crossing Savannah Common. Sheftall Sheftall could not swim across the creek, so the elder Shaftall stayed with him. They were part of a group of 186 officers and men taken by the British. In addition to the Sheftalls were Philip Minis, David Sarzadas (a lieutenant in the Light Dragoons of Georgia), Abraham Seixas (a lieutenant in the Georgia brigade) and David Nunez Cardozo (first sergeant to grenadiers). Cardozo later received a wound in his leg in the attempt to retake Savannah.

The prisoners were plundered by the Highlander Regiment. Sheftall, his son and Major Low surrendered to Lieutenant Peter Campbell, who only disarmed them. When they discovered they had Mordecai Sheftall, they had him specially guarded because he was "a very great rebel." He was guarded by a sentry with a drawn bayonet. The British commissary general, Bresler, tried to get Mordecai to tell him where American provisions were hidden so he could feed "American prisoners who were starving." Sheftall knew this was a falsehood because he had seen to the feeding of the Americans that morning. Bresler tried to break his spirit by telling him Charleston was taken ten days earlier. Again, Mordecai knew this was a lie because he had received a letter from his brother in Charleston three days earlier. Bresler became angry and had Sheftall imprisoned with drunken soldiers and Negroes. He was in danger of being bayoneted (skivered) by a New York Tory three times.

Mordecai was protected by a Sergeant Campbell. Sheftall was kept without food for two days until he was rescued by a Hessian officer (Zaltman) because they could speak the same language. He allowed Sheftall to write to Ms. Abigail Minis, who sent him some food. Sheftall Sheftall was permitted to stay with his father. A Colonel Innes gave him leave to go to Mrs. Minis's house to get a shirt she had washed for him. Upon his return, he was transferred to the prison ship *Nancy*. His rations included two and one-half pints of water, one-half gill of rice and seven ounces of boiled beef per day.

He was sent on board a prison ship to Antigua in the West Indies.[39] Mordecai kept a manuscript of his captivity. He and three other prisoners kept regular meetings of the Union Society while on board, and he was elected president by the others. From the ship, he and four others were sent to a common jail, where they endured many privations until they were freed on parole. The men were able to send letters to the colonial board of war[40] and were later exchanged. (Sheftall was exchanged for a British general.) The men were brought to Sunbury, Georgia. Sheftall Sheftall was exchanged earlier, and the father did not know where the boy was. He was permitted to send a letter to his wife, Frances, who had moved to Charleston after the men were captured.

After the Sheftalls were exchanged and freed, the son, now 18, was appointed flag master of the mercy ship *Carolina Packett* by the board of war in Philadelphia. He was to carry money and provisions to General Moultrie to feed the populace in Charleston. The young Sheftall received £1,367.18s.1d for distribution as well as flour and provisions. In 1782, Mordecai Sheftall took a shipload of supplies to Savannah. Throughout the war, the Sheftalls were recognized as rebels. In the "Disqualifying Act" of 1780,[41] passed by Great Britain, Sheftall's name was near the top of the list. After the war ended, he received a grant of land in the "Georgia continental establishment" for his service. Neither he not his heirs ever received payment for the money he advanced to feed Georgia troops. In 1796, he was a delegate for Chatham County to the Georgia general congress. Mordecai died on July 6, 1797. Sheftall Sheftall later practiced law in Georgia.

A Jew, David Emanuel,[42] was the sixth governor of Georgia after his military and political service. The family originated in Germany and came to Pennsylvania, where David was probably born in 1744. During the fighting, he was a scout and soldier throughout the Revolution. At one time, he was taken prisoner by a band of loyalists who turned him over to the British, who planned to execute him. (He was a scout a the time.) Emanuel jumped into the midst of a group of tethered horses and then into a swamp, and his pursuers were unable to find him. By morning he reached the army of General Twiggs (patriot).

Later, when Georgia was overrun by the British, he led 30 patriot families to an area below Augusta, where they built cabins and made guerilla attacks against the loyalists. The Tories called the area "Rebel Town." After the war, Emanuel served in the Georgia legislature representing Burke County for many years. In 1797, he was president of the Georgia senate, and on March 3, 1801, he was governor of Georgia. It is not clear if he was elected or had the position as president of the senate. This story leaves some questions unanswered. During the eighteenth century, most legislators, governors and judges had to take their oath on the Bible including the New Testament. Emanuel was a magistrate in 1781 and a justice for Burke County in 1782. The answer may lie in his conversion to the Presbyterianism, although this is not certain.

Among the sad stories accompanying the fall of Charleston was one involving Reuben Etting,[43] who was a 19-year-old Baltimore bank clerk. Etting enlisted and was soon in the defense of Charleston. When it fell, he was taken prisoner. The English guards learned he was Jewish and gave him pork as the main source of his diet. Etting, an Orthodox Jew, refused to eat and lost weight. He was finally exchanged, but he died shortly after he was exchanged of "starvation and consumption."

It is difficult to learn how many Jewish Tories were killed in the war. Isaac Hart[44] of Newport was killed on Long Island. The Harts, including Isaac, Samuel, Moses, Samuel Jr., Jacob and Naphtali were loyalists. The Hazzan Touro was a loyalist. He stayed when the British occupied Newport and left when they left the city. Touro led the small number of Jews who stayed during the British occupation of New York. At war's end, he left for Jamaica, where he died. Most Polocks in Newport were loyal, and Myer Polock refused to take the oath of allegiance to Rhode Island. Other Jews who remained in Newport during the British occupation were the Elizers, Hyam Levy, Moses and Simon Levy and Moses Seixas. Some in this group may have been Tories, neutralists or crypto–Whigs. Philip Moses took the oath of allegiance in Newport. He then moved to Charleston, where he was in the defending force. After the British took Charleston, he swore allegiance to the Crown.

In 1776, an act of the assembly of Providence[45] declared that "persons suspected of being dangerous or disaffected [must] take or subscribe the Oath of Allegiance and Abjuration, and on refusal officers may proceed against them for confiscation of property." (This act was repealed in 1783.) in 1780,[46] the Rhode Island assembly deprived three in the Hart family of their rights and property. Isaac Hart[47] was given land on Long

Island by the Crown to replace his losses in Newport. While trying to protect his grant, he was fired upon, bayoneted 15 times and beaten with a musket. Hart died several hours later.

Another Jew, Moses Michael Hays, a patriot, refused to sign. He stated that as a Jew he was not permitted to vote in Rhode Island and that the oath was not required of all residents of the colony and that no congress recognized the position of the Jews. Hays was never bothered after his stance, and he left Newport when the British occupied the city. He eventually moved to Boston and became wealthy as a maritime insurer.

Several Jews reached high rank in the Continental Army. One was David Salisbury Franks.[48] He was born in Philadelphia and moved to Canada when the British conquered Canada in the French and Indian War. Franks lived in Montreal, where he was arrested on May 3, 1775. A statue of George II was defaced, and a sign was placed on the bust stating, "This is the pope of Canada and a fool of England" (written in French). The people wanted the perpetrators to be hanged. Franks responded that in England men are not hanged for such small offenses. He expressed sympathy for the colonials and was involved in a fistfight with a French-speaking Canadian because of the damage done to the statue. The Canadian struck Franks, and Franks knocked him down. The French Canadian complained to the "conservators of peace of the district of Montreal" about Franks's words. Franks was jailed under a £10,000 bond, and he remained in jail for 16 days. When the American General Montgomery captured Montreal on November 13, 1775, Franks advanced to the continental troops 500 Johanes,[49] a Portuguese coin, as well as needed provisions for the soldiers. He was repaid in continental paper. After the failure of the patriot army to take Quebec, General Wooster appointed Franks paymaster to the workers at the garrison in Montreal. He used his own money when the American treasury was empty.

Franks joined the continentals in their retreat from Canada, and he remained with that army until after the defeat of General Burgoyne at Saratoga in 1777. In 1778, he was appointed aide-de-camp to General D'Estaing (French) until the general failed to retake Newport. Franks returned to Philadelphia, where he became aide-de-camp to General Benjamin Lincoln at Charleston. After the failure to save Charleston, Franks became aide-de-camp to Benedict Arnold at West Point. One of his duties was to look after the safety, welfare and health of Mrs. Arnold. In Arnold's "family," Franks was called "the nurse."[50] Franks described her as having attacks of nervousness, at which time she blurted out everything that was on her mind. Therefore, Arnold never told her of his scheme. He also knew she had "warm patriotic feelings."

Before Arnold's treason, he was court-martialed in Raritan, New Jersey, on June 1, 1793. He was charged with eight specific incidents of misconduct while in Philadelphia (Arnold was injured at the battle of Saratoga, and Washington gave him control of Philadelphia after it was retaken. It was a "cushy job" to allow his wound to heal). It was here that he met and married his second wife. After Philadelphia, he was transferred to guard West Point. Among the charges at his court-martial in New Jersey was his use of his new power to improve his financial condition; the use of militia for menial duties for his benefit; the use of government equipment for his personal use; and his use of his influence to get a ship out of Philadelphia while that city was occupied by the British and to dock at a port held by the patriots. When Franks was called to testify, his testimony was generally in Arnold's favor. The general was found guilty of the charge related to the ship, and the court-martial board ordered General Washington to reprimand Arnold. (It should be remembered that Washington thought of Arnold as a son he never had. After Arnold's treason, he turned that paternal affection toward Lafayette.)

Following Arnold's flight and treason at West Point, Colonel Varick and Major Franks were court-martialed at their request to clear their names. On November 2, 1780, the court-martial board met at West Point. Prominent officers testified as to the integrity and innocence of Arnold's aide. General Knox, in sworn testimony, stated that neither Varick nor Franks knew of Arnold's plans to flee. Colonel Varick, in a search of Arnold's quarters after his flight, found a copy of "Plans and Profiles of each breastwork at West Point." Varick delivered these to General Washington. The two were acquitted, but Franks sent another investigation request directly to Washington. This was carried out, and again he was acquitted of all charges. To further exonerate the two officers, Arnold sent a message to Washington, after he was safely within British lines, that Varick and Franks knew nothing of his plans to join the British and give up West Point.

In 1781,[51] Franks was appointed a courier from Robert Morris and Jay in Madrid and Franklin in Paris. Franks was later a member of Jefferson's retinue at the Treaty of Peace in Paris. In 1784, he was again dispatched to Europe with ratification of the peace treaty. In 1785, Franks was made vice-consul at Marseilles after he tried for a higher position. He acted as secretary to the delegation for the peace treaty with the emperor of Morocco. He carried this pact to our ministers in Europe and then to the U.S. secretary of state (1787). He was also secretary to the delegation meeting the Creek Indians. Finally, he was assistant cashier of the Bank of the United States. Jefferson[52] described him to Madison as "light, indiscreet, active honest and affectionate." Both Jefferson and Madison believed "he talked to much" and couldn't be trusted with confidential information. Furthermore, he lost his self-control around women. For his services in the war, Lieutenant Colonel David Franks[53] received 400 acres of land in 1789. Another who reached the rank of lieutenant colonel was Solomon Bush[54] in the Pennsylvania militia, who was wounded in battle. He survived and left the service with that rank. Isaac Franks of New York also reached that rank. Colonel Isaacs of the North Carolina militia was wounded at the battle of Camden and was taken prisoner. He was later exchanged.

The Franks[55] family of Philadelphia were old, wealthy members of Philadelphia's leaders. Several had lost their Jewish identity through intermarriage with the leading gentiles. The family had been purveyors to the British army and navy in the American colonies for two generations. David, an uncle of David Salisbury Franks, supplied the British army in the French and Indian War. At the start of the Revolution, the family had branches in Philadelphia (David), New York (Jacob), and London (Moses, a partner in Nesbitt, Drummond and Franks). David was appointed to supply provisions to British soldiers held in American prisoner-of-war compounds starting in the winter of 1775. His appointment was acceptable to British General Howe. Franks was suspected of Tory sympathies. His daughter, Rebecca, was openly Tory. In October 1778, he was thrown in jail by federal authorities and charged with writing a letter to his brother Moses in England, which "expressed intentions against the safety of liberty of the United States." The following month, he was removed from his position of commissary to British prisoners.

Franks was tried and found innocent by the supreme court of Pennsylvania, and he was freed. He next tried to get money back that he had advanced to feed the British, but the company in London and General Sir Henry Clinton turned him down. His requests[56] to pass the lines to New York to collect money were also turned down. He was able to get a letter to Major André in New York to help him get his money. He was kept under surveillance beginning in December 1779, and in October 1780, Franks was rearrested by Pennsylvania state authorities on the charge of corresponding with the British in New York and undermining American currency by paying for the feeding of British prisoners in paper money rather that specie, which was demanded by congress. Franks was ordered to leave Pennsylvania for New York by the executive council and to put up £200,000 in security that he would not return to the United States during the war. In 1782, his daughter, Rebecca, married Sir Henry Johnson and moved to England. Franks applied to the British government for compensation for his losses as a loyalist. He received lump sums of £125 and £100 per year. He later returned to Philadelphia and died in the yellow fever epidemic in 1793.

After the British left Boston for New York early in the war, there was little warfare in New England except for the failed attempt to take Newport by General Sullivan and General D'Estaing. However, English forces under General Tryon[57] and General Benedict Arnold carried out attacks on Connecticut towns along Long Island Sound. There were several Jewish officers who led Connecticut militia to try to repel the raids, including Solomon Mears and David Pinto. In addition to David, the Pinto family supplied Abraham, William and Solomon to the patriot cause. Abraham was wounded, and Solomon was taken prisoner and sent to England, but he returned and joined Washington's army. Solomon was one of the founders of the Order of Cincinnati in Connecticut. In 1780, Solomon was an ensign in the Seventh and later the Second Regiment of the Connecticut line and served in the Hudson Highlands. While the Pinto family's roots were Jewish, by the time of the Revolution they had given up any religious affiliation and were probably deists. In addition to the Pintos, Michael Judah was in Captain Gregory's company of the Connecticut line. Mordecai and Abraham Marks were active patriots, but their brother Nehemiah was a Tory.

Moses Levy,[58] born in Philadelphia in 1757, joined the Continental army. During Christmas 1776, he was with Washington when the remnant of the American army crossed the Delaware. He fought at Trenton and Princeton, but he remained in the Pennsylvania militia. While in active service, he found time to obtain admission to the Pennsylvania bar in 1778. Levy was a member of the state legislature. Finally, he ended his legal career as president judge of the district court for the city and county of Pennsylvania. Philip Moses Russell[59] joined the army in 1776 and he was a surgeon's mate with the Second Virginia Regiment at Valley Forge. Russell developed camp fever, which affected his sight and hearing, but he continued to care for the sick and wounded until he was forced to resign. General Washington was aware of his work and thanked him for his care of the injured and his courage in battle.

A story is told of a Polish Jew at Valley Forge. He lit a menorah (candelabra to celebrate the eight days the oil lasted to clean the temple) to celebrate Hanukkah. The lighted menorah was seen by Washington, who asked about it. The Jew told the general the story of the Maccabees and Washington recounted the story to Michael Hart and his family when he was a guest in their house while his army was on the way to Millbrook, New Jersey, for winter quarters (1778–1779). He was there during Hanukkah and gave the three Hart children silver coins (Hanukkah gelt [money]). It is a nice story, but only a story.

To complete the Pennsylvania story, there was a Mr. Gomez, aged 68,[60] who formed a company under his command. When told by a member of congress that he was too old to serve, his reply was, "I can stop a bullet as well as a younger man." Perhaps more important than individuals who served in the line was Joseph Simon. He and his partner Henry had a factory that turned out rifles for Washington's army. This was the best rifle used by either side.[61]

The state of Delaware issued a broadside renouncing allegiance to George III on August 9, 1778: "I do firmly swear or affirm that I do not hold myself bound to yield any allegiance or obedience to the King of Great Britain and his heirs or successors and that I will be true and faithful to the Delaware State and will support and maintain the freedom, independence and constitution thereof against all open enemies and secret traitorous conspiracies and will disclose and make known to the commander in chief for the time being or some judge of justice of this state all treasons and traitorous conspiracies, attempts or combinations against the same or the government thereof which shall come to my attention." Among the signers were Samson Levey and Moses Levy. This was a lot of words for a small state, but it should be noted that the soldiers of Delaware (and Maryland) in the continental line could be counted on to hold their place.

The following is a list of some of the men in the Virginia line[62]: Isaac Israel, Andrew Moses, Moses Franks, Francis Goldman, Joseph Hart, Benjamin Jacobs, John Isaac, Juda Levi, Ezekiel Moses, Samuel Myers, Levin Philips, George Solomon, David Stein, Lewis Steinberger and Henry Samuel, but there weren't this many Jewish men in the whole state of Virginia. This is further proof that one cannot tell one's religious background from a name.

The description of the Jews in the American Revolution is by no means complete. For those who are interested in more complete lists of Jews in the Revolution, the author suggest *Unrecognized Patriots* by Samuel Reznick; *Eyewitness to American Jewish History* by Eisenberg; *The Levy and Seixas Families of Newport and New York* by N. Taylor Phillips; *Pilgrim People* by Lebeson; *United States Jewry* by Marcus; *The Jews of the United States* by Joseph L. Blau; *History of the Jews in America* by Deborah Pessin; *The American Jew as Patriot, Soldier and Citizen* by Simon Wolf; *The Colonial American Jew* by Marcus and *The History of the Jews in America* by Pete Wiermik.

Privateers

The primary purpose of the privateer was to make money for its stockholders. A secondary purpose was to damage the enemy's commerce. In a country like Great Britain, whose great wealth depended on commerce, the loss of shipping and cargoes to privateers represented a serious threat to its prosperity. The cost of insurance on English ships jumped precipitously and reached a point where merchants' profits decreased even if the ship made port successfully. It is believed that more that 600 British[63] ships were taken or destroyed by privateers at a cost of $18,000,000 to the owners. The number of privateers of American origin increased from 136 ships with 1,360 cannon in 1775 and 1776 to 323 ships with 4,845 guns in 1782.

While great sums of money could be returned to shareholders on a successful trip, money could also be lost if the privateer was taken by an enemy privateer or destroyed by an English man-of-war. (Aaron Lopez, a wealthy merchant in Newport, lost his fortune when his ships were taken or destroyed by the British.) The crew of a privateer represented all levels of society. There were doctors, lawyers, army officers, politicians, merchants and ministers on board, who were anxious to build a fortune or repair one destroyed earlier. When naval officers could not get command of a government vessel, they frequently accepted a privateer until a ship became available. Many naval officers preferred a privateer because their profits were greater.

Early in the war, the government took a substantial part of the profits of an enemy ship taken by a United States naval vessel. (This was ended later in the war.) A privateer shared all of its profits among the officers, crew and shareholders. If an American naval vessel was taken by the British, its crew were treated as prisoners of war unless they were shown to be British born. These men were considered to have committed treason and were hanged. The crew of a privateer were frequently considered pirates despite their letter of marque.

The Jews of the United States represented a fraction of one percent of the population, but they were involved as shareholders in 4 or even 6 percent[64] of privateers. In November 1775, Congress legalized the capture or destruction of a ship belonging to an inhabitant of Great Britain. This meant that a large, slow merchantman was fair game and could easily be taken if not convoyed by the navy. There was one major expense that shareholders had to undertake. The government forced them to put up a bond, sometimes as high as $80,000,[65] to prevent misconduct on the part of the crew (piracy).

Isaac Moses of Philadelphia[66] was a major owner and shareholder of several privateers. He owned the *Chance*, a Philadelphia schooner with six guns and a bond of $10,000. It sailed on July 30, 1779. The *Havannah*, a Pennsylvania schooner of six guns, was bonded by Isaac Moses and Solomon Marachi. Its owners were Robert Morris, Isaac Moses and Hyamen Levy. Robert Morris was the financial "dictator" of the government. His activities are discussed later. The *Marbois* out of Pennsylvania was a brig with 16 guns, bonded by Isaac Moses and Robert Morris and owned by Isaac Moses and Matthew Clarkson of Philadelphia. The *Cornelia* was a sloop of four guns bonded by Isaac Moses and owned by Isaac Moses and Matthew Clarkson.

Small ships with few guns were limited to offshore exploits of a week to several weeks. These ships were preferred by naval officers so they could be near shore if a command suddenly opened up. Other ships either fully or partly owned and bonded by Isaac Moses were the *Black Prince*, the *Mayflower*, the *Two Rachels* and the *Fox*. In 1782, with the war all but over, Alexander Smiley and Michael M. Hays (Jewish) put up a bond of $80,000 on a privateer. Other Jews involved in privateering were Sampon Simon,[67] who owned the *Hardy*, the *Polly*, the *Union* and the *Sampson*. Hayamen Levy owned two, and Jacob Franks and Judah Hays had interests in several ships involved in the same activity.

There were also some Tories involved in privateering. The Hart family in Newport sent out ships to prey on American shipping. The *Elizabeth*,[68] owned by Naphtali Hart, was captured by an English privateer because it carried molasses sugar for Spanish Haiti (in violation of the navigation acts). Occasionally a ship could be captured by an allied privateer.[69] This frequently resulted in years of litigation before a ship was returned.

Early in the war, the Lopez family of Newport had many ships under sail. The family was permitted to send the schooner *Hope* to pick up their stock in Jamaica and continue on to New Bedford, Massachusetts. The ship was apprehended by an English ship and brought to a port. The next morning the schooner left port while the English ship "guarding" it was still at anchor. This time it was captured by two American privateers (Captain Brooks and Captain Griffith). The ship was taken to an admiralty court in Connecticut on August 22, 1778. Lopez appeared at court with a deposition from the lower house of the Rhode Island assembly proving he was a patriot. Judge Jake awarded the *Hope* to the captains. Lopez appealed to the Continental Congress who found in his favor. The captains were ordered to pay Lopez $280 for court costs, but they refused to accept the verdict. In 1781, Lopez sued Ezekiel Williams, marshal of the admiralty court, for £3,000, but the case was dismissed. In 1782, Lopez sued in the Hartford County superior court, who awarded him the *Hope.* Finally, in September 1783, Lopez again received possession of the *Hope.*

When one considers the financial support of the Revolution, the name Haym Salomon comes to mind. It is difficult to separate fact from fiction in a discussion of his contribution to the war. In the early part of the nineteenth century, his son, Haym M. Salomon, petitioned Congress for money his father had given or lent to the government. During the 1930s, the Great Depression and the ranting of Adolph Hitler caused a resurgence of anti–Semitism in America. Leading American Jews of the period looked for someone the Jews could look back to with pride in the founding of the United States. As an objective student of colonial history, it is difficult for me to grasp how a penniless person could come to America in 1775 and within five years be able to reach such financial heights. The Revolution was not like the wars of the twentieth century, where defense contractors earned millions serving the war effort.

Salomon (or Solomon or Solomons) was born in Lissa, Poland,[70] in 1740. His family was very poor. After he reached America they wrote him despairing letters asking for financial help and for him to take and raise several of his nephews in the United States. Before coming to America, he had traveled around Europe and obviously had an ear for language. It was said he could speak Polish, Russian, Yiddish, German, French and Italian. He was not involved in the Polish Revolution[71] of 1770, and he did not know Pulaski and Kosciusko, two Poles who came to help the American Revolution. (For a lowly Jew to know two Polish noblemen is unbelievable.) He arrived in 1775 and listed his occupation as distiller. In 1776, Salomon opened an office in New York as a broker and commission merchant. In 1776, Leonard Gansevoort of the Provincial Congress, recommended him to General Schuyler as sutler to his troops moving north to Lake George. Salomon was back in New York City that same year when he was arrested by General James Robertson (September 1776) for "anti–British activities" and placed in the provost prison. (He was supposedly a member of the Sons of Liberty, but this is questionable.) His ability with languages made him valuable to the Hessian Lieutenant General Heister.[72] Salomon became purveyor to the Hessian officers.

Salomon's imprisonment seemed not to have been too strict because he was able to engage in private business as well as to marry Rachel, age 15, the daughter of Moses Franks (who may have been a Tory) in 1777.[73] During his imprisonment he was able to help French and American prisoners of war escape, and he encouraged Hessian officers to resign. He may have been freed and rearrested as a spy in 1778 by Sir Henry Clinton.

Supposedly he was contacted by General Washington to set fire to British warships and storehouses in New York City. He attempted to carry out this order. Salomon was sentenced to death, but with a bribe of gold, he was able to escape to Philadelphia in August 1778. (The story of the bribe and escape was in a letter by Salomon to his brother-in-law, Major Franks.[74] "Major" was his first name.) Upon his arrival in Philadelphia, he requested any job to support his family. In his flight, he left his wife and infant son in New York as well as £6,000 sterling.[75]

In Philadelphia, Salomon started as a merchant and sold tobacco, sugar, tea and dry goods. He also sold real estate and slaves[76] on commission. By the end of 1780, Salomon was a broker for paper money. Ben Franklin raised foreign money in Europe for the American cause, and Salomon became a broker because of his knowledge of the value of foreign money.[77] Another step up the financial ladder came when he became broker for the consul general of France and treasurer for the French army.[78] He converted French bills into cash to buy supplies for French troops. It was about this time that Salomon started to lend money to American luminaries so that they could remain in Congress and help the war effort. James Madison, Thomas Jefferson, General St. Clair, Baron Steuben, General Kosciusko, General Mifflin, Edmund Randolph, Colonel Mercer, James Wilson and James Ross borrowed money without interest from Salomon. James Madison, in his diary, said he hated to visit the "Jew Broker" because he refused any interest on his loans. Madison claimed that Salomon told him, "The price of money is so usurious that he thinks it ought to be extorted from none but those who aim at profitable speculations."

Salomon was a great believer in newspaper ads and advertised in New York and Philadelphia. In the Pennsylvania *Journal*[79] on February 28, 1781, his ad listed, "A Few Bills of Exchange on France, St. Eustatius and Amsterdam to be sold by Haym Solomon, Broker. The said Solomon will attend every day at the Coffee House between the hours of twelve and two, where he may be met with, and any kind of business in the brokering way, will be undertaken by him; and all those Gentlemen who chuse to favour him with their business may depend on the greatest care and punctuality."

On May 10, 1781, Robert Morris became superintendent of the office of finance. It was his job to keep the army and the government afloat despite a lack of funds. He also had to bring inflation under control. At this time, one dollar in specie could bring $500 to $1000 in continental paper.[80] The Continental Congress did not have the power to levy taxes, loans from abroad were needed to feed, clothe and arm the army. In Robert

Morris' diary on August 27, 1781, is this entry: "Sent for Haym Salomon, the Jew Broker."[81] On September 14, 1781, he wrote, "Conferences with Salomon respecting exchange, Money, etc." On July 11, 1782, he entered this: "Consulted with Salomon on ways and means of raising money to answer the present demand of the public and to provide for the first of August." The following day he wrote, "H. Salomon came respecting bills, etc. The broker has been useful to the public interest and requests leave to Publish himself as Broker to this office to which I have consented as I do not see that any disadvantage can possibly arise to the public service but the reverse and he expects individual Benefits therefrom."

On August 16, Morris asked Salomon to sell 20 dry hides and potash for the best advantage of the United States. Ten days later, Salomon told Morris that there was no market for bills of exchange and that he could not raise money for Morris. Morris's diary mentions Salomon 114 times before Salomon left for New York. Morris knew Salomon to be honest, reliable and energetic. He sold bills of exchange at the highest rate, and the money was used to pay the army. Salomon's commission on paper that passed through his hands was one-quarter to one-half of one percent.

A story is told that a messenger reached Salomon in 1779[82] with word that Washington's army was on the verge of mutiny because they had not been paid. Salomon went to the Jews at prayer on Yom Kippur and raised $400,000. Salomon was supposed to have given $240,000 of his own money, but there is no proof of this incident, just as there is no proof of his lending large sums to Pulaski and Kosciusko. He is also reported to have supported the Spanish ambassador, Don Francesco Randon, out of his own pocket. Salomon also sent £1,000 to his family in Poland. At another time, he sent a gold necklace[83] to his mother. She was not to sell it, and when she died, it was to be returned to him. He provided clothes for his father, but this may have been a burial shroud. As a founding member[84] and trustee of the congregation Mikveh Israel, he donated £300 to the building of the synagogue in 1782. This donation was verified when the synagogue was dedicated. Salomon was given the honor of opening[85] the doors for the first time. At one point there was a serious problem in Philadelphia related to specie and continental dollars. Salomon donated $2,000 to the poor of Philadelphia[86] to carry them until money became available.

Salomon was in charge of all the money given by France and Holland to the U.S. government. He handled 150 million livres and took one-fourth of one percent as his brokering fee. He was a friend and advisor to agents, consuls and ambassadors of the countries allied to the new country. Salomon handled large sums of specie for the army[87] and the hospital at Rochambaud. The broker paid our large sums to Chevalier De La Luzerne, Marbois, the consul general, and De La Forest, an agent of the French government. Salomon was appointed banker and treasurer to the French forces in America. He was in the office of the paymaster general, which he handled without recompense.

In an ad in the Pennsylvania *Journal*,[88] Salomon listed himself as "Broker to the Office of finance, to the Consul General of France and treasurer of the French army [all true]. He sold on commission Bank stock Bills of Exchange of France, Holland and Spain and other parts of Europe and the West Indies. Buys and sells Loan office Certificates, Continentals and state money of any state, Paymaster and Quartermaster general's notes. His commission is ½ percent. He can procure money on loan for a short time and gets notes and bills discounted. Those living at a distance will get their business transacted with as much fidelity and speed as though they were present. He will sell on commission tobacco, sugar, tea and other stores, and he has proper storage place for them. He has extensive connections in Europe and the United States." This ad was as true a picture of his activities as anything written about him.

The picture gets fuzzy, however, when Salomon's outlays of money are described. He advanced more than $200,000 to Morris in hard currency,[89] but was it his money or money received from brokering paper for the government? It was also said that Salomon either lent of gave the government $700,000, but it was not his to give or lend. This money was deposited in his name from brokering paper. The money belonged to the government, and he turned it over when asked. Salomon's financial activities as described by the Bank of North America[90] occupy 15 pages in double columns of a bank ledger. At times his specie balances were between $15,000 and $50,000. The bank charged to his account and paid to Robert Morris more than $200,000. The bank described the funds given to leaders of the war effort. Salomon gave Morris $10,000. He also gave money to Jefferson, Wilson, Ross, Duane and Reed. (Was this the money he lent to them without interest as described earlier? Was it his money or money from his brokerage account?)

When the war ended, he joined Jacob Mordecai[91] in partnership (1784), and they had an office in Philadelphia and one in New York. The duo advertised themselves as factors, auctioneers and brokers. This was short lived because Salomon died in 1785 at the age of only 45. Did he leave substantial estate or was he poor? His account showed $353,744.45[92] in government obligations and Continental paper, which were sold for a pittance. He may have been a debtor of the government because the administration of his estate was turned over to the Bank of North America. The papers in his estate[93] depreciated so that his property was valued at $44,731 with debts of $45,292. Another story claims that the value of his estate shrank due to poor management by his executors. There is also a story of a bad investment in the *Sally*, a ship whose cargo and hull were valued at 40,000 florins. (This is not explained in his papers.)

His public securities and papers were as follows[94]:

58 Loan Office Certificates	$110,233.65
19 Treasury Certificates	$18,259.50
2 Virginia State documents	$8,166.48
40 Commissioners documents	17,870.37
Continentals liquidated	$199,214.45
	$353,744.45

These were all paper at a time of inflation, uncertainty, and the growth of counterfeiting. In the last year of his life, Salomon may have been aware of problems with his estate because there is a listing of "Sales at Auction by Order and for aid of Mr. Hyman Solomon" (February 9, 1789):

1 Feather bed, pillows—4 blanketts [*sic*]	£ 4.12.6
1 desk—bookcase	£ 3.18
1 dressing table	£ 4.10
1 gin case	£ 8
Quilts, pillow case, pillow sheet	£ 3.14
1 traveling box	£ 5
	£17.7.6
Commission of 5% / Total received	£16.08

Another explanation is that he may have planned to leave Philadelphia to move to New York and he did not wish to carry these personal items.

There were other Jews[95] who helped raise money to keep the war going. Benjamin Levy of Philadelphia, Benjamin Jacobs and Samuel Lyon of New York signed bills of credit in 1779. Isaac Morris of Philadelphia donated £3,000 to the colonial treasury. Hyman Levy donated money to keep troops in the field. Manuel Mordecai Noah of South Carolina, who was on Washington's staff, donated £20,000. Isaac Moses subscribed[96] £3,000 to the Bank of Pennsylvania to supply provisions for the continental army for two months. In 1775,[97] when the army set out to annex Canada, he and his partners raised $20,000 in specie and took continental paper in return.

VII

From Immigrant to American Citizen

Anthropologists tell us if man has instincts, the first one is self-preservation. A large number of Jews who came to English and Dutch colonies in North America escaped from the Inquisition, the massacres and the pogroms of middle and eastern Europe. When Columbus left Spain on his first voyage of discovery, the Jews left Spain to avoid conversion to Catholicism. These Jews moved to North Africa, Italy, Greece and the Turkish Empire, and some went north to Western Europe and later Eastern Europe, but in every case they were aliens in all the lands they inhabited. They were squeezed out of all trades and could not own land. As a result, they turned to commerce,[1] and very soon they had an international network of trade based on relatives, friends and men from the same area of Spain. They were not citizens in Christian Europe or in the Moslem states of the Levant. As such, they could carry on trade between the two areas.

The world of trade expanded to sub–Saharan Africa (for slaves) and to the West Indies and South America (for sugar and tobacco). Much of this expanded trade was in Dutch hands and brought great wealth to the low countries. When Menasseh Ben Israel made formal application for the readmission of Jews to England, Cromwell had his eyes on the carrying trade and wished to move it from the Dutch to English hands. The protector felt the Jews could help in this plan because of their wide dispersal. In a few years, at the time of the Restoration (Charles II), the London Corporation complained that the "Jews monopolized the foreign trade." In 1692, Sir Josiah Child, an English economist of great prestige, called for the naturalization of Jews in England to improve English commerce. He observed the wealth of Holland, which he attributed to the Jews.

In 1712, in an essay in *The Spectator*, Joseph Addison wrote, "They are, indeed, so disseminated through all the trading parts of the world, that they become the instruments by which the more distant nations converse with one another, and by which mankind are knit together in a general correspondence. They are like the pegs and nails in a great building, which, though they are but little valued in themselves, are absolutely necessary to keep the whole frame together." Judge Charles P. Daly corroborated Addison's words. He noticed that "they were shut out of other vocations and had to turn their energies to trade. Their cosmopolitan character led them to see what was needed to promote international trade. Their quickness and sagacity resulted in discovery of how trade is facilitated. Widely spread through many nations—trade and commerce brought favorable results to them and to the world. Their important part has never been adequately acknowledged."

Not all Jews were rich international merchants. The great majority were Spanish Jews who fled the Inquisition and left their estates behind, or Jews who fled the massacres in Poland, Ukraine and Lithuania. They converged on Holland, which was more accepting than other countries of Europe. The new inhabitants were not permitted to enter the "mechanical arts" (guilds) or the retail trade for fear they might contaminate the Christians with whom they would be in contact. Soon there were too many poor Jews for the Jewish community to support, which explains the activities of Menasseh Ben Israel. The poor Jews moved to England and to the possessions of Holland in the West Indies and South America. The ones in England soon overpowered the capacity of the English Jewish community to find a means of support for them. Like the Jews of Holland, those of England went to the West Indies and the eastern seaboard of North America. They recognized the financial benefits of international trade, but they did not have the resources to finance shares in a ship.

Most Jews reached American shores free of debt. They were usually sponsored by their wealthy kin in London and Amsterdam. Some however had to indenture themselves for passage as many gentiles were forced to do. Isaac Moses[2] indentured himself to Edward Somerville for passage to the colonies: "This indenture made the nineteenth day of May, in the thirty-first year ... [of] George the Second ... and in the year of our lord, 1758, Between Isaac Moses of Hanover, gold and silver refiner of the one part, and Edward Somerville of London, merchant of the other part, witnesseth

That the said Isaac Moses ... doth covenant ... with Edward Somerville ... that he the said Isaac Moses ... as a faithful covenant servant ...

serve the said Edward Somerville ... in the plantation of George (Georgia) ... for the space of three years ... in the employment of a gold and silver refiner[.]

...Edward Somerville ... will provide for and allow the said Isaac Moses necessary cloaths, meat, drink, washing, lodging" (The indenture could be avoided if Isaac paid the costs within one month of arrival. If either side violated the contract, the fine was £20.

Jews did not approve of other Jews being indentured to Christians. They worried that the servant would have to eat non-kosher food and work on the Sabbath. Several Jews would therefore wait at the port to purchase the Jew's indenture from the ship's captain, or a single Jew might purchase the indenture from its owner: "Received of Mordecai Sheftall the sum of eight pounds eight shillings in full for the within mentioned Isaack Moses' servitude December 11, 1758."

The Jewish community paid the fee because of the Jewish concept of "redemption of captives."[3] This idea might refer to the ransoming of Jews in the Mediterranean trade. Jewish sailors could be picked up by Christian or Moslem "privateers" and held captive or threatened with slavery. The Jews in the ship's home port contributed to a fund to redeem the Jewish captive.

Jews indentured themselves to other Jews for passage. Isaac Solomon indentured himself to Aaron Levy for £19.10s paid by Levy to E. Duthil and Company for freight from Rotterdam. The indenture was for four years. Levy was a merchant and land agent and carried his servant to Philadelphia, Lancaster and Northumberland. After completion of the term of servitude, many freed servants became respected members of society and married well. While there were many more single men than women, occasionally a wealthy man like Elijah Etting, with five daughters, was happy to find a free, single, healthy Jew.

Jonas Philips came as an indentured servant from Germany to Charleston in 1756. After completion of his indenture, he moved to New York, where he married Rebecca Marchado and became a leading citizen. Their daughter, Rachel, married Michael Levy of Virginia, and one of the offspring of this union was Uriah Philips Levy, who became a commodore in the navy. Another son, Jonas Philips Levy, commanded the U.S.S. *America* in the Mexican War and became captain of the port of Vera Cruz.

Indentured Jews, like the gentiles, sometimes fled the home of their owner. Abraham Peters and Wolf Samuel[4] came to Maryland as indentured servants. On April 1, 1775, Peters escaped servitude to Mr. Purdue along with seven others. He was described as a 28-year-old bearded Jew, a cripple who spoke Dutch. Wolf escaped from his master, Stephen Boyd, and found work as a supervisor to 94 blacks. He studied English one hour per day, for which is owner paid the teacher. Boyd had paid $26 for his passage in return for three years of work.

The navigation acts of 1660[5] hit Jewish merchants in England severely because all imports and exports had to be carried on English ships with English seamen. The Jews in England were not considered to be Englishmen, but for a substantial "fee" the Jewish merchant could receive a letter of endenization. This was a level below a naturalized Englishman, but it allowed Jews back into trade. The restrictions were made stronger when parliament established a board of trade and plantations,[6] which forbade any person not native or born in England, Ireland or the British plantations from involvement in trade or the occupation of merchant or factor in any plantation. ("Plantation" here meant a colony or large area.) In February, 1696, three Jews on behalf of merchants presented a petition to the House of Commons that the bill would be ruinous to many families. French Huguenots in Carolina and New York presented a similar petition. As a result, the objectionable restrictions were removed.

These rules were not too limiting to the Jews and other alien colonists in America because they were still unable to be involved in trade. By the mid–eighteenth century, Americans and Jews could purchase shares in ships and cargoes as a result of the naturalization act, which allowed men not living in England to become English citizens. In time, Jews in New York had a major involvement in New York, the West Indies, Africa and European trade. When a ship came to port, Sephardic agents placed ads in the New York *Gazette*. Naphtali H. Myers, on January 1, 1750, advertised an "Assortment of European and East India goods, very cheap for ready money or short credit." On May 4, 1752, an ad placed by Abraham Pereira Mendes described "A parcel of Likely young Negroes, Pimento, Old Copper, Coffee etc. At The House in Smith's Fly, lately in the occupation of Roger Pell, Innkeeper. If any person has a mind to purchase any of the Goods mentioned, they may enquire of Mr. Daniel Gomez." On June 24, 1751, another ad read: "Just imported from Liverpool to be sold on board the *Snow Nancy*... Several white Servants; also sundry sorts of Earthen ware in Casks and Crates, Cheshire Cheese, Loaf sugar, Cutlery Ware, Pewter, Grind-stones, Coals and Sundry other Goods too tedious to mention, by Abraham Van Horne, Daniel and Isaac Gomez or said Master." In Rivington's *Royal Gazette*[7] (New York) on November 3, 1779 (New York was occupied by the British) was this ad: Lyon Jones, Furrier From London ... has for sale ... muffs, tippets, ermine cloak linings, etc. etc. ... ground squirrel muffs and tippets ... black martin and martin throats ... gentlemen's caps and gloves lined with fur. The highest price is given by him for grey and ground squirrel skins." (A "tippet" was a shawl, frequently made of fur.)

By the middle of the eighteenth century, Jews were major ship owners, and their ships were seen all over the world. Between 1757 and 1776, Sampson Simpson[8] was an important Jewish trader. Simpson sent ships to the West and East Indies, and he was also in the whaling trade. He owned the schooners *Hardy* and *Sampson*, the scow *Union* and the brigantine *Polly*. Ships registered to Jewish owners in the port of Philadelphia[9] between 1730 and 1775 included *The Barbados Factor* (50 tons), *Charming Sally* (60 tons), *Hannah* (40 tons), *Polly* (40 tons), *Dolphin* (50 tons) and *Charming Polly* (50 tons), which belonged to Joseph Marks. Nathan Levy and David Franks owned the *Drake*, *Sea Flower* (30 tons), *Myrtella* (100 tons), *Phila* (105 tons) and *Parthenope* (95 tons).

Perhaps the most important ship owners and traders were Aaron Lopez and his father-in-law, Jacob Rodrigues Rivera.[10] Lopez was involved in the triangular trade[11] from Rhode Island to Jamaica to London and back. From Rhode Island he sent horses, cattle, meat, vegetables and candles to Jamaica, which supplied molasses (to produce rum) and sugar to be taken to London. London supplied manufactured goods to be carried to Rhode Island. Occasionally, his ships went to Jamaica and returned to Newport with the products normally sent to England. Rhode Island and Massachusetts had the greatest number of distilleries for rum from West Indian molasses. The captains of his ships had to be good businessmen. If they could sell the cargo and pick up other products, they received a commission on their sales as well as a salary.

Lopez and his father-in-law were heavily into the slave trade after 1764 (see chapter IV on slavery). he was never heard to express feelings of doubt or guilt about the practice. Lopez also made spermaceti candles[12] (spermaceti candles were made from the head matter of whales). This became the largest industry in Newport. Candle manufacture led to whaling, and Lopez had investments in 20 whaling ships. During the Revolution, the British seized five of his ships, and this may have thrown him into insolvency[13] at the time of his death in 1782." On one of the whaling trips, the captain and crew received ⁴⁄₈ of the profit; the owner of the ship, ²⁄₈ for the vessel and ¹⁄₈ for supplying half of the provisions. Lopez received ¹⁄₈ for the other half of the provisions.

Lopez had first choice in purchasing the whale head matter at a fair price plus a commission on selling the whale oil. One trip brought 34 casks of spermaceti white oil, which represented 1,190 gallons of material for candles. In 1768, Lopez[14] was involved in transporting pig iron from

Nicholas Brown and Company of Providence, Rhode Island. In 1769, Lopez purchased more than 80 tons. He purchased iron to sell locally and to ship to the West Indies. It was also used as ballast on sailing ships. It is believed that in his heyday, Aaron Lopez owned 30 ships out of 150 that sailed from Newport.

An important product for the Jews locally and to be shipped to the West Indies was kosher meat.[15] At the end of the seventeenth century there were no butcher shops kept by Jews, although Asser Levy was sworn in as a slaughterer of animals in 1660. There were no signs saying "KHR." Part of the problem was the inability to get rid of the nonkosher parts of the carcass. In the eighteenth century, the slaughter of cattle was in the hands of a few butchers licensed to the mayor of New York. Kosher slaughtering was supervised by the trustees of the synagogue. In 1753, their fee for supervision came to £25.4s.9d. The ritual slaughterer received 50 cents for each large animal slaughtered for export. Jews contracted with Christian butchers to allow the *shohet* (ritual slaughterer) to kill and inspect the animals and seal the parts that Jews could eat. These pieces were sold at certain hours by certain butchers. In this way, they would not be mixed with the nonkosher meats that the butcher sold at other times.

These butchers had as customers all Jews who obeyed the rules pertaining to kosher meat. The butchers paid the congregation for this monopoly, and they paid the shohet $420 for his compensation. He also received $130 from the congregation. The butchers also gave the shohet small pieces of meat, like the tongue, which were kosher. These he could sell to members of the congregation. In return for his compensation, the shohet promised to supply enough meat for the congregation; he would place seals on the proper parts of the carcass, remove the seals when he believed the beef had become unkosher; and would place a seal on the *Crantz* (perhaps fat from the forequarters of the animal, which was kosher) fat when requested by the butcher or the congregation. Beef became unkosher if it was not consumed within a certain period of time after slaughter.

The shohet was elected by the congregation. If not reelected, he turned over the tools of his trade and could not slaughter for the congregation. If a butcher sold unkosher meat as kosher, he was fined $25 per offense by an ordinance passed by New York City.

Ports with a Jewish congregation sent kosher meat to the West Indies and South America[16] in barrels that carried a statement that the contents were kosher. The congregation Shearith Israel in New York levied an export tax on each barrel, which was branded and sealed, and the meat carried a lead seal. The Library Company of Philadelphia was involved in this export: "I testify by this that I have kill de meat and examine the same, as being *shohet* of this place, and that in consideration of that, all our brothers, the Home of Israel, may eat the same.

"In witness thereof, I sign my hand, Philadelphia, the ... 17" (Meat that was salted after slaughtering remained kosher because it was safe to eat.)

Newport,[17] with its large Jewish population, sent kosher food to the West Indies: "I, the undersigned, certify that the 40 kegs of beef and two geeze [geese] picked [pickled?] that are shipped by David Lopez ... from this port to Surinam marked ... Kosher ... are *Casser*, and that any Jew may without the least scruple eat of them, as they are prepared according to our holy law, and that is true I sign this with my hand ... date ... in the Holy Congregation *Jeshuat Israel*."

Generally speaking, the Jews were interested in overseas trade because they were free of local control.[18] They dealt with their relations in many ports. Jews could send reports in English, Hebrew, Yiddish, Spanish, Portuguese or Dutch. They learned from relatives what was needed and where, and they carried the cargo where needed. They could carry chocolate, cocoa, coral, textiles and slaves. The Jewish traders carried armaments in wartime and tea in peace.

They were known to have paid bribes, written wrong shipping orders and sent ships to different ports than stated in their papers. They were therefore frequently involved in court cases. Some became insolvent, and some were jailed. In trade, Jewish merchants were represented in much greater frequency than their presence in the total population. In one year, their ships carried 40 percent of the trade to Jamaica, 24 percent to Barbados, 24 percent to London, 9 percent to Rhode Island and Boston and 3 percent to Guinea. During the French and the Indian War, Jews were actively interested in privateering. Sampson Simson owned four ships with 26 guns, and Hayman Levy had two ships with 14 guns. The Franks and Hays families were also involved. All in all, the Jews owned 3.8 percent of British privateers.

The owner or owners of a ship made the most profit because of the hazards of sailing and foreign privateers. They were frequently the major merchants of the port who bought and disposed of the cargo. In Philadelphia, the major merchants were David Franks[19] and Barnard and Michael Gratz. David was born in New York City and married an Episcopalian, Margaret Evans, and his children were raised in the faith of their mother. Barnard and Michael were born in Silesia (Prussia) and had to leave because of Frederick's decree that only one child per Jewish family could remain in Prussia. Barnard married a Jewish girl from New York and was deeply involved with the congregation. He helped bring a shohet to Philadelphia and was involved with the purchase of a Jewish cemetery. Barnard left Prussia to join his cousin, Solomon Henry, in London. He was advised to join David Franks in Philadelphia in 1754. Gratz received £21 per year from Franks as salary. They bought and sold cargoes in port.

David Franks[20] was also an insurance broker. In a letter, Philip Cuylor asked for insurance on £400 worth of goods on board the *Charming Rachell* from New York to Liverpool. Franks sent the policy with a premium of £71 (in 1758 when the Seven Years' War was being fought). When the ship was captured and taken to Louisberg, Cuylor sent a note to Franks to be paid. He needed the money soon and was willing to accept a discounted amount. Franks probably paid because he had to keep his good name in business. Franks[21] was in the triangular trade and sold slaves from his ship out of Guinea. Michael Gratz[22] seemed more adventurous than his brother. He left Europe for the East Indies, returned to London, and then planned to go to Philadelphia. Barnard advised him about what to do with what was left of his capital after losses in Asia. He was to pay their cousin, Shelomo, £19 sterling which Barnard owed him. Next, he suggested 18 to 20 silver watches worth 45 to 55 dinars each (dinar was an Oriental coin); some new-fashioned watch chains; 20 dozen women's shoes made of *calamanco* (a glossy woolen fabric) and worsted of all colors; and few dozen women's mittens of black worsted. He was told to have the stock insured and was also advised to ask Moses Franks what he thought he should bring if he had more money. After he came to Philadelphia, Michael[23] took a trip to the West Indies. He found an important market for kosher meat and fat to the Jews in the Caribbean. To meet kosher requirements, meat could not be sent fresh if the trip lasted more than three days. He obtained a Hebrew certificate from Abraham J. Abrahams of *Shearith Israel* in New York that the Jews of Barbados and other islands could eat the meat sent down. The animal was slaughtered properly, then the meat was boiled, salted and placed in barrels and sent out. There was no shohet in Philadelphia at this time, and one wonders how Michael got around this barrier.

The Gratz brothers acted as middlemen for Jewish merchants in the small communities of Pennsylvania. Meyer Josephson[24] of Reading was one such customer. In 1761, he wrote for 1,000 pounds of leather at 13 cents a pound. In 1763, he asked for good deerskins. One year later, he requested saddlery ware which he could sell at a profit. Josephson believed that saddlery from London was more expensive than that manufactured in Birmingham (England). he requested 30 pounds of kosher cheese from London and finally 500 to 600 hides weighing 14 to 15 pounds each. In another letter, he asked for six deerskin trousers with a flap rather than a slit with buttons, because farmers preferred flaps.

Josephson included gossip in his letters. He described his newborn daughter who was as pretty as a Polish maid. His wife would be nursing his daughter, so that would save him £20 (apparently for a wet nurse). The Gratzes must have been friends as well as business associates because Josephson told them of Mordecai, a Jew, who had committed a crime and would have to stay until the court met in May. Josephson hoped he could keep him out of jail, but he would have to feed and lodge him until the court convened. No Jew had ever been in jail in Reading. Apparently Josephson had several stores in town and requested the Gratzes to find a Jew to manage a store for one-half of the profits.

The Gratz brothers were two of nine Jews who signed the nonimportation agreement[25] in 1765, which stopped international trade for them, so they turned to western trade, which carried great risks. The Pontiac (Indian) War resulted in the death of many traders, and the Indians took or destroyed much of the merchandise. One Jewish company lost £86,000 in trading goods. The Gratz brothers dealt as far west as the Illinois country and sent merchandise to Fort Chartres, Kaskaskia and Cahokia (Kaskaskia and Cahokia were taken by George Rogers Clark in the Revolution.)

Jews in the larger cities were frequently joined in the companies by gentiles. The Gratzes were partners in companies that owned hundreds of thousands of acres in Western Virginia and the upper Ohio Basin. Their wealth and land holdings made them known in London,[26] and they had influence in the English court. Although Jews were in partnership with gentiles,[27] they depended on other Jews in the more intimate aspects of business. Michael Gratz asked Isaac Da Costa to investigate the credit standing of Mr. Braiford and William Kelsall and Company who had signed bills of exchange. The profit to purveyors of British troops in the French and Indian War was enormous if parliament paid its bills. The Franks family and the Gratzes supplied blankets and leggings to Americans in the war.

However, it was land speculation in the west that produced untold wealth. David Franks[28] and several others purchased two tracks of land from the Indians in 1774. The land extended from the Mississippi River along the Illinois River to present-day Chicago and from the Mississippi River below Kaskaskia to the mouth of the Ohio River. The land was purchased for colonization. They could promise the settlers protection by the colony of Virginia and the king of England if they could get the lord chancellor in London to accept their petition. Governor Dunmore of Virginia urged the acceptance of the petition (probably for a piece of the action). The petition stated:

> Humbly showeth that your petitioner having seen the opinions of Lords, chancellors, Camden and York; relative to the Titles, derived by his Majesty's Subjects from the Indians or Natives ... and being farther induced by motives of extending the British Trade into the Indian Country, and by equitable fair, and open dealing, to bring over the Natives to a due Sense of a peaceable and well regulated Commerce; as well as to avert the Evil Consequences, that might ensue to his Majesty's good subjects from the great numbers of irregular and Lawless emigrants, that are about seating themselves upon the lands of the Natives, without having obtained the consent of those Natives and Natural Proprietors ... be productive of Indian Insurrections ... The fatal consequences of which, have been experienced by many thousands of his Majesty's subjects. Your Petitioners ... at an expense of many thousand pounds ... very great fatigue ... in a most fair, open, and public manner purchased by Fee Simple ... two several tracts ... of Lands as by the Indian Deed of conveyance... That your petitions are, at very considerable expense, making settlements upon their purchase ... useful British subjects whom your petitions are transporting to that country ... may soon become useful and beneficial to their parent country, as well as to His Majesty's Colonies in America ... expedite the civilization of those Indians ... the settlers becoming a good barrier to Cover the Frontiers of the several Contiguous Colonies.... Your petitioners therefore pray, that your Lordship be pleased to take ... their settlements in to the protection of your Lordship's Government of Virginia. (Nothing came of this, because the American Revolution started the following year.)

Philadelphia was home to other Jewish families who had their fingers in many pies. Isaac Moses[29] was a New York merchant who left the city when the British occupied it in the Revolution. He became the wealthiest Jew in Philadelphia, and his estate at one time was estimated at £115,200. Moses personally gave £3,000 to pay continental troops during the Revolution. He was engaged in privateering along with the Gratz brothers, Abraham Sasportas, Moses Cohen and Samuel Judah. Moses and Company turned over $20,000 in specie to help pay for the invasion of Canada. in return, he received that amount in worthless continental paper. His partners were Samuel and Moses Myers. When the company failed, it owed £150,000 to creditors, so the partners sold their personal belongings to help pay the debt.

Practically all Jewish merchant shippers,[30] sometime in their career, were forced to make settlements on their debts or go into bankruptcy. A bankrupt Jewish firm owned by Israel Abrahams and Nathan Nathans of Newport requested of their creditors that they be let out of jail because they had surrendered all of their assets. Isaac Elizer[31] was placed in jail when he declared bankruptcy. He offered to give up his entire estate to his creditors and petitioned for his freedom so that he could work to feed his large family. This was possible because Rhode Island had an "Act for the Relief of Insolvent Debtors" (1756). Some Jews turned to illegal practices when their businesses went sour. Emanuel Lyon[32] and Isaac Jacobs purchased a stock of goods on credit from a group of gentiles. When they fled, their creditors put up a reward of $500 for the two men. Isaac solomon[33] took the name William Jones. He was a forger and sold worthless stock but was caught and sent to Australia.

Several notches below the merchant shippers financially were the merchants in the small and large communities. They purchased from the shipper or from a middleman the commodities they sold to the locals. They sold guns,[34] brassware, rum, wine, cocoa, chocolate, ironware, glass, cloth, skins and furs. Jonas Philips[35] owned a *vendue* store (auctioneer). He advertised "to the highest bidder, an assortment of merchandise, the property of a merchant leaving the Dry Goods Business. At his store, Philips had sundry Dry Goods, Brandy, Geneva [an alcoholic beverage from grain and flavored with juniper berries], mamsy, Frontenac and Claret Wines. Also sweet oil, new raisins, best French and Carolina Indigo, mace [an aromatic spice], cinnamon, nutmeg, pepper, Beaver and Raccoon skins—all very cheap—for ready money only."

Jewish women[36] went into business of necessity. Usually, they were widows with families to support or spinsters without an estate. Esther, widow of Isaac Pinheiro, inherited his business. She sailed in her sloop *Neptune* and brought sugar and molasses from Nevis. In return, she carried to the island lumber, fish and European goods. Some women had to work in industry and made cloth, clothing, soap and candles. Other women worked on farms, and still others managed plantations with slaves. Some women opened small stores in the front room of their house and purchased their inventory from local middlemen. Others opened boarding homes, and some of their boarders were poor Jews paid for by the Jewish community. Women also ran taverns.

The concept of the Jewish peddler with his sack of salable items on his back was common in the early nineteenth century. Sometimes the peddler later went on to open a store and became a major merchandiser. However, there were peddlers[37] in the colonial period, and they were frequently licensed by the state. "By The Supreme Executive Council of The Commonwealth of Pennsylvania:

Whereas Solomon Raphel, the bearer hereof, intending to follow the business of peddler within the Commonwealth of
Pennsylvania, hath been recommended to us as a proper person for that employment and requesting a license for the same.
We do hereby license and allow the said Solomon Raphael to
employ himself as a peddler and hawker within the said Commonwealth, to travel with one horse and to expose and vend
divers goods and merchandize until the twenty-first day of
March next. Provided he shall, during the said term, observe
and keep all laws and ordinances of the said Commonwealth
to the same employment relating. Given under the seal of the
Commonwealth, at Philadelphia, the twenty-third day of
March, in the year of our Lord one thousand seven hundred
and eighty seven.

B. Franklin, president

Attest: James Tremble for John Armstrong, Junior, secretary

Most Jews in trade were in the retail business, and fathers indentured their sons to relatives or friends to learn the business. Andrew Hays
of Montreal indentured his son, Lazarus, to his uncle Samuel David.[38]

Apprentice of said master will and faithfully shall serve, his
secrets keep, his lawful commands every where gladly do, hurt
to his master he shall not do, nor willingly suffer to be done by
others.... The goods of his said master he shall not imbezel or
waste.... [H]e shall not at any time depart or absent himself
... demean himself toward his said master ... during the term
of four years....
   The master ... shall and will teach and instruct ... the best
way and manner that he can. And shall ... allow unto his said
apprentice meat, drink, washing, lodging and apparel ... and
all other necessaries in sickness and in health....
   An at the expiration ... one new set of apparel ... to wit coat,
waistcoat and breeches, hat, shoes and stockings with suitable
linen....

Another indenture contract involved Solomon Morache to master
Isaac Hays.[39] In addition to the usual terms, the boy promised not to commit fornication or matrimony. He was not to frequent taverns, ale houses
or playhouses and was to behave as a faithful apprentice. The young man
promised not to play cards, dice or other unlawful games. The master
promised the usual requirements, and he was to provide evening schooling in the winter. He also paid his apprentice £3 in the second year, £5
in the third, £7 in the fourth and £12 in the fifth (this payment plan was
very unusual). Another unusual addition to the protocol stated that if the
apprentice went to the West Indies after completion of the indenture, the
master would consign ten tons of provisions to him.

Unhappily, not all apprentices learned their trade. Jonas Philips,[40] age 20, came to Charleston as an indentured servant. After three years he went to Albany. He tried to go into business with the British army, but failed, declared bankruptcy and fled to New York City.

In Europe, Jews were excluded from artisan guilds.[41] In the colonies, Jews were admitted with other qualified people. Some Jews achieved prominence in their skill. Myer Myers[42] was admitted to the silver and gold smiths' society and was elected its president. "A Massive silver tureen made in New York City circa 1760 by Myer Myers,[43] one of the most distinguished of the eighteenth century American Silversmith." At sale, the tureen sold for $800 (in 1920). Myers was described as a man of high character and was held in esteem by his fellow craftsmen. He was a most capable and finished workman. Among the pieces he produced were the six crowns of the law (the Torah scrolls in the Newport synagogue). "These pieces are beautifully wrought ... and exhibit a degree of intricate workmanship considerably above the average of the period in America." (A crown was placed on top of each handle of the Torah scroll.) Myers[44] also made ceremonial objects and baptismal bowls as well as alms bowls for churches. During the Revolution, he smelted down household items for bullets. Myers left New York during the British occupation and returned in 1783. He was involved in a lead mine in Middletown, Connecticut, with his brother-in-law, Solomon Simson, and Michael Gratz.[45] His training in metallurgy was important in the Revolution. The state of Connecticut wished to appoint him to direct smelting around Middletown for bullets.

Moses Michael Hays[46] was a trained watchmaker. In 1771, he put aside his trade and went into business with Myer Polok in Newport. When they lost money, they applied to the Rhode Island court for relief as insolvent debtors. Hays spent the Revolution in Boston after the English occupied first New York, then Newport.

According to the mercantilist theory, the mother country manufactured and exported necessary objects to the colonies. The colonies exported agricultural goods, furs and naval supplies to the mother country. Manufacturing was not approved in the colonies, and the colonies were far behind Great Britain in the development of an Industrial Revolution. Nonetheless, there was some manufacturing in the colonies in which the English could not or would not wish to become involved. The spermaceti industry was introduced into Newport by Jacob Rodrigues Rivera.[47] Spermaceti[48] was used to manufacture candles that provided brighter light than tallow candles. Rhode Island became the center of candle making in the thirteen colonies. Candles from Rhode Island were sent throughout the colonies and to London.

The two chief spermaceti manufacturers were Lopez and Rivera in Newport and the Browns in Providence. There were 17 factories in Rhode Island, and there was never enough head matter to supply their needs. The New England candlemakers[49] formed the United Company of Spermaceti Candlers in 1761. The group allocated specific amounts to each member and tried to control production, the price of raw material and the price of the candles. Manufacturing spread to Providence and Boston. Distribution fell to New York companies such as Isaac Stoutenburg and Company and Sampson and Solomon Simson and Company.

The production of castile soap was introduced by James Lucena, who brought the secret of castile soap manufacture from Portugal. Potash manufacturing was introduced by Moses Lopez.[50] The ashes of burned trees (to clear the land) were leached and boiled to produce potash, which was used in the manufacture of glass and soap and to bleach textiles. Samuel De Lucena moved to Norwalk, Connecticut, where he obtained equipment for potash manufacture and requested a monopoly for 20 miles around the factory. Abraham De Lucena, his father requested in a letter to the English board of trade and plantations that they hire him to make potash in Nova Scotia. He claimed it would clear the forest, increase the population of the area both for cutting timber and using the land. He said he could produce enough potash to make England independent of foreign suppliers.

Jacob Marks[51] was involved in copper mining and smelting. He offered to sell 50 tons of copper to Alex Hamilton in 1794. Copper was used for minting money and by ship builders to make sheets to cover wooden hulls. This kept sea worms from digging through the wood and kept rats off the ship. In 1792,[52] Jacob Franks built lumber mills in what would be Green Bay, Wisconsin. Abraham Touro opened a shipyard in New Bedford, Massachusetts. Newport, Rhode Island, was the site of 22 distilleries and four sugar refineries. There were also furniture factories and five rope walks (a long path where ropes were made). Abraham De Leon[53] produced Georgia wine, Joseph Ottolenghe started silk manufacturing, Joseph Simon made guns in Lancaster and Solomon Marache made earthenware and glassware.

Daniel Gomez[54] was a major fur trader. In 1717, he built a trading post home fortress on 2,500 acres of land in Ulster County, New York. It was described locally as the "Jew's house." He left for Philadelphia, but his son remained. Gomez had an apprentice, John Jacob Astor, from Germany. Gomez dismissed Astor because he had no head for the fur business. Moses Michael Hays joined Myer Polock in Newport, and they built ships for the China trade. In 1750, Newport was the site of the Scotch

Snuff Manufactory.[55] Lazarus Isaacs[56] was a glasscutter and engraver who went to work for William Henry Stiegel at the Elizabeth Furnace in Lancaster.

During and after the Revolution, Jews were important in brokerage houses.[57] There was a need for people to handle bills of exchange and foreign money. Moses Cohen was the first to open a house. As a side occupation, he had the first employment agency. Workers left their names for 18 cents and would be notified of job openings. These operations failed to bring enough income to Mr. Cohen. One ad said, "Moses Cohen, Broker, has for sale upon the lowest terms for cash or public securities, wholesale and retail various colored *ell* [measurement of cloth, 45 inches], wide Persians Barcelona and flag handkerchiefs, *Baizes* [cotton material made to resemble felt] and *duffels* [a fabric for blankets], durants, calamancoes, Irish poplins, Fine wild boar and shallons and morens Platellas, Brettanias, Bowlasses. Mens and boys maccarony and fantail hats." "Samuel Hays, Broker: at his office in Front St. ... does business in Bills of Exchange on Europe and the United States.... By long residence with the late Haym Salomon, he has acquired a perfect knowledge of this business."

Haym Salomon, Isaac Franks and Benjamin Nones were in the brokerage business. Franks also dealt in black slaves. None of the brokers became rich, and Salomon left his family in dire straits when he died in 1785. The economic chaos after the Revolution with many circulating forms of money caused many bankruptcies. M. Noah, S. Nathan, B. Nones and M. Hornberg declared bankruptcies between 1787 and 1791. Another form of brokerage was in Revolutionary land grants. Veterans of the Revolution received grants of land as bounties for enlisting. These were purchased for a substantial discount by brokers. This in turn put the brokers in land speculation. Cohen and Isaacs[58] of Richmond owned thousands of acres in what would be Kentucky by bartering for land granted to veterans by Virginia.

Between the end of the Revolution and the turn of the century there was a severe economic depression. The independent United States was cut out of English commerce, and the other European powers still observed the mercantilist theory. Jews left shipping and went into small manufacturing for local use.[59] Myer Marks was a hatter, Abraham Cohen made trunks, and Moses Judah made jewelry of gold and silver as well as silk clothing. Isaac Katz was a cooper (barrel maker), John Moss engraved glass, and Jacob Myers and Michael Katz worked in leather. Isaac Moses was a shoemaker, and Henry Moses was a saddler and coachman. Jonas Philips could not get an auctioneer's license in Philadelphia, so he held auctions across the Delaware River and provided a coach to take people to the ferry.

There were Jewish inventors as well. Jacob Isacks,[60] a Newport merchant, claimed he could convert salt water into sweet by a chemical process. He wanted a reward and patent for his discovery. His letter was turned over to Thomas Jefferson who, as secretary of state, was in charge of patents. Jefferson believed the process was worthless. This opinion was concurred with by Dr. Isaac Senter (a Revolutionary War physician). Senter believed Isacks used either alkaline salt or calcareous substances. Senter advised him that these were dangerous and that the only safe way was by distillation. Isacks[61] tried the distillation process. He placed sea water in a still with a tube of tin that passed through a cask of cold water. He was able to produce 22 pints of fresh water from 24 pints of sea water in four hours using 20 pounds of seasoned pine. The water was pure, but the taste was disagreeable.

Abraham Cohen[62] sent a letter to Jefferson claiming he had perfected a mineral water with a higher gaseous content than in any natural water. He needed about $15,000 to build a hall with fountains of his water. Cohen wanted Jefferson's name to push its acceptance. Jefferson refused him gently and advised him that the physicians of Philadelphia would be a better endorsement.

In most parts of the Old World, Jews were not permitted to own land. Therefore, Jews were not farmers and for the most part remained in cities. There were exceptions, however. Francis Salvador[63] was sent from London (1775) to South Carolina to manage land owned by his father and father-in-law. He was reported to have 30 slaves and to grow indigo. Moses Lindo, also from London, was involved in indigo production (1756).[64] He placed ads in the South Carolina *Gazette* (1756) that he wished to purchase indigo. Lindo was appointed "Inspector General of Indigo, Drugs and Dyes for the province." He experimented with indigo to produce shades of blue dye.

Mordecai Sheftall[65] of Savannah was a rancher whose brand was "5S." Abraham and Abigail Minis owned the A.M. Ranch. Aaron N. Cardozo[66] and his sons, Moses and Abraham, owned a farm in Bowling Green, Virginia. Moses was also the jailer in Powhattan County. Abraham De Lyon[67] in Georgia was involved in viniculture (wine).

Jacob Mordecai,[68] a first-generation Jew, opened the Warrenton, North Carolina, Female Seminary in 1808. Jacob was born in Philadelphia of an unusual couple in 1762. His father, Moses, born in Bonn, Germany, moved to England. He married Elizabeth Whitlock, who converted to Judaism. Jacob joined the Philadelphia Rifle Company in 1774 (at age

12?). This group was part of an escort of representatives to the First Continental Congress. He next joined David Franks, commissary for British prisoners of war held in Pennsylvania. Moses Mordecai died in 1781, and his widow married Jacob J. Cohen of Richmond. Jacob Mordecai lived with them when they moved to Warrentown. He married Judith Myers of New York and opened a country store. Judith died in childbirth with their seventh child. The widower married her half-sister, Rebecca Myers, who gave him six more children.

A household with 13 children required a substantial income. His Christian neighbors accepted the family, the only Jews in town. Mordecai over speculated in tobacco and lost heavily. His neighbors turned over to him a boarding house built for a male academy. In 1808, the town leaders asked Jacob to be headmaster of a school for girls. He gave up his store and placed an ad in the Raleigh *Register*[69] on August 1, 1808; "an Institution for Female Improvement ... My object not merely to impart words and exhibit things; but chiefly to form the mind to the labour of thinking upon and understanding what is taught ... to cultivate taste for neatness in their persons and propriety of manners.... In my seminary will be taught the English Language grammatically, Spelling, Reading, Writing, Arithmetic, Composition, History, Geography and use of the Globes. The plain and ornamental branches of Needle Work—Drawing ... and Instrumental music. Terms—For Board, Washing, Lodging and Tuition (Drawing and Music excepted) $105 per annum." For an extra fee, students received instruction in drawing and vocal and instrumental music. The tuition did not include books, paper and writing material. The girls' families supplied sheets, blankets and hand towels.

In the first year,[70] Jacob and Rebecca taught all courses. The Jacobs children worked on the infrastructure of the school. Jacob bought a slave woman to help the girls stay clean. The school expanded as more girls enrolled. In 1811, a fire accidentally set by a girl burned down the school. Mordecai then purchased a large house for a school and dormitory. Most of the girls were Christian, but this seemed not to make any difference. Several of his children became teachers to help with the increased enrollment. By 1810, 60 girls were enrolled. In July of that year were 80 girls; 55 were boarders from outside Warrentown. There were 90 students in the third year. The girls came from Washington, Richmond, Petersburg, Philadelphia and several large towns in the Carolinas. The number of girls increased to more than 100. He sold the school in 1819 and moved to a farm near Richmond. Mordecai died in 1838. From this distance, one wonders why he decided to start this school in view of the fact that there is no evidence of his having any special training. Since his education was probably similar to that of Jewish boys of that period, he probably got along by personality and a quick mind.

Teaching was never a lucrative profession. Teachers had to do other things to support their family. In 1762, Abraham I. Abrahams[71] was hired in New York as a teacher. He was to keep a public school in the community building. Abrahams taught Hebrew and how to translate it into English. He also taught English and the three Rs. Abrahams was also a volunteer rabbi and ritual circumciser. At one point he traveled to Newport to circumcise four adult Lopezes. The teacher was also a merchant and manufactured snuff and distilled liquor.

The Jews in the colonial period made up one-tenth of one percent of the population of the colonies and even less in the federal period. As such, Jewish merchant shippers and businessmen had to deal with the larger gentile population to support themselves. In turn, this led to joining Christians in commercial ventures. Cohen and Isaacs[72] were the largest Jewish merchants in Richmond, Virginia. They purchased land grants from Revolutionary War veterans and were in business with Daniel Boone, who surveyed land for them and found choice places in Kentucky to buy land. On December 24, 1781, Boone acknowledged the receipt of 24 warrants on land for 10,000 acres and his pay of £6 specie. He promised to locate "as good (land) as the country will admit of." In a letter to his partners in Richmond he described his expenses of listing warrants, entry fees, copies, surveyor's fees, registry fees plus chains and markers.

Isaac Moses[73] left New York for Philadelphia when the British occupied New York. In Philadelphia, he was associated with Joseph Reed and Robert Morris in starting the first bank of the United States. He gave a bond of £3,000 as part of the total of £300,000 to support the bank. The main purpose of the bank early in its history was to supply provisions for the continental army.

Judah Hays[74] and Moses kept a receipt book of their financial transactions. There were many Jews listed as well as the gentile men with whom he traded: Theodore Van Wyck, Abraham Van Deussen, Thomas Ludlow, Jr., John Dikeman, Beverly Robinson, William Beekman, Peter Jay and Stephen De Lancy. The book included expenses which provided an understanding of the cost of living. Samuel Clossy, an eminent physician of the time, received £15.7s to treat Hays in his last illness. He paid out 16s for "one dozen beer," 35s in freight charges for a pipe of wine from Madeira (a "pipe" was a wine cask containing 125 gallons of wine).

Judah Hays lived in a house owned by John Jay. He paid £125 plus the cost of taxes and repairs (this seems excessive for New York City at the time). After Judah died, his family moved to a rental from Mary

Brockholst for £25. The rent on a stable was £8 per year. The tax on the Jay house was £7.11.8, and there was an additional assessment of £3.15.10 to pay for the minister, the poor, street lamps and a watch tax (police). (The tax for a minister suggests New York State had an established church in 1765, unless this tax supported all Protestant religions.)

The Hays family purchased 24 lottery tickets for £48. A notation lists £80 for a slave, Aaron, and £20 for four years of service from an indentured servant, John Camble. Female servants, not indentured, earned 17s per month. Mrs. Hays paid Isaac Marschalk £1.3.0 for Passover baked goods. The receipt book of Isaac Moses[75] is more complete. He paid Tuckey Echley, a female, £36 for 20 months of wages, £5 to A. A. Van Ottingen for killing poultry (the name's not Jewish, so the Moses family did not eat kosher food), 45s for a cord of wood, 14s.6d for cleaning the chimney, £1.10s to a barber for shaving, £1.14s for brandy, 12s to teach his daughter music, £1.3s for three barrels of beer, £1.4s for two loads of wood, 4.2s.4d for milk and David's schooling, £2.16s for whitewashing, £6.5s.2d for shoes for the family, £4 for one-quarter tuition for his sons, 12s to shoe and doctor a horse, £1.12s for shaving for one quarter (three months), 34s for one case of gin, £1.8s.6d for six bushels of corn, £2 for pigeons (eating or racing?), and 46s for one barrel of flour.

After the Revolution,[76] there was a marked economic downturn, and Jews left the occupations of merchant—shipper and storekeeper. They turned to positions of doctors, lawyers, auctioneers, accountants, hardware sellers, and so on. They left shipping because of the constant warfare between England and France and the undeclared war of the United States and France at the end of the century which left them open to attack by privateers. Jews left the Caribbean because of war, hurricanes and epidemics. Most doctors were apprentice trained, but some went to medical schools in Europe.

Law students were indentured to read the law in the office of a settled lawyer. For example, Mordecai Sheftall[77] of Georgia was indentured for three years to study under Thomas V.P. Charlton (a Christian). Among other things, Sheftall was warned not to "commit fornication, nor contract Matrimony.... [A]t Cards, Dice or any other unlawful game he shall not play ... nor haunt Ale-Houses, Taverns or Play-Houses.... [S]aid Master ... teach, or cause to be taught or instructed ... in the Trade or Mystery of the Law Professor—and procure and provide for sufficient Meat, Drink, Lodging and Washing, fitting.... Thomas V.P. Charlton, covenants and agrees not to require the said Mordecai Sheftall to attend to any business or to do, or perform anything appertaining to the study or profession of Law on the Jewish Sabbaths or any other Days consecrated to That religion." The last part of the contract is unusual in that a master would not care to be bothered by the religion of the apprentice. Perhaps the Sheftall name carried great weight in Georgia. Sheftalls were present at Savannah's start; they were active patriots in the Revolution and owned a large acreage for their ranch.

In the early colonial days, the settlers had little or no use for doctors or lawyers. Gabriel Thomas[78] wrote in 1690, "Of lawyers and physicians I shall say nothing, because this country is peaceable and healthy. Long may it so continue and never have occasion for the tongue of the one nor the pen of the other—both equally destructive of men's estates and lives." In some colonies, lawyers could not receive fees, and in some they were banished. Lawyers could not enter Georgia during the control of the trustees. In New England, ministers were expected to make judicial decisions. Boston, in its early years, had two lawyers. One was banished, and the other left because he could not earn a living.

The Revolution caused unsettled conditions, however, and the number of lawyers grew. The law was closed to Jews before the Revolution. After the war, Maryland and North Carolina still kept Jews out. Isaac Miranda sat on the bench in Pennsylvania only after he converted: "An apostate Jew or Fashionable Christian Proselyte." In New Amsterdam, Solomon Pieterson, a Jew, was listed as an attorney in 1654. Asser Levy Van Swellen "became a lawyer" after he stood up repeatedly to Stuyvesant and the authorities. He later represented Protestants in court. When the English occupied New York, no Jews were permitted to practice as was the condition in the home country.

The American Constitution ended this ruling, however. Pennsylvania, South Carolina and Georgia were the only states that had Jewish lawyers before the nineteenth century. In 1774, Moses Franks of Pennsylvania was a member of the London inns of court. Moses Levy was the most famous early lawyer in Pennsylvania. He was admitted to the bar in 1778. His name was mentioned when Jefferson was looking for an attorney general, and he had two brothers admitted to the bar. By the turn of the century, Daniel Levy, Samuel D. Franks and Joseph Simon Cohen were in practice in Philadelphia. Moses Myers, Abraham Myers and Chapman Levy practiced in South Carolina, and Lyon Levy was a justice of the peace.

There were no laws against Jewish physicians. The earliest Jewish physician was Jacob Lumbrozo, who came from Portugal to Maryland in 1656. Dr. Samuel Nunez Ribiero was court physician in Portugal. He escaped and went to England, then to Savannah, where he stopped an epidemic in that city. It was his work that caused Oglethorpe to disobey the trustees in London and allow the Jews to stay. Dr. Siccary, a Portuguese Jew, is said to have introduced the tomato to Virginia. Isaac Levy practiced in the "Illinois County" of Virginia. In 1742 two Jewish physicians, Dr. Woolin and Dr. Nunez, practiced in New York. Woolin was an army surgeon in Europe for four years. Other Jewish physicians in New York were Jacob Isaac, Andrew Judah and a Dr. Levy. Dr. Isaac Abrahams graduated from Columbia (King's) College in 1774. Dr. Joel Hart graduated from the Royal College of Surgery and helped found the Medical Society of the county of New York. In the first New York City Directory, Dr. Barnet Cowan, Saul Israel ("a curer of deafness") and Hyman Isaac Long were mentioned. In the Jewish Cemetery in New York there was a tombstone of Walter J. Judah, who died in 1798 while treating patients during the yellow fever epidemic. "Zealous he was of his labor, the labor of healing, Strengthening himself as a lion and running swiftly as a hart to bring healing To the inhabitants of this city, treating them with loving kindness when they were visited with the Yellow Fever. He gave money from his own purse to buy for them beneficient medicines. But the good that he did was the cause of his death."

Several Jewish physicians served in the Revolution. Philip Moses Russell served with the Second Virginia Regiment at Valley Forge. Dr. Levy Myers was apothecary general of South Carolina. Dr. Sarzedos was mentioned. Dr. Solomon[79] was a surgeon to the continental line, and Dr. Moses Sheftall was a surgeon in the Chatham Regiment. David de Isaac Cohen Nassy was a physician and pharmacist in Surinam. He left the island for Philadelphia and reached it in time to help with the yellow fever epidemic. Nassy opposed Dr. Benjamin Rush's excessive bleeding treatment at a time when Rush was the icon of Pennsylvania's, if not America's, medicine. Nassy treated his patients mildly and had more success. Most Jews were poor and could not leave Philadelphia. However, the number of Jews lost to the disease was less than the number of Christians, proportionately, due to the ministrations of the Jewish doctor.

Isaac Abrahams, son of the *mohel* Abraham Abrahams,[80] graduated from King's College and became a physician. Dr. Moses Sheftall of Georgia,[81] after completing his training, traveled to Philadelphia to study under Dr. Benjamin Rush. At this time, Rush was a professor of medicine at the University of Pennsylvania. In addition to his teaching students at the university, he had 10 to 15 doctors like Sheftall who paid him for the right to study under him. Rush also was able to carry on a busy medical practice.

Sampson Simson,[82] a graduate of Columbia in 1800, became a physician and was one of the founders of Mount Sinai Hospital in New York.

Simson[83] was the commencement speaker at Columbia and gave his address in Hebrew (he turned to Gershon Mendes Seixas, hazzan of Shearith Israel and a trustee of the institution, to help him with his Hebrew.): "It is more than 150 years since Jews came here, then under the control of the Dutch. New Amsterdam was exchanged for Surinam, all inhabitants came under English control. One synagogue was built and we served God for 70 years.... [I]n 1776 every Israelite stood up to separate. We still stand up against any allegiance to foreign government."

During the eighteenth century, there was a union of interests between the Jews and Christians. Early in the century,[84] Jewish children were taught in Hebrew schools under the control of the synagogue. Other Jewish children were taught by a *rebbe*, an itinerant teacher who stopped in a small community and taught a group of boys largely for room and board. The textbooks were prayer books and Hebrew scriptures. They also learned the three Rs,[85] which was enough to prepare them for business. Toward the end of the century, Jewish parents became Americanized and recognized the need for higher formal education if their children were to succeed in the new country which allowed them to achieve any position of which they were capable.

Some rich Jews were able to send their children to private secondary schools which were under the control of gentiles. From these schools boys were able to attend college. There were about 25 colleges[86] in America before 1800. Most were founded to prepare boys to become clergymen of a particular Protestant sect. The number of graduates from a school varied from one to five. By 1800, Harvard and Yale may have graduated 25. Before the Revolution, the legal profession was closed to Jews. Early medical schools, like the University of Pennsylvania and Columbia, were joined by Harvard and Dartmouth before the end of the eighteenth century, and Jews were permitted to matriculate. However, before 1800 fewer than 100 doctors were graduated by these schools. During the colonial and federal periods the only colleges with Jewish students were Yale, Brown, the University of Pennsylvania, Franklin (and Marshall) and Columbia. There were no Jews in Harvard until 1800, but the commencement speakers had to give an oration in Hebrew until 1817.

A number of wealthy Jews became benefactors of the universities. Several members of the Isaacs family, along with Jacob Rodrigues Rivera, were supporters of Yale. Although Brown had no Jewish graduates before 1800, there were several Jewish benefactors (for example, Israel Joseph, Michael Lazarus, Benjamin Andrews, Benjamin Hart and Moses Lindo). Moses Lindo's[87] donation of £20 had a significant effect on Brown's leaders. It was "Voted that the children of Jews may be admitted into this institution, and entirely enjoy the freedom of their own religion without any restraint or imposition whatever. And that the Chancellor and President do write to Mr. Moses Lindo of Charleston, South Carolina, and give him information of this resolution." There may have been Jews in Princeton; at least some of the students had Jewish names: Noah Hart in 1763, Joshua Hart in 1770, and Israel Harris, 1790. The University of Pennsylvania had the largest enrollment of Jews: David and Moses Franks, David Judah, Moses and Nathan Levi and Michael Simpson. Moses Levy graduated in 1772 and was admitted to the bar in 1778. He would become one of the foremost lawyers in America. Franklin college in Lancaster had four Jews in its first class: Jacob and William Franks, Hyman Gratz and Richea Gratz, a woman. The Gratzes were children of Michael Gratz, a wealthy merchant in Philadelphia.

During this change in Jewish attitude toward higher education, many Christians turned to the study of Hebrew outside of the universities. An ad in Dunlap's[88] *American Daily Adventure* (June 4, 1793) stated: "J.M. Ray of Edinburgh, lately Paris will give a Hebrew class and study of languages. Will give a comprehensive view of Eastern, Western and Modern languages—Philosophy, oratory and Poetry as the Hebrew; Chandee, Syriac, Samaritan, Ethiopic, Arabic, Persian, Greek, Latin, English, French and Modern languages.... Hebrew is key to the New Testament and Old and pagan theology and Mythology and all Antiquities and is the easiest language to learn so mere English scholars learn it in a few months."

In the Pennsylvania *Gazette* appeared this ad: "Emanuel Lyon, late of London, intends to teach a few gentlemen the Hebrew Language in its purity.... It is another tongue very necessary to be understood by the Studious.... Mr. Lyon will translate the Hebrew into English or Dutch."[89]

The acceptance of Jews into higher education and the growth of businesses involving Jews and Christians led to socialization and intermarriage. Approximately 16 percent of marriages of Jews were to non–Jews in the colonial period.[90] About 87 percent of those who married gentiles were assimilated into the larger society, although some gentiles converted to Judaism. In many cases, Jews lost their "Jewishness" by the second or third generation, and these grandchildren became Protestants. By 1800, less than half of the grandchildren of early settlers were Jewish. When Jews married Christians, the Jews did not try to convert them.[91] (There was a fear of Christian neighbors, and there were no rabbis who were required to teach gentile wives.) Jews were not a proselytizing religion. Once married, there were no divorces because America lacked a rabbinic court able to give a divorce.

At the time of the Revolution there were about 2,500 Jews in the colonies. In 1790,[92] in the first census, there were 1,300 to 1,500 Jews in a population of 3,929,000 Americans. Why the decrease? In New England, Jewish peddlers lost their association with New York Jews and disappeared. In Newport there were ten Jewish households. Moses Michael Hays and his family lived in Boston. Moses Wallack was head of a household of ten, but the family converted. There was one Jewish household in New Hampshire. In Maine, Susman Abrams married a Christian. In Connecticut, David Judah and Jacob Pinto left Judaism. In New York there were 40 Jewish households with 242 people. Most were American born. Some Jews, like David Hays, lived in Westchester County. In Philadelphia there were about 25 Jewish families with a smaller number in Lancaster and Easton. In Baltimore there were 30 Jews. Outside of Baltimore, one Jewish family lived in Frederich County and another in Washington County.

In Richmond there were 20 Jewish families. There was a Jewish family in Norfolk and one in Petersburg. In Charleston, South Carolina, there were 53 Jewish families with about 200 Jews. There was a large influx of Jews, mostly males, into South Carolina. Most came from Germany, followed by England, France, Holland, Bohemia, Poland and the West Indies. Their congregation, Beth Elohim, was the largest in America. By the turn of the century there were 400 Jews in Charleston. Georgetown had the second largest Jewish population in South Carolina. Jews were in Camden and the Cheraw district. Many Jews from Savannah, Georgia, migrated to Charleston. The remaining Jews formed the congregation Mickve Israel. In the census, there were 12 Jewish families in Savannah.

Jews were less than 0.04 percent of the population, and they lived in six communities (New York, Charleston, Philadelphia, Richmond, Newport and Savannah). The Sephardic Jews were the earliest immigrants, but by 1720 the greater number of Jews were Ashkenazi. However, all six centers followed the Sephardic ritual. The meaning of the terms *Ashkenazi* and *Sephardic* are clouded in history. In the Book of Obediah (20),[93] the smallest book of the Old Testament, there is a reference to "Sepharad," probably "Sardis," the capitol of the kingdom of Lydia. In the Middle Ages, Sepharad served as the Hebrew designation for Spain. The Sephardic Jews were the offspring of the Jews expelled from Spain in 1492, who lived in the Near and Middle East. They spoke Ladino, a dialect of a Romance language written with Hebrew letters. Most Sephardim in America were Marranos who continued to live in Spain after the expulsion. When the Inquisition became overwhelming, they emigrated to

Holland, then England, then America. They threw off their Catholicism to become open Jews. The term *Ashkenazi* is supposed to refer to the great-grandson of Noah. How that relates to the people of Eastern and Middle Europe is another mystery. Unlike the single tongue of the Sephardim, the Ashkenazi spoke German, Polish, Ukrainian, Dutch and English. They had one unifying tongue, Yiddish, which was mainly Low German plus words of the country where they lived.

Whatever their background, the Jews in America, after their problems with Stuyvesant, were aware of their special existence in Ameirca[94] compared to the Jews of Europe. They loved and appreciated British America, then the United States. In Europe, Jews[95] were aliens or strangers who lived in a community (*kahal*) separate from the rest of Christian society. Christian governors and kings recognized the control the kahal had over the individual Jews. It supplied sustenance, shelter and protection to the individual Jew and may well have been responsible for their survival. The leaders of the kahal judged its members in civil and minor criminal matters. The kahal was an intermediary between the king and his Jewish subjects, particularly for the collecting of taxes. In many countries, the Jews "belonged" to the king, and their presence depended on royal grants. They had a charter, a "priviligium,"[96] to settle in certain areas, carry on certain businesses and collect taxes from the Jews for use of the Jewish community and the "outside state." Jewish rabbinical courts were the legislative, executive and judicial branches of the community and could turn to the outside state to enforce their decisions. A Jew could leave the kahal's control if he converted.

In their early settlement in America, Jews attempted to maintain a kahal. The scarcity of Jews in any community led them to belong of necessity to one congregation.[97] They were controlled by leaders who refused to bury them in sanctified ground, perform proper marriage ceremonies, train their children, supply ritually slaughtered meat and provide the social intercourse needed by any human. If Jews migrated to the frontier, the leaders lost control, or if the population grew and two congregations formed, the leader's control was diluted. The powers of the leaders of the kahal depended on the voluntary commitment of the members. The most serious threat to the individual was excommunication, but this was not terribly serious to the individual who sought acculturation. He eventually became Americanized and accepted the Protestant sect held by most of his Christian neighbors. After the Revolution, he became an American citizen,[98] rather than an alien tolerated by the majority.

For those who wished to be part of the Jewish community, activities centered around the synagogue. Through the synagogue[99] they helped the needy, gave religious instruction which was free to the poor, supplied interest-free loans, gave money to widows and orphans of the congregation, supplied medical care to the disabled and paid debts of those in debtors' jail.

The Sephardic and Ashkenazi synagogue rites were not too different. Hebrew was used in worship, and the prayers were similar. The Torah was equally important in both, and the structure of the service was similar. The architecture of the synagogue was Sephardic. There was a gallery above the main floor for the women, and on the ground floor where the men prayed, there was a podium where the Torah was read. The Torah was housed on the eastern wall in an ark. In Sephardic rites, the hazzan stood on the podium during services. The Ashkenazi reserved the podium only for the individual who read the Torah. The Sephardim read the morning blessing of Thanksgiving at the synagogue, whereas the Ashkenazi recited it at home.

The synagogue was used by the Sephardim more often for rituals than among the Ashkenazi. In periods of mourning, the Sephardim had the mourners in the synagogue, while the Ashkenazi stayed at home to mourn except on Saturday, when they went to the synagogue. The Sephardim built a *succoth* (feast of the tabernacles) at the synagogue, and the Ashkenazi built the hut at home. The Sephardim had a congregational seder at Passover in the synagogue; the Ashkenazi held theirs at home. On the eve of Yom Kippur, the Sephardim purged themselves of sin at the synagogue; the Ashkenazi, at home. The Sephardim named their children after living people; the Ashkenazi, after a dead loved one. The Sephardim believed they were descended from the nobility of ancient Jerusalem; the Ashkenazi, from commoners. The Sephardim traced their heritage to the House of David.

The Ashkenazi felt that the Sephardim were too easygoing in their attitude toward religious observances and that they compromised in ritual and practice. The Ashkenazi were stricter in religious practices such as fasting, family purity and dietary observances. Intermarriage between the two Jewish groups was frowned upon until Isaac Mendes Seixas married Rachel Levy in 1740. Their child, Gershon Mendes Seixas, became hazzan at Shearith Israel and led the Jewish community of New York for 40 years. (His formal education ended at age 14, and he had no real rabbinical training.)

The Sephardim were the first Jews to reach America, although there were some Ashkenazi with the first group of 23 in New Amsterdam. The rituals up to that time and until the end of the eighteenth century remained Sephardic in the houses of worship.[100] The two groups differed in the pronunciation of Hebrew, they had a different mode of chanting, and the content of the chants differed. However, their basic theology and laws were similar. The Sephardim had been Marranos for several generations before they left Iberia. As such, they lost touch with much of the Hebrew lifestyle and knowledge of the Torah.[101] They tended to bypass many Jewish principles of religion and life. It was only with increasing Ashkenazi migration that knowledge of Jewishness came to America. The Jews of Middle and Eastern Europe kept their religion in Europe despite the hardships placed upon them by the greater society. Manuel Josephson, in a letter to Moses Seixas, told him the congregation had to read a part of the Torah each week, which was commanded by Jewish law. He described the necessity of blowing the *shofar* (ram's horn). However, the congregation did not own a shofar, so Josephson advised them they could borrow one from another congregation.

The Sephardic Jews looked down on the Ashkenazi Jews and tended to marry gentiles rather than Ashkenazi. The Sephardim were more likely to lose their religion and slip into the greater population. There was a larger number of single men than women, so Jewish men tended to marry outside of the religion. Sometimes these Jews chose to be married in civil courts. They retained their religion while their children were frequently brought up in the religion of their mother. When a mixed couple wished to marry, they might request the congregation to allow a proper Jewish ceremony.[102] It was at this juncture that the leaders of the congregation worked to prevent intermarriage.

The Jews were not proselytizers and did not welcome converts into their midst. In a letter to Shearith Israel in New York[103] (1788), James Foster wished to convert. He was refused by the New York congregation, so he asked for a letter of introduction to the Jews of Amsterdam, who might accept him: "giving me such letters of Recommendation as Shall Serve to introduce me to an A Quaintance with the Jews of Amsterdam where I hope to get my desire in part fulfilled ... to make use of Ruth's Reply to Naomi." (Ruth, a non-Hebrew, was married to Naomi's son and wished to follow her mother-in-law's religion.)

In 1763, Shearith Israel forbade the acceptance of proselytes or marriage with proselytes. English Jews[104] had promised civil authorities that they would not try to proselytize in England, which is one of the reasons King John forced the Jews out of England in 1290. The Jews in the colonies still had no rabbis and therefore lacked the authority to accept proselytes. The main fear of the leaders was eventual assimilation and loss of Jews. When a member (Moses Nathans of Philadelphia) married a gentile without Jewish ritual, and his wife wanted to convert and be married with the Jewish ritual, the congregation sent the history to the Spanish-Portuguese synagogue in London for adjudication. Their response is not available in the records of the Philadelphia congregation, but the couple was finally wed in the Jewish ritual.

The conversion of men to Judaism required circumcision and a certificate of conversion. Jacob Bar, son of Abraham Abinir, underwent this ritual. "We acknowledge[105] by the signature of our hands as under that the Doctor Emanuel son of Jonah circumcised the proselyte Jacob son of Abraham our father on Sunday after the section 'Life of Sarah' [part of the Torah read that Saturday] the thirteenth day of the month marcheshvan in the year 5580 since the creation, also that he took the ritual bath in the presence of three witnesses on the Monday after the section (And Jacob went forth) of *Kislev*, wherefore we have signed.

Doctor Emanuel son of Jonah M.D.

Jacob son of Elizer....

Solomon son of Jacob

Manuel Philips, M.D., certified that he had circumcised Jacob Bar Abalan Abinir. He stated that Jacob is "a member of our holy religion (The Hebrew) he being fully sensible of the truth of the Jewish faith and the Unity of the Divine Being." The *parnas* (leader of president) of Shearith Israel signed a certificate that the doctor was known to him as a *mohel* (ritual circumciser) and "qualified to perform the covenant of circumcision and that full faith is to be given to his declaration."

Circumcision, performed on the eighth day after birth, was a covenant of the child with God. Children born in communities without a mohel had to wait until one came through town. Aaron Lopez's son Joseph,[106] born in 1754, waited until age three, when Abraham I. Abrahams came to Newport and performed the operation. Dr. Rush,[107] a Presbyterian, described a circumcision. The mohel pulled forward the foreskin and held it with silver forceps and cut off the skin. He then tore the inner skin with his fingers and pushed it back so only the glans penis showed. He sucked some of the blood and spit it into a glass of wine. He sprinkled it with dragon's blood (a red resin or exudates of the palm tree or its fruit). He then covered the penis with lint wet with *Balsam copaica* and then a plaster of wax and oil. Rush learned that as a result of the operation, Jews were less subject to venereal disease. If they caught the disease, they did not develop its complications (phimosis, paraphimosis and chancres). (As an aside, it should be noted that Napoleon outlawed the sucking of blood because, on occasion, the child developed an infection from the mohel's mouth. In some areas of the West Indies, a spider's web was placed on the wound to stop the bleeding. Occasionally, however, the child developed tetanus from the web.)

The limited number of available partners for marriage led to intermarriage with relatives, frequently first cousins. Several generations of intermarriage resulted in a big, close family which provided their social life, including visits, parties and family reunions. In Rhode Island, Leviticus[108] 18:6, was used in laws concerning kinship and marriage. For example, there could be no marriage to a granddaughter. Mosaic law forbad the marriage of a nephew to his aunt. The Talmud allowed an uncle to marry his niece, however. Marriages in prohibited degrees were voidable by English common law. There was no penalty except voiding the marriage. Rhode Island allowed special privileges to Quakers and Jews and had allowed intermarriage as permitted in Jewish beliefs and practices (act of assembly, 1764).

The marriage between Jews required a *ketubah*,[109] or agreement of marriage. "Agreement of Levy Solomons of Albany, New York recites his proposed marriage to Katherine Manuel and agrees to support her with 'decency and sufficiency' and to allow her a virgin dowry of 200 *zuzim*. Consent of Katherine Manuel thereto. $800 amount of marriage portion of bride consisting of silver, dresses, household linen, etc. increased by gift of Levy Solomons. In event of decease of Levy Solomons, with or without issue, bride to regain marriage portion of $1,200 in reverse case, Levy Solomons to be sole heir of his wife, in accordance with Jewish law, Signed ... 1801."

Jonas Philips,[110] father of a bride, invited Dr. Rush to the marriage of his daughter. Dr. Rush described the rite:

> At one o'clock 30 to 40 men assembled in Philips' common parlor. The ceremony started with a Hebrew prayer by an old rabbi (Jacob R. Cohen). The whole company followed the recitation. They covered their heads with hats as soon as the prayer began. After the prayer, a piece of parchment, written in Hebrew, contained a deed of settlement (*Ketubah*) to which the groom subscribed in the presence of four witnesses. In this deed he conveyed part of his fortune to her. Then they erected a beautiful canopy (*huppah*), composed of white and red silk, supported by four men with poles held in white gloved hands. The bride came down with a retinue of women. Her face was covered with a veil which reached halfway down her body. She was led by two bridesmaids to go under the canopy. Two men placed the groom directly opposite her. The priest chanted a prayer followed by the company. He then gave the bride and groom a full glass of wine. They sipped a bit followed by the

company. He then gave the bride and groom a full glass of wine. They sipped a bit followed by another prayer. The priest took the ring and directed the groom to place it on her finger. Then the father of the bride got wine as did the bride and groom. Then the groom took the glass and threw it onto a pewter plate placed at his feet. When it broke into small parts, there was a shout of joy and this ended the ceremony. Rush asked the meaning of the canopy, drinking wine and breaking the glass. The canopy as used because marriages in Europe occur outside, and the canopy protects them from the wind and rain. Both taking wine from the same glass means mutuality of their goods; breaking the glass was to teach them the brittleness and uncertainty of human life and the certainty of death. Therefore temper and moderate today's joys.

Marriage outside of the faith presented a problem to the congregation. Benjamin Moses Clava[111] married out of the religion by a civil official. He did not help in the building or maintenance of the synagogue. When he died, the problem came up as to where and how to bury him. They initially decided that he and other similar persons in the future could be interred, but without washing and shrouds to his body. He was to be placed in a coffin and buried as such. A decision was made by a religious court appointed from the congregation. The court decided that the dead man was to be buried in a corner of the cemetery without washing, shrouds or ceremony. Shrouds were to be put in the casket, but not draped on him. Some members went against the ruling and cared for the body properly and buried him. The case was described and sent to a rabbi, Saul Lowenstamm, in Amsterdam. In a somewhat similar case, the son of Ezekiel Solomon, born of a gentile mother, was not circumcised. The congregation decided to bury him in a Jewish cemetery, but starting from sixty days in the future no uncircumcised male was to be buried in a Jewish cemetery.

The kahal issued instructions on how to treat the dead and dying.[112] The leaders stated,

> [I]t was prohibited to move a dying person from his place or to remove a pillow from under him or to place anything under him and not to give anything to him unless directed by the Physician and do nothing to hasten death. If there is any noise, sound, motion that may retard death—stop it. If there is salt on the tongue it may be removed. It is prohibited to prepare anything to be used after death until the person is dead. A person with the patient may pray to Almighty—there are cases of recovery from this. There are suitable prayers to be said by the patient and those around him in the *Sepher Haim*. When death is near, bystanders to form a circle around him and keep his

body covered, even his hands and open a window. When life is almost spent, say "Hear O Israel and blessed be his name" and say it seven times. Each person at death rends some part of his garment. For at least one quarter hour the corpse must not be touched. A fine feather is placed on the mouth to notice if any Breath remains. The eyes must then be closed and jaws tied up then laid straight on the ground facing the side on which the door of the room is, first observing to remove everything offensive from the corpse, cover it with black cloth and place a lighted candle at the head. Symptoms of death: rattles in throat when lips are (closed) and white and nose is sharp, the Hands and Feet Cold as Death and the eyes fixed.

To the non-Jew, the burial practices of the Jews seemed strange. "The Jews in Charleston, among other peculiarities in burying their dead, have these: After the funeral dirge is sung, and just before the corpse is deposited in the grave, the coffin is opened, and a small bag of earth, taken from the grave, is carefully put under the head of the deceased; then some powder, said to be earth brought from Jerusalem and carefully kept for this purpose, is taken and carefully put upon the eyes of the corpse, in token of their remembrance of the holy land and of their expectations of returning thither in God's appointed time.... They generally expect a glorious return to the Holy Land, when they shall be exalted above all the nations of the earth."

Many congregations had a "Society Gemilut Hasadim"[113] (a mutual benefit society). It spread donations to the needy—not necessarily part of the congregation. It supplied donations in money and fuel and provided medical assistance when called for. The society superintended all funerals in accordance with the rites and customs of the Jews. It rendered religious consolation to the mourner and contributed to "brotherly love and kindly feelings in the community." The group gave £1.4.0 to everyone in mourning. (*Abelot* means mourning. This became *abel* money.) If one was sick, he was entitled to attendance by fellow members to assist him in nursing. If he died, the society supplied enough men to complete a *minyan* (ten men are needed to pray). The society owned a hearse, tools and instruments like the bier, spades, shovels and picks. This society was replaced in 1802 by a similar group. In this society, the donors worked in secret, and their names were not given.

The hub of the Jewish community was the meeting house or synagogue.[114] The congregation did not have rabbis, but it paid cantors or hazzans, shohets and sextons. A burial ground which was consecrated was purchased before the congregation thought of renting or buying a house for a synagogue. Teaching children was done at home[115] by parents, private tutors or private schools for a secular education. After 1755, the Shearith Israel school taught in English and gave instruction in the three R's. Girls did not go to synagogue school until 1793, but they received an education at home in the "womanly skills." They were literate through home teaching.

The congregation cared for the needy, taught the children and maintained the Jewish laws of *Kashruth* (eating kosher food). The support of the needy could become expensive, particularly if they were sick. Myer Myers[116] kept a list of expenses incurred in the treatment of his family by Dr. Middleton, who was an eminent physician in New York. The congregation could choose a less expensive physician to care for the needy. The cost of Dr. Middleton's services is presented to describe medical costs of the period. Middleton was called to see Tom, one of Myers's slaves in 1771. In 1773, the doctor treated Tom for syphilis with mercury. In 1775, Tom was treated for worms with powdered tin and a purge. In 1772, Myers was treated for dysentery. The doctor treated one of Myers's children, Joseph, and gave him a smallpox inoculation. Middleton treated Myers's second wife for a kidney infection after childbirth. He treated the child Samuel for two months in 1772. He may have had "dysentery or a heart problem." Myers's daughter, Judie, was treated for a stomach upset. Joseph was treated for dysentery in 1773. Judie was seen from February to August for a stomach disorder. The doctor saw Moses for a month for a stomach disorder. He treated Judie for headache, stomach disorder and fever. Middleton treated Mrs. Myers after the birth of twins for a nervous disorder. Both children died of the "galloping ague" (malaria). The total cost of these visits was £30.

Most settled communities were troubled by itinerant beggars[117] and tried to move them out to the next community. They would supply food, clothes and a small amount of money to get them to the next city. In 1773,[118] Ribi Tobiyah of London was supported for two weeks in New York. He requested enough money to get to Philadelphia. He received $8. In 1774, the congregation agreed to send Aaron Bosquolo to Curaçao as soon as possible. They gave him provisions and paid his passage costs as well as the costs of boarding him until he left.

The Jewish community tried to keep its "dirty linen" away from the general public. Michael Hays of New York and Myer Polock of Newport[119] were in dispute with the Hart family over the ownership of the *Rising Sun*. The case was turned over to three Jewish merchants for arbitration rather than turning it over to an admiralty court.

The positions of *parnas* (president) and *hatanim* (usually two men who supported the president; they would help him pick the next president, usually one of themselves) carried great prestige. As will be described later, these positions required a great deal of time. Consequently, those who the congregation wanted were often too busy to take the position. One method placed six names in a hat, and two were chosen for one year. If a busy merchant refused the honor, he paid the congregation £5.

The need to assure the community of kosher food[120] required a constant watchful eye over the shohet. Judah Jacobs accused the shohet, Moses Lazarus, with mixing kosher and unkosher tongues. The shohet killed four oxen according to the proper technique. He then brought home three tongues. When he discovered his mistake, he returned to the slaughterhouse and brought home a tongue without a mark and "make it kosher" (the ox may have been killed by a gentile butcher). He also sealed a lamb (put a seal on it which meant it was killed properly) killed by a butcher. The shohet appeared before a court of the synagogue led by the parnas. He claimed Manual Myers purchased all of his tongues. He discovered that he had taken home four unkosher tongues. When he discovered his error, he brought the meat to Michael Varian, a butcher, who would sell the tongues for him. His story was corroborated by Mr. Myers. The court found in favor of the shohet, and he kept his job. However, if he made another mistake concerning slaughtering or sealing, he would lose his position.

The need to maintain *kashrut* affected a smaller and smaller population. Peddlers living on the frontier, single men without families, those who had married out of the religion and people who simply did not care ate *treyfa* (unkosher food). Peter Kalm,[121] a Swedish visitor, noticed the difference between American and European Jews: "They ate pork and dressed like their neighbors. They were beardless. The women curled their hair and wore French finery. Men wore no head covering unless it was a wig, which many married women gave up." (A married woman had to keep her head shaved clean, so, she wore a wig—a *sheitel*).

The earliest congregation in American was Shearith Israel. The day-to-day actions of the members were found in *Minute Book of the Spanish and Portuguese Congregation Shearith Israel*[122] in New York from 1728 to 1760. The date 1728 is the year that it was decided to build a synagogue. (In 1695, a rented house was used as a synagogue.) Building started in 1729 and finished in 1732. The synagogue was on Mill Street. In 1706, rules and restrictions were made by the elders of the congregation to preserve peace, tranquility and good government. At this time it was found necessary to revive these rules and add amendments:

1. There shall be elected a *Parnaz* and two *Hatanim* as assistants for good government. The *Parnaz* chose two *Hatanim*. The *Par-*

naz and his two assistants then have power to choose another *Parnaz* and assistants yearly.

2. The men elected will govern the congregation according to their consciences.

3. Anyone in the congregation abusing another pays a fine of 20s for synagogue use. If they refuse to pay, the congregation will help the *Parnaz* collect the fine.

4. If a *Parnaz* is elected and refuse to serve, he was fined £5. *Hatanim* who refuse to serve are fined 40s for synagogue's use.

5. If a dispute arises and the *Parnaz* and *Hatanim* cannot solve it, an indifferent person whom they choose will decide.

6. No bachelor can be elected *Parnaz*. A married man must serve as a *Hatan* before he can be elected a *Parnaz*.

7. In the event of a poor person coming here—the *Parnaz* may give him 8s per week for up to 12 weeks. The *Parnaz* is to hurry them on to another place and get them the necessary items for the journey up to a value of 40s for an individual. In the case of a family, the *Parnaz* calls his assistants to help decide how much is to be spent for upkeep and for their necessities for departure. Those poor in the congregation will receive as much as the *Parnaz* and assistant think fit.

8. Offerings are gathered every three months by the *Parnaz* as well as by selling *Mitzvots* (readings from the *Torah*). In the future, the *Parnaz* and his assistants shall tax men's seats, but not more than 15s per seat and not less than 5s. *Mitzvots* are given out by the *Parnaz* for the whole year.

9. Those admitted as *Yechudin* (first class) shall submit to the foregoing articles.

10. The *Parnaz* causes the reading of the articles in the synagogue twice a year in Portuguese and English.

Articles for Officers

Officers may not pretend ignorance of what is at their charge to observe. We have resolved that:

1. The *Hazzan* attends at the synagogue twice a day on weekdays and three times a day on the Sabbath and feast days to perform prayers and also if *Bodeck* [examines slaughtered animals to see that they are kosher] is indisposed shall assist in his place for which he receives his salary of £50 plus six cords of walnut wood per year, Passover caks [*matzohs*]—all paid out of the *Tsedaca* [treasury].

2. Benjamin Elias will receive £20 per year as *Bodeck* plus 2 cords of wood and *matzohs*.
3. *Bodeck* will kill at several places and enough for the whole congregation. Every six months he is examined by the *Hazzan* and another *Bodeck*. His salary is £20 per year.
4. The *Shamaz* [beadle] attends the synagogue and calls together members at the usual hours. He calls to *selichot* [a set of prayers at a certain time] those people whose names are given to him by the *Parnaz*. He keeps synagogue candles and lamps clean and makes the candles. He keeps the cistern supplied with water. He receives £16 plus two cords and *matzohs*.
5. Those officers who neglect their duties, the *Parnaz* and assistants fine him what they think would fit, but not more than £3. If the offense is great, all members are called to vote. The *Parnaz* has two votes, and the majority rules.
6. Salaries are for this year. At the beginning of next year, the *Parnaz* and his assistants are to confirm [or] *anneil* [deny] these terms concerning salaries and they will sign their names.

The cornerstones used for the foundation of the synagogue were auctioned off—except the first stone, which was awaiting the decision of Abraham de Mucata of London to whom it was offered. "If he refuses, it will be sold in public, and the buyer's names placed in the record." Three stones were sold the first day for £7, £6 and £5.12s. Later de Mucata refused the first stone, so it was sold at auction for three *pistoles* (a *pistole* was a Spanish gold coin worth sixteen to eighteen *shillings*).

"Anyone called to the *Torah* and if he refuses is fined 30s for the *Tsedaca*.

On June 19, 1731, there will be an increase in salary of the *shohet* from £15 to £18 per year. If he fails in his duties, he is fined 5s each time.

The *Hazzan* receives £50 per year."

The names of donors for building the synagogue were listed (most names were Sephardic, including David Lopez, who donated £3 [November 13, 1729]).

Money offered for the *shulchan, banca* and *Hechal* in the synagogue [parts of the interior of the synagogue]:

Abraham Franks of London £8.0. Asher Levy of London £8.0 plus other Ashkenazi names (August 30, 1730).

Some expenses of the synagogue:

Wax for one year	£6.8s.1/4d (for making candles)
Oil for *Tamid*	£4.16s (Lamp that burns 24 hours)

Expenses on new *Beth Haim*	£3.14s.3d
Wood and *matzohs* for officials	£9.15s.6d
Sundry expenses (cleaning, repairs)	£4.14s.10½d
To J. Navalro for painting the synagogue several times	£15.15s.3d
To poor of the city and outside[,] sending people away	£53.4s.1d
Salary of the *Hazzan*	£50
Salary of the *Shamash*	£16
Salary of *Shohet* and *Bodeck* for three months	£5

In 1734 an expense for hiring "a negress" to clean the Synagogue was £2.2s.6d.

In 1737, the congregation found itself short of money. To make the expenses, the synagogue wrote a new rule stating that everyone that carried on trade in the county "shall pay 40s if his public offerings do not amount to that much. If less, his offerings will be used to reach 40s. Those whose amount is more than 40s will not be charged. Those who refuse to pay will be separated from the congregation until they pay if able to pay."

Solomon Myers, deceased, served as shohet and bodeck for many years. "His widow, Judith, and family are to receive £30 per year plus matzoh and 8 cords of wood," the records noted.

On April 14, 1747, to help support the synagogue, the congregation levied "a tax for 18 months on every person capable of paying in quarterly payments. Refusal to pay over four quarters result in removal from the congregation. he will not be called to the Torah and not be looked upon as a member of the congregation. The amount each is taxed is in a book open to all. He who pays the tax gets a seat in the synagogue." Among the "big-givers": Mordy Gomez, £14; Jacob Franks, £14; and Joseph Simson, £7. The total tax was £268.6s.8d.

On April 15, 1747, it was noted that David Mendez Machado would teach Hebrew to the children from 9 A.M. to noon and from 2 to 5 P.M. on Thursday. "He will receive 8s per child per quarter plus one load of wood from each child. He will teach free those who cannot pay. The parnaz or one of the *adjunto* [committee to help parnaz] will visit the school each week."

On September 4, 1747, a list of debts was published (this technique was used to shame the individual into paying): Abraham Myers Cohen, £3.16s; Benjamin Pereyra, £0.6s.9d; Judah Mears, £7.17s.0d; the widow of Jacob Levy, 0.3s.9d; and Isaac Polock, £6.1s.7d. The total debt was £103.6s.11d.

On October 9, 1747, it was decided that no kosher beef would be sent away "by any of this congregation without applying to the Hazzan for a certificate. The price is 6s per 20 half barrels."

In 1750, to raise money, four persons were appointed to set the price on each seat in the synagogue. The price was 15s to £3 per seat. "If this is not enough to pay the balance, the four may raise the price of the seats." Isaac, Benjamin and Gordy Gomez each paid £4 (this to shame others to raise their price). The total raised was £100.16.0.

In 1751, the congregation hired William Sanders Masson to add a wall to the cemetery. The wall would be 50 feet long, 9 feet high and 2 feet thick. He would also build a new front and repair the old wall—price £110.

In 1752 it was decided that for a dead person who in life stayed away from the synagogue or who was never a benefactor of the congregation, his body, his wife's body and any children under 13 would not be buried in the cemetery "without leave and license ... obtained from the elders." "The elders are called together and vote—the majority will decide whether the corpse is buried inside or outside the walls."

Beef for shipping overseas had to be kosher. It was placed in casks which were branded (K.S.H.I.) *casher*. If the meat was prepared locally, the fee per cask was three pence. If prepared out of the colony, the fee was six pence. Meat prepared and exported without a brand was deemed unkosher. Any beef or fat taken on Friday or before a holiday for export was fined 40s per offense.

In 1753, it was ordered that Rachel Campanal was to receive £20 per year because of her age and infirmities. Widow Hayes would receive 6s per week but only after officers had been paid. "Widow Abrams and family to be shipped off. All expenses for provisions are on the ship. Captain Miller will take her off. The entire expense is not to exceed £50. On October 10, 1755, one S.H. who created disturbances in the synagogue and spoke badly of the congregation in the community. He is expelled from the congregation, and none of the congregation is to communicate with him. This notification is to be made every three months until he has satisfied the congregation."

"In 1755, £20 is added to the salary of the hazzan on condition he opens a school in his house every day except Friday afternoon, Holy Days and Fast days and teaches poor children free with a note from the Parnaz. He is to teach Hebrew, Spanish, English, Writing and Arithmetic. In the summer his hours will be from 9 to 12 noon and 2 to 5 P.M. In the winter, his hours will be 10 to 12 noon and 2 to 4 P.M. Parnas and Elders to visit school once a month to check the children."

In 1756, the parnaz was permitted to spend up to £150 for salaries and £20 for charities without having to discuss it with the board of trustees. At the start of the year each member was assessed £2. Later additional assessments were made according to the income of the members. Other income came from contributions, rental of seats and penalties between £1 and £20. The hazzan who taught school could receive up to £80 per year; sexton, £40; shohet and bodeck (one person had both positions), £40 plus free residence, wood and his instruments of office. School cost each pupil £8 per quarter and there was no charge for poor families. Widows received £40 per year. Every man was to be called to the Torah each year, for which he paid $20. Those who refused the honor were expelled from the congregation.

In 1757 this note was made according to Leviticus, thou shalt reprove thy neighbor and not suffer him to sin: "Some Jews living in the county trade on the Sabbath, eat forbidden meats and 'other Heinous Crimes.' Those committing these sins will be removed from the congregation and not buried in our cemetery. Those who change will be returned to the fold.

Our hazzan retired due to ill health. We requested a hazzan from the Portuguese Synagogue in London. The salary to be £50 per year. We agree to pay the expense of passage."

In 1759, Judah Israel was appointed *Shamas*. "His duties include constant attendance in the synagogue at prayer times; he is to make candles; keep the Tamid light; and to clean the synagogue. He will attend at marriages, circumcisions and funerals. He will receive £10 per year salary plus £7.10 to buy wood and matzohs. He will live in a house rent-free. At the time of baking matzoh, he must make available any part of his house the parnassim think necessary. He will take in anyone for board and lodging as ordered by the elders. The elders will pay for board."

In 1759, plans were laid for a bathing house of stone (ritual bath—*mikveh*). In 1760, "S.H. made proper submission for injuries to the congregation. He promised not to do it again. He was fined £25 and promised to give up a book written against our society. Therefore, he is readmitted to the congregation. In 1760, £10 added to shamas salary. For which he will keep bath in good order and clean and heat the water when necessary. For needed wood 50s per year." In 1760, Judah Hays complained about the seating available to his daughter. The elders provided that the bench on which his wife sat would be lengthened for his daughter. Hays refused to accept this, and for his contempt he was fined 40s. "Until he pays the fine and agrees to the seating for his daughter, he is out of the congregation. He was given 10 days to reconsider."

In 1761, it was decided to whitewash the wall of the cemetery every spring.

In 1763, Jacob Franks paid the 40s fine for Judah Hays.

In 1764, there is a mention of a rabbi (however, the first real rabbi came to the United States in 1840). The rabbi is allowed £7.10s for wood. He will pay £4 per year for house rent.

In 1765, Mrs. Navarro will be allowed a doctor.

In 1765, Rabbi Joseph Israelis to be sent to Newport to take passage to Surinam. If he doesn't go, he stays at his own expense.

In 1768, when a man is called to the Torah, a minimum amount to be given is 6d.

In 1769—On the petition of Levy Moses for himself, wife and children in prison £5 is to be given to them.

In 1770, Mrs. Deborah Gomez, widow of Isaac, made application for the vacant ground for her grave next to her husband in the cemetery—granted.

In 1771, Dr. Anderson's bill for £5 for care of Rachel Campanal is to be paid.

£4.12.1 to be paid for charges sending away Moses Mial, a poor lad, to St. Croix.

A review of the handbook illustrated several parts:

1. The congregation was too small and probably too poor to support the synagogue and the paid officers. They probably had a mortgage on the temple as well as on the house of the hazzan and shamas. The money was raised from "selling" seats, readings of the Torah, contributions and fines.
2. The control of the congregation was in the hands of a select few. The parnaz chose his assistants, the hattanim, and one of them became parnaz after one year. This group was chosen from the yehudim, the upper class of members.
3. They supplied charity to their "own" and tried to move others on to the next community.
4. Toward the end of the century, basic education was supplied to the boys.
5. The congregation often had to look to other congregations to raise money.

Shipping kosher meat[123] to the south and to the West Indies was an important industry in New York, and they had to be certain it was properly prepared. The parnaz believed at one time that the hazzan did not see the meat, and he did not know whether it was killed properly. The shippers might have kosher certificates for ten casks and ship out 50. It was decided that the shipper had to go to the hazzan's house. The hazzan would put brands on the casks at his own convenience. The hazzan was not to trust anyone to brand the meat. All meats were branded in his presence because this was the only way to avoid fraud. The hazzan would write out and send a list of the casks shipped and to whom they were consigned. At times pieces of pork were found in casks of mackerel. These were declared forbidden and would remain so until further information was sent about this matter.

Occasionally, the congregation found itself without a leader due to death or the inability of the hazzan to support his family. When this happened, the congregation would send a letter to the London congregation asking them to find a hazzan—"a Young Man of good Morals and strictly religious with the Advantage of an agreeable Voice and Capacity for teaching of Hebrew, and translating it into English as well as Spanish ... in reading the Prayers and the Law, as also for instructing the poor Boys." Often the congregation in London could find no one they could endorse, but they promised to keep looking. The individual's passage and expenses would be paid by the New York congregation, and there would have to be a contract for a certain number of years. London asked if New York would accept a married man with a family and whether £50 offered was exclusive of offerings and Perquisites (1758). In a letter back to London the congregation said, "We have no objection to a married man, but would choose one, rather if with a small family and not attended with much Charge.... The Salary of Fifty Pounds Sterling, is exclusive of voluntary offerings, Marriages and other things of that Kind."

The hazzan was needed for the usual duties of leading the congregation in prayer, teaching the boys, performing marriages and conducting services at funerals. An important part of his duties was the supervisor of meats for exporting. A letter from Kingston, Jamaica, stated, "that you are without a hazzan. You are shipping meats either without certificate or without specifying in accompanying certificates the exact number of casks.... There is no *somer* [inspector] in the slaughter-house, and that he used to give certificates for meat which he was not able to warrant to have been properly slaughtered, *porged* (examined closely and carefully) and made casher.... Also, if it should be found that salting has been omitted in the meat, putting in the salting (afterwards) leaves it *trefah* [unkosher] nevertheless. You should see to it moreover, that no goy (gentile) has a concern with the meat, as otherwise it will be trefah." The need for a hazzan was so important that the congregation wrote letters to the congregations in St. Lucia and Jamaica.

During the federal period,[124] the governing of the congregation changed. Instead of small groups keeping control in their circle, the vote for all officers went to all members, and changes in the constitution were similarly voted on by all men. The position of the hazzan changed. He became a representative of the congregation to society. Gershon Mendes Seixas, hazzan of Shearith Israel, became a trustee of the Humane Society and of Columbia University, where he later was a member of the board of trustees. He met with other ministers to fix days of fasting and thanksgiving.

In 1790, the constitution of Shearith Israel changed and excluded those who intermarried from the rights and privileges of the congregation. Excommunication, which meant complete isolation from all Jews, ended at the turn of the century. Care of the poor became a duty of groups within the congregation rather than of the congregation as a whole. (In Charleston, a group of Jews formed a society to care for orphans outside of the congregation.) After the Revolution there was a splitting of Ashkenazi and Sephardim. In 1783, Charleston had separate cemeteries for the two groups. This also happened in Philadelphia. When a separate Ashkenazi congregation was formed, those who attended the Sephardic temple were expelled.

The congregation was generally successful in keeping their affairs out of the courts. On rare occasions, a problem was too severe to keep from the general society. In 1756, a member of the congregation named King[125] accused the entire board of elders (leading members of the congregation) with assault and battery. The case was heard in superior court before three judges and 12 jurymen: "One S... H... made disturbances in the synagogue and made scandalous remarks about us in the city." He was not a member of the congregation, and no one was to converse with him or have any business with him. The publication of this order was to be posted in the synagogue every three months until he gave satisfaction to the congregation. S.H. was Solomon Hays, a merchant and shohet. he publicly accused Daniel Gomez of a usurious rate on a loan. Hays also openly told of two Jews, born in Holland and living in Albany, who could not be in business but were. he also accused members of the congregation of trying to proselytize Frances, the wife of Isaac Isaacs.

There was an open dispute between Hays and Moses Gomez. This followed a dispute in the women's gallery on Yom Kippur about whether to keep a window open or closed. When Moses Gomez went upstairs and took the sash out of the window, Solomon Hays confronted him in the synagogue yard. Hays was evicted forcibly, and the board fined him 20s. Hays accused the board of assault and battery and went to court. The jury found the elders not guilty, and Hays had to pay the defendants' lawyer's fee. Later, the Hays family had another run-in with the elders, but this time, it was kept in the community. The family was told to make concessions to the elders in one month, or their names would be erased from the list of Jews.

A far more serious situation developed when Shearith Israel excommunicated a transgressor. He appealed to the secular authorities for reinstatement, and the resultant court battle widened the religious rights of the individual against the rights of the group.

Although most Protestant sects could be incorporated to purchase property and protect individual members from being sued or taken to court by others, Jews were not given this protection until 1784. At this time the New York legislature allowed for the incorporation of "religious societies."[126] Changes in the attitude of Jewish individuals toward the ruling class of the congregation led to changes in the constitution (1790). They elected a board of trustees for the property and finances of the congregation. Individuals could not be sued, and more individuals were willing to accept office. The new constitution stated "that every man living and professing to be a Jew, not married contrary to the rules of the religion and over 21, not a bound servant, could be a member equal to others. Anyone who signed the constitution would be a member. If an individual did not sign within the appropriate period, he would later have to make a formal application and pay a fee."

A stranger had to live in the community for three months to apply for membership and pay two-and-a-half Spanish milled dollars. Anyone who applied and was accepted had privileges equal to the others. Finally, once a year before Rosh Hashonah (new year) all members were to meet to elect the parnas and his adjunto (board). The potential officers came from a list of previous parnases or adjunto members. There would be three in the adjunto, and officers would serve one year. In addition the constitution had the usual prohibitions. "Any Yehude[127] [by this time any Jew] violating any Jewish religious laws by eating *Trafa*, Breaking the Sabbath or any other sacred day—shall not be called to the *Sepher* [recitation from the scroll of law] or receive any other *Mitzva* [synagogue function] or be eligible to any office in this congregation." (It should be noted that there was no fine for these violations. By the end of the century, businessmen had to remain open on Saturday to compete with gentiles. The "blue laws" prohibited their operating on Sunday.)

In 1803, the cost of running the synagogue was published[128]:

Hazzan's salary	$500.00
Shohet's salary	$250.00

Lead	$5.00
Shama's salary	$125.00
Wood	$33.75
Clerk's salary	$70.00
Wax, oil, coal	$150.00
Negroe's [*sic*] salary	$125.00
Pension to J. Moses, Sr.	$150.00
Pension to Sarah Israel	$150.00
Taxes on property	$62.50
Interest on mortgage (7%)	$350.00
	$1,871.25

Debts owed to synagogue:

S. Nathan's note	$57.25
B. Seixas' note	$191.61
Alex Zuntz's note	$87.37
J. A. Abrams' note	$20.37
Joshua Levy's note	$750.00
Simeon Levy's note	$42.62
Balance in Treasury	$276.16
Collector's list	$637.00
Sale of seats	$1,125.00
Rents from tenants	$76.00

In the list of notes held is one from Alexander Zuntz, who was a Hessian Jew who came over with the British army in the Revolution. During the British occupation of New York for most of the war, he replaced Gershon Mendes Seixas as hazzan when Seixas and most Jews left New York. As was not uncommon, Jews in the Hessian and British army preferred to remain in the new United States than to return to Europe.

Congregations

The first Jew in Philadelphia was Jonas Aaron[129] in 1703. In 1738, a child of Nathan Levy died, so he needed a sanctified burial ground. He purchased a plot which became the first Jewish cemetery in Philadelphia. The congregation Mikve Israel began in the 1760s,[130] and they opened a synagogue in Cherry Alley in 1771. Most of the congregation was German, but they celebrated Sephardic rituals. Their organization was somewhat different from Shearith Israel in New York. The members selected a board of five who chose a president. He was not to be quarrelsome or tyrannical, but he had to be God fearing and give justice to the best of his conscience and ability. Everyone was expected to obey his orders in the synagogue. In the event of a quarrel, the one in the center of the quarrel had to go to the president and board of five to settle the argument. If he failed to appear, the president could remove his seat in the synagogue. When a new group of officers was elected, they could not show him any courtesy until t he problem was thoroughly investigated.

The president could call the board to meet when he felt it to be necessary. In a quarrel in the congregation, when a man felt he was unfairly treated by the president, the individual could bring his case to the board of five. If they felt unable to solve the problem, they summoned a group of householders. If a person desecrated the Sabbath, he received no religious courtesy in the synagogue until he heard his sentence and acceded to it, which usually involved a fine.

A *minyan* of ten men was needed for services, which represented an inconvenience for most merchants. Individuals were appointed to fill in a minyan for morning and afternoon services. Failure to appear brought a fine.

A stranger in town was not welcomed unless he was known by some members of the congregation.

If an individual separated from the congregation and then died, his heirs had to pay for a plot at a price decided by the president and board. If a stranger died in town, his heirs paid for a plot unless they were impoverished.

The American Revolution caused the population of Jews in Philadelphia[131] to go from 300 in 1775 to about 1,000 in 1782. The British occupied most seaports, and the Jews, predominantly patriots, fled to Philadelphia, where the members felt they could build and support a synagogue. The first drive for contributions collected £897 (Haym Salomon promised one-third and paid £304). The Lopez and Rivera families sent £62.12s.6d. Gershon Mendes Seixas, the displaced New York hazzan, donated £11.5s.0, a rather princely sum for a hazzan. Their first site for the building was near a German church. The Germans complained, and the Jews sold the site and moved to a new area. They raised more money by selling four cornerstones and two posts for $370.

On June 19, 1782, the building was started. It was to be 30 feet by 36 feet. Space was left behind for a schoolhouse, ritual bath and hazzan's house. On the cast wall was the ark for the scrolls. Facing the ark was the reader's table. Along the north, west and south walls was a women's balcony. The synagogue was dedicated on September 13, 1782, after they asked for and received donations from Newport, Lancaster, Surinam, Cap François, St. Thomas and St. Croix.

When the war ended, the Jews from the major seaports left Philadelphia. In 1783, the Jews of Philadelphia formed the Ezrath Orechun (Society for Destitute Strangers), the first Jewish charitable organization of its type in America. The congregation, diminished in numbers after the war, turned to the gentiles for help to maintain the synagogue. Ben Franklin donated £5. He was followed by Hilary Baker, William Bradford, Thomas McKean, David Rittenhouse, Fitzsimons, Rush, Biddle and Ingersoll. The Jews next petitioned the legislature to hold a lottery. This was granted in 1790. They hoped to raise £800.

In 1799, a Portuguese gentile visited and described the synagogue in Phildelphia[132]:

> Today I went to the Jew's [sic] synagogue (on Cherry Street above Third). It was 10 o'clock and the religious service was over. The room is square with benches all around it. On one of the walls there was a kind of a chest which was open so that I could see what looked like some silver lamps inside. It was lined inside with white silk and had red curtains fringed in gold. The outside of this chest had little or no decoration. At the top there was a coat of arms of glided and painted wood above which was a sort of crown. The shield was blue with gold letters in Hebrew. Further on there was a small bank. In the middle of the room I saw a high table covered with a red cloth and beside it chairs facing the chest. The floor space occupied by the table, which was higher than the rest of the room, was surrounded by a wooden railing, as was also the area around the chest. Beneath this were two steps covered with carpet.... He [one of the priests] invited me to come back on Saturday at 9 o'clock in the morning, or Friday at night.

The congregation in Newport was described earlier. It started in the seventeenth century and disappeared, only to be reborn and then shrink again after the Revolution. The permanent contribution of Newport was its synagogue.[133] The land for the synagogue was purchased in 1759 in Griffin Street for £1,500 in bills of credit of the colony, so-called old tenor, which is about $187.50 today. The congregation sent appeals to congregations in New York, Jamaica, Curacao, Surinam and London for donations. All responded, and New York raised £149.0s.6d. On August 1, 1759, ground was broken for the synagogue and school.

Peter Harrison, a student of Christopher Wren, was the architect. The architecture[134] did not resemble European synagogues. It was built according to the Palladian style, derived from the classical period using columns, pediment and cornices. The architect tried to stress symmetry, proportion and balance. The style was disrupted, however, by the addition of a schoolhouse which the Jews insisted had to be there.

By 1761, they ran out of funds and sent out a second appeal. An urgent appeal went to New York, but there is no proof they responded. It was finally completed in 1762 and dedicated on Hanukkah (festival of lights) on December 2, 1763, by Isaac de Abraham Touro. Of interest, there was a small secret staircase from the reading desk to a secret passage to the basement. It was a reminder of Marrano escape passengers from the Inquisition. There was a school building adjacent to the synagogue with stairs that led to the women's gallery. There were also sexton's quarters with an oven to bake matzohs.

The synagogue had three Torahs. One was from the congregation in Holland. The second was brought by the original 13 Jewish families who moved to Newport (1658). The third was from the Portuguese synagogue in London. The synagogue had a seating capacity of 79. At its dedication there were 60 to 70 Jewish families in the city. In 1771, there were about 121 Jews. Touro was the hazzan, but he was not a rabbi. The temple had to be supported like the others—by dues, contributions, seats and calls to the Torah. Donations were usually given in multiples of *Chai* (life). (Chai was spelled by the eighth and tenth letters of the Hebrew alphabet. These added up to 18.)

Dimensions[135] inside the synagogue were 42 steps from east to west and 34 from north to south. The women's gallery and ceiling were supported by five columns on the north-to-south side. On the west side behind the *Tebah* (the reading platform) were two columns. There were ten windows on the first floor plus three in the gallery. The parnaz had a seat on the north side, and the elders sat on a bench on a raised platform in an enclosure. The hechal had a rail in front with four brass candlesticks. The two tablets with the ten commandments upon the hechal were surmounted by three crowns. The hechal with the tebah and parnaz's seat were painted white. The perpetual lamp hung from the ceiling in front of the hechal. Five brass chandeliers were suspended from the ceiling with varying numbers of candles. On the columns on the west side were mahogany boxes for donations. There was also a list of who supplied funds for the erection of the temple (New York, Jamaica, London, Philadelphia, Curaçao and Surinam).

Charleston had a Jewish community at the end of the seventeenth century, and they built a synagogue in 1750.[136] Their integration into the city and their acculturation produced a synagogue that resembled a church[137] and was called the Portuguese synagogue of Charleston.[138] A translation of the Hebrew name was "the House of the Lord and mansion of peace." In 1790, a new synagogue for Charleston was consecrated. The ceremony was attended by Governor Moultrie. At the turn of the century, Charleston had the largest Jewish population. They supported the arts and resembled their Gentile neighbors completely. Intermarriage and loss to the Jewish community was common, however. In 1820, a reform unit of Judaism was introduced into Charleston: the "reformed society[139] of Israelites for promoting the true principles of Judaism." Its concept was to join Judaism and Americanism. Their leaders believed Jewish services as carried out were alien, not educational, unintelligible, too long, with too much Hebrew and not enough English. They opposed swaying in prayer and the sale of synagogue honors. The new reform group was led by Isaac Harley and Abraham Morse.

A Jewish group existed in Savannah, Georgia, shortly after its founding. As was usual in Jewish congregations, the cemetery came before the synagogue, and it consisted of two lots out of town, almost adjoining. The smaller lot was said to belong to the Sheftall family. The larger area was for the rest of the Jews. The synagogue in Savannah could hardly be recognized as Jewish. They had a choir[140] with organ music played by a music director who came from a church. The Jews of Savannah[141] were well accepted by the community. The Georgia *Gazette* described them as progressive and patriotic and said that they advanced the city's interests. All the Jews of Savannah were patriots, and many fought in the Revolution and contributed money to the Revolutionary cause.

In the federal period, Richmond[142] had the sixth largest Jewish community, Beth Shalome, which was organized in 1789. According to its constitution, every free man living in the city for three months and at least 21 years old could be a member of the congregation. Most were Ashkenazi, and the ritual was in Hebrew with an English translation written by Isaac Pinto. (The English translation was based on a Spanish translation of the original Hebrew.) In 1789, the congregation had 29 male members representing a population of about 100. The community also had other Jews not affiliated with the congregation.

The first Ashkenazi[143] synagogue was organized in Philadelphia in 1802 by the Hebrew German society. Their separation from the Sephardic community caused by ethnic and cultural beliefs.

In their homes and synagogues they were Jews. Unlike the Jews in Europe, however, the American Jews felt a need to be part of the whole community. Their small numbers represented no threat to their neighbors, and they were accepted for the most part. Very early in the eighteenth century, "the Jewish rabbi[144] and his congregation contributed funds to build the original parish church of Trinity in this city" (New York, 1711).

In the eighteenth century, the Jews recognized a need for an orphanage,[145] not necessarily Jewish. The Jewish community donated £63.8s.4d. The Jews turned far a field because of a rumor of a Jewish community in China.[146] In 1795, a letter was written in Hebrew by Alexander Hersch and Joseph Simson of New York City to the Chinese Jews. They wanted to know the numbers of the group; from which of the original tribes the members came; how long after the destruction of the temple they had reached China; whether they had books of the Torah, what other books they had; whether they lived peacefully and in what occupations they were involved. The reason for the letter was a description of China by the Abbi-Jean-Baptiste-Gabriel-Alexandre-Grosial. The Abbi had never been to China, but he believed the Chinese Jews lived in the province of Honan. There was no answer.

Early in their stay in America, Jews were solely interested in making a living. After that, they recognized a need to be involved in politics to protect their gains. When Washington was elected, many Christian groups sent greetings and well wishes. Nineteen months[147] later, the president received a similar letter from five congregations. The delay in their response was due to infighting among the congregations to determine who would write the letter. (Philadelphia was finally chosen). He returned a letter thanking[148] them and hoping God would return to them the blessings they asked for him. The Jews, almost to a man, supported Jefferson. They knew he composed the disestablishment[149] act of Virginia, which prohibited a state-supported church. His lieutenant, Madison, introduced the first amendment to the United States Constitution, which prohibited a national religion in the country. There were about 600 Jews in New York City, and they were involved in the founding and supporting of the Tammany Society in 1794. Noah Jackson later became the Grand Sachem of the society.

Throughout the period under discussion, the Jews represented less than one percent of the population, and they lived predominantly in large seaport communities. Many Christians in the hinterlands never saw a Jew, unless he was a peddler. In the cities they were seen and, for the most part, accepted. Elisa Williams (1713) said,[150] "Christian nations are grafted on the tree of Abraham. The promises and Threatening that were propounded to the people of Israel are propounded to us also." Timothy Cutler (1717) said, "God did not deal with the Jews any differently than with other nations—it was only that others failed to see the steady hand of Providence behind second causes." In Thomas Brockway's sermon on Thanksgiving for victory over England, he said the events they experienced differed significantly from Israel's victory over Canaan because

"England came not against the covenant people of the Lord. We had no such national covenant to plead, as had the Jews." Jonathan Edwards recognized the covenanting in the Old Testament by the Jews, and like them, he said, "New Englanders were God's People." Williams wrote, "The Jews gracious and moral alike, covenanted with their God and were alike called the People of God, A Chosen Generation, a royal Priesthood, an holy Nation, a peculiar people." Williams claimed Christians were in covenant just as the Jews: "All Christians Gentiles were grafted onto the root of Abraham so God's promise extends to them and their seed." Ezra Stiles (1752) probably knew more Jews more intimately than anyone else of that period. He said, "Israel has been unique among the nations of the world Because the Jews alone lacked the idea of immortality and future retribution, God ruled them through" an "equal distribution of justice under the Mosaic plan, rewarding them in this world for their virtue and vice." After the victory of the British over the French at Quebec, Stiles stressed the similarities between Britain and Israel, not just as exemplars of God's universal moral government, but also as peculiarly chosen nations with divine historical missions.

Notes

Introduction

1. Johnson, Paul, *A History of the Jews* (New York: Harper Perennial Press, 1987), pp. 78–84.

2. Birmingham, Stephen, *The Grandees* (New York: Harper and Row, 1971), pp. 26–45.

3. Swetschinski, Daniel M., "Conflict and Opportunity in Europe's Other Sea: The Adventure of Caribbean Jewish Settlement." *American Jewish Historical Quarterly*, December 1982, pp. 212–240.

4. Faber, Eli, *The Jewish People in America*, Vol. I, "A Time for Planting: The First Migration 1654–1820" (Baltimore: Johns Hopkins University Press, 1992), pp. 5–10.

5. Johnson, Paul, *A History of the Jews* (New York: Harper Perennial Press, 1987), pp. 231–241.

6. Feingold, Henry I., *Zion in American* (Albany: State University of New York Press, 1986), pp. 227–230.

7. Yerushalmi, Yosef Haym, "Between Amsterdam and New Amsterdam," *American Jewish History*, LXXII:2 (December 1982), pp. 122–140.

8. Johnson, Paul, op. cit., pp. 273–281.

9. Ibid., pp. 172–176.

10. Ibid., pp. 177–79, 205–208.

11. Ibid., pp. 304–307.

12. Feingold, Henry I., *A Midrash on American Jewish History* (Albany: State University of New York Press, 1982), pp. 4–6.

13. Swetschinski, Daniel M., op. cit., pp. 212–240.

14. Maslin, Simeon J., "1732–1982 in Curaçao," *American Jewish Historical Quarterly*, Vol. 72, (1882–1883), pp. 160–161.

15. Gutstein, Linda, *History of the Jews in America* (New Jersey: Chartwell Books, 1988), pp. 11–13.

16. Marcus, Jacob R., *The Colonial American Jew* (Detroit: Wayne State University Press, 1970), pp. 138–142.

17. Ibid., pp. 153–157.

18. Johnson, Paul, op. cit., pp. 209, 211, 213, 278.

19. Ibid., pp. 209–213.

20. Ibid., pp. 273–283.

21. Fishman, Priscilla, *The Jews of the United States*, "Striking Roots" (New York: Quadrangle Press), p. 17.

22. Schappes, Morris U., *A Documentary History of the Jews in the United States* (New York: Schocken Books, 1971), pp. 142–144.

23. Hershkowitz, Leo. "Some Aspects of the New York Merchant Community," *American Jewish Historical Quarterly*, 1976–1977, pp. 10–34.

24. Marcus, Jacob R., *American Jewry Documents—Eighteenth Century* (Detroit: Wayne State University Press, pp. 200–201.

25. Vater, Manasseh, "Naturalization Roll of New York (1740–1859)," *American Jewish Historical Quarterly*, Vol. 37 (1947), pp. 369–389.

26. Hollander, J.H., "The Naturalization of Jews in the American Colonies under the Act of 1740." *American Jewish Historical Quarterly*, Vol. 4, 1896, pp. 103–117.

27. "The Jew Bill." *American Jewish Historical Quarterly*, Vol. 26 (1918), p. 244, notes.

28. Baron, S.W., *Steeled by Adversity* (Philadelphia: Jewish Publication Society of America, 1971), pp. 93–96.

29. Marcus, J.R., *Early American Jewry* (Philadelphia: Jewish Publication Society of America, 1951–1955), pp. 20–21.

30. Wolf, Simon, *The American Jew as Patriot Citizen Soldier* (Philadelphia: Levytype, 1895), p. 26.

31. Faber, Eli, *A Time for Planting* (Baltimore: Johns Hopkins University Press, 1992), p. 6.

32. Blau, Joseph L., *The Jews of the United States* (New York: Columbia University Press, 1963), pp. 20–23.

33. Birmingham, Stephen, op. cit., pp. 50–51.

34. Faber, Eli, op. cit., p. 19.

35. Karp, A.J., "Jewish Experience in America," *American Jewish Historical Society* (Waltham, Mass., 1969), p. 164.

36. Wiernik, Peter, op. cit., pp. 214–216.

37. Herrwitz, Samuel J., and Herrwitz, Edith, "The New World Sets an Example for the Old," *American Jewish Historical Quarterly*, Vol. 55 (September 1965–1966): 1, pp. 41–42.

38. Tindall, F., Davis, N.D., and Friedenberg, A.M., "Documents Relating to the History of the Jews in Jamaica and Barbados in the Time of William III," *American Jewish Historical Quarterly*, Vol. 24 (1916), pp. 25–29, 33–35.

39. Wiernik, Peter, op. cit., pp. 144–146.

40. Notes (*American Jewish Historical Quarterly*, Vol. 28 (1922), p. 238.

41. Friedenwald, H., "Material for the History of the Jews in the British West Indies," *American Jewish Historical Quarterly*, Vol. 4 (1896), pp. 50–57.

42. Ibid., p. 88.

43. Op. cit., pp. 46–48.

44. De Bethancourt, Cardozo, "Notes on the Spanish and Portuguese Jews in the United States, Guiana and the Dutch and British West Indies during the Seventeenth and Eighteenth Centuries," *Publications of the American Jewish Historical Society*, Vol. 25 (1925), p. 10.

45. Marcus, J.R., op. cit., pp. 83–85.

46. Ibid., pp. 88–90.

47. Ibid., p. 86.

48. Adler, Cyrus, "Jews in the American Plantations between 1600 and 1700," *American Jewish Historical Quarterly*, Vol. 1, 1892, pp. 105–108.

49. De Bethancourt, Cardozo, op. cit., p. 37.

50. Cone, Herbert G., "The Jews of Curaçao," *American Jewish Historical Quarterly*, Vol. 10 (1902), pp. 142–149.

51. Philips, N. Taylor, "Items Relating to the History of the Jews of New York," *American Jewish Historical Quarterly*, Vol. 11 (1903), pp. 149–152.

52. Friedman, Lee M., "Some Reference for the Jews in the Sugar Trade," *American Jewish Historical Quarterly*, Vol. 42 (1953), p. 309.

53. Marcus, J.R., *The American Jew 1585–1990: A History* (New York, Carlton Publishing, 1995), pp. 8–9.

54. Wiznitzer, Arnold, "Crypto-Jews in Mexico in the Sixteenth Century," *American Jewish Historical Quarterly*, Vol. 51 (1962), pp. 170–179.

Chapter 1

1. Friedman, Lee M., *Early American Jews* (Cambridge, Mass.: Harvard University Press, 1934), p. 53.

2. Birmingham, Stephen, *The Grandees* (New York: Harper and Row, 1971), pp. 53–58.

3. Gutstein, M.A., *History of the Jews in America* (New York: Bloch, 1936), p. 18.

4. Friedman, Lee M., *Pilgrims in a New Land* (Philadelphia: Jewish Publication Society of America, 1948), p. 5

5. Friedman, Lee M., *Early American Jews* (Cambridge, Mass.: Harvard University Press, 1934), pp. 49–52.

6. Gay, Ruth, *Jews in America* (New York: Basic Books, 1965), pp. 6–7.

7. Op. cit., pp. 54–60.

8. Oppenheim, Samuel, "The Early History of the Jews of New York," *American Jewish Historical Quarterly*, Vol. 18, 1909, pp. 52–70.

9. Birmingham, Stephen, *The Grandees* (New York: Harper and Row, 1971), pp. 59–84.

10. Hertzberg, Arthur, *The Jews in America* (New York: Simon and Schuster, 1989), pp. 23–30.

11. Gutstein, M.A., *History of the Jews in America* (New York: Bloch, 1936), p. 14.

12. Scheppes, Morris U., *A Documentary History of the Jews in the United States* (New York: Schocken Books, 1971), pp. 15–16.

13. Oppenheim, Samuel, "The Early History of the Jews of New York," *American Jewish Historical Quarterly*, Vol. 18, 1909, p. 21.

14. Gay, Ruth, *Jews in America* (New York: Basic Books, 1965), p 10.

15. Op. cit., p 23.

16. Friedman, Lee M., *Early American Jews* (Cambridge, Mass.: Harvard University Press, 1934), pp 52–60.

17. Op. cit., pp. 27–28.

18. Ibid., pp. 29–33.

19. Marcus, J.B., *The American Jew: A History* (Brooklyn: Carlson, 1995), pp. 15–20.

20. Blau, Joseph L., *The Jews in the United States* (New York: Columbia University Press, 1913), pp. 25–29.

21. Marcus, J.B., *Early American Jewry* (Philadelphia: Jewish Publication Society of America, 1951–1955), p. 23.

22. Gay, Ruth, *Jews in America* (New York: Basic Books, 1965), p 11.

23. Faber, Eli, *A Time for Planting* (Baltimore: Johns Hopkins University Press, 1992), pp. 32–34.

24. Oppenheim, Samuel, "The Early History of the Jews of New York," *American Jewish Historical Quarterly*, Vol. 18, 1909, pp. 24–26, 35–37.

25. Feldstein, Stanley, *The Land That I Show You* (Garden City: New York, Anchor Press/Doubleday, 1970), p. 74.

26. Rosendale, Simon W., "An Early Ownership of Real Estate in Albany, New York, by a Jewish Trader," *American Jewish Historical Quarterly*, Vol. 3, 1895, pp. 61–66.

27. Friedman, Lee M., *Pilgrims in a New Land* (Philadelphia: Jewish Publication Society of America, 1948), p. 34.

28. Sachar, H.M., *A History of the Jews in America* (New York: Knopf, 1992), pp. 15–16.

29. Karp, A.J., "Jewish Experience in America," American Jewish Historical Society (Waltham, Mass.: 1969), p. 46.

30. Huhner, Leon, "Asser Levy," *American Jewish Historical Quarterly*, Vol. 5, 1897, pp. 16–23.

31. Kohler, Max J., "Civil Status of the Jews in Colonial New York," *American Jewish Historical Quarterly*, Vol. 5, 1897, pp. 82–94.

32. Theberties, Charles, "Duke of York Takes New York," *American Jewish Historical Society*, Vol. 4, 1895, pp. 38–46.

33. Blau, Joseph L., and Baron, S.W., eds., *The Jews of the United States 1790–1840* (New York and London: Columbia University Press, 1963), p. xviii (Preface).

34. Kohler, Max J., "Civil Status of the Jews in Colonial New York," *American Jewish Historical Quarterly*, Vol. 5, 1897, pp. 90–92.

35. Baron, S.W., *Steeled by Adversity* (Philadelphia: Jewish Publication Society of America, 1971), pp. 89–90.

36. Gay, Ruth, *Jews in America* (New York: Basic Books, 1965), pp. 12–14.

37. Phillips, N. Taylor, "The Congregation *Shearith Israel*," *American Jewish Historical Quarterly*, Vol. 5, 1897, pp. 126–131.

38. Dyer, A.M., "Points in the First Chapter of New York Jewish History," *American Jewish Historical Quarterly*, Vol. 3, 1895, pp. 46–60.

39. Janowsky, Oscar I., *The American Jew: A Composite Portrait* (New York: Harper and Brothers, 1942), p. 32.

40. Ibid., p. 60.

41. Kohler, Max J., "Civil Status of the Jews in Colonial New York," *American Jewish Historical Quarterly*, Vol. 5, 1897, pp. 96–104.

42. Baron, S.W., *Steeled by Adversity* (Philadelphia: Jewish Publication Society of America, 1971), p. 91.

43. Hershkowitz, Leo, "Some Aspects of the New York Merchant and Community," *American Jewish Historical Quarterly*, 1976–1977, p. 28.

44. Marcus, J.B., *The Colonial American Jew* (Detroit: Wayne State University Press, 1970), p. 63.

45. Faber, Eli, *A Time for Planting* (Baltimore: Johns Hopkins University Press, 1992), pp. 32–36.

46. Hershkowitz, Leo, "Wills of Early New York Jews (1704–1740), *American Jewish Historical Quarterly*, Vol. 55, 1965–1966, pp. 170, 187, 204–205.

47. Hershkowitz, Leo, "Some Aspects of the New York Merchant and Community," *American Jewish Historical Quarterly*, 1976–1977, pp. 10–34.

48. Schappes, Morris V., *A Documentary History of the Jews in the United States* (New York: Schocken Books, 1971), pp. 13–20.

49. Ibid., pp. 92–93.

50. Dunn, Mary M., and Dunn, Richard Z., eds., *The Papers of William Penn, Vol. 1, 1644–1679* (Philadelphia: University of Pennsylvania Press, 1981), pp. 91, 226, 43; Vol. V, pp. 37–41, 424.

51. Bronner, Edwin B., and Fraser, David, eds., *The Papers of William Penn, Vol. 5* (Philadelphia: University of Pennsylvania Press, 1986), pp. 215–218.

52. Kelley, Joseph J., Jr., *Pennsylvania: The Colonial Years, 1681–1776* (New York City: Doubleday and Co., Inc. 1980), p. 31.

53. Jenkins, Howard M., ed., *Pennsylvania—Colonial and Federal: A History 1608–1903* (Philadelphia: Pennsylvania Historical Publishing Association, 1903), p. 354.

54. Marcus, J.R., *The Jew in the American World* (Detroit: Wayne State University Press, 1996), p. 37.

55. Wolf, Edwin, II, and Whiteman, Maxwell, *The History of the Jews of Philadelphia* (Philadelphia: Jewish Publication Society of America, 1957), pp. 10–11.

56. Rosenbach, Abraham S.W., "Notes on the First Settlement of Jews in Pennsylvania, 1655–1703," *American Jewish Historical Quarterly*, Vol. 5, 1896, pp. 191–196.

57. Rosenbach, Abraham S.W., "Notes on the First Settlement of Jews in Pennsylvania, 1655–1703," *American Jewish Historical Quarterly*, Vol. 5, 1896, pp. 191, 198.

58. Wolf, Edwin, II, and Whitman, M., *The History of the Jews in Philadelphia* (Philadelphia: Jewish Publication Society of America, 1957), pp. 14–15.

59. Marcus, J.R., *Early American Jewry, Vol.*

II (Philadelphia: Jewish Publishing Society of America, 1955), p. 19.

60. Necarsulmer, Henry, "Early Jewish Settlement at Lancaster, Pennsylvania," *American Jewish Historical Quarterly*, Vol. 9, 1901, pp. 29–34.

61. Hertzberg, Arthur, *The Jews in America* (New York: Simon and Schuster, 1989), p 32.

62. Hart, Gustavio, "Notes on Myer Hart and Other Jews of Easton, Pennsylvania," *American Jewish Historical Quarterly*, Vol. 5, 1897, pp. 127–129.

63. Ibid., pp. 130–132.

64. Gay, Ruth, *Jews in America* (New York: Basic Books, 1965), pp. 21–24.

65. Birmingham, Stephen, *The Grandees* (New York: Harper and Row, 1971), p.3.

66. Faber, Eli, *A Time for Planting* (Baltimore: Johns Hopkins University Press, 1992), pp. 39–40.

67. Byars, William V., "The Gratz Papers," *American Jewish Historical Quarterly*, Vol. 23, 1915, pp. 2–12.

68. Marcus, J.R., *American Jewry Documents: Eighteenth Century* (Cincinnati: Hebrew Union College Press, 1939), p. 65.

69. Marcus, J.R., *Early American Jewry* (Philadelphia: Jewish Publishing Society of America, 1951–1955), pp. 2–9, 14–20.

70. Scharf, J. Thomas, and Wescott, Thompson, *History of Philadelphia, 1609–1804* (Philadelphia: L.H. Everts, 1884); *Freeman's Journal* (Philadelphia), Jan. 21, 1784, p. 1438.

71. Marcus, J.R., *Early American Jewry* (Philadelphia: Jewish Publishing Society of America, 1951–1955), p. 154.

72. Birmingham, Stephen, *The Grandees* (New York: Harper and Row, 1971), pp 164–175.

73. Scharf, J. Thomas, and Wescott, Thompson, *History of Philadelphia, 1609–1804* (Philadelphia: L.H. Everts and Co., 1884), p. 1420.

74. Faber, Eli, *A Time for Planting* (Baltimore: Johns Hopkins University Press, 1992), pp. 104–109.

75. "Yellow Fever Epidemic of Philadelphia 1793," *American Jewish Historical Quarterly*, Vol. 35, 1939, pp. 285–287.

76. Morais, Sabato, "Mickve Israel Congregation of Philadelphia," *American Jewish Historical Quarterly*, Vol. 1, 1892, pp. 13–19.

77. Marcus, J.R., *Early American Jewry* (Philadelphia: Jewish Publishing Society of America, 1951–1955), p. 146.

78. *Colonial Records of Pennsylvania: Minutes of the Supreme Executive Council of Pennsylvania, Vol. 15, 1781–1783* (Philadelphia: Theo Fenn, 1853), p. 367.

79. *Pennsylvania Archives First Series—Vol. X 1783–1788* (Philadelphia: Joseph Severns, 1854), p. 731.

80. Marcus, J.R., *American Jewry Documents: Eighteenth Century* (Cincinnati: Hebrew Union College Press, 1959), pp. 114–115, 130–134.

81. Ibid., p. 142.

82. Op. cit., p. 84.

83. Faber, Eli, *A Time for Planting* (Baltimore: Johns Hopkins University Press, 1992), pp. 109–113, 127.

84. Sharfman, I. Harold, *Jews on the Frontier* (Chicago: Henry Regnery, 1977), p. 62.

85. Friedenberg, Albert M., "The Jews of New Jersey from the Earliest Times to 1850," *American Jewish Historical Quarterly*, Vol. 17, 1908, pp. 33–36.

86. Kull, Irving S., ed., *New Jersey: A History* (New York: American Historical Society, Inc., 1930), pp. 97, 321–378.

87. "Notes on Early Jews in Middlesex County, New Jersey," *American Jewish Historical Society*, Vol. 33, 1934, pp. 251–252.

88. Friedenberg, Albert M., "The Jews of New Jersey from the Earliest Times to 1850," *American Jewish Historical Quarterly*, Vol. 17, 1908, pp. 36–41.

89. Winkel, Peter, "Naturalization in Colonial New Jersey," *New Jersey History* Vol. 109, 1–2, 1991, pp. 27–53.

90. Schappes, Morris V., *A Documentary History of the Jews in the United States* (New York: Schocken Books, 1971), p. 123.

91. Marcus, J.R., *The Colonial American Jew* (Detroit: Wayne State University Press, 1970), p 137.

92. Munroe, John A., *Colonial Delaware: A History* (New Jersey: KTO Press, 1978), p. 166.

Chapter 2

1. Auerbach, Jerold S., *Rabbis and Lawyers: The Journey from Torah to Constitution* (Bloomington: Indiana University Press, 1990), pp. 3–8.

2. Meyer, Isadore S., "Hebrew at Harvard," *American Jewish Historical Quarterly*, Vol. 35, (1939), pp. 147–155.

3. Friedman, Lee M., *Pilgrims in a New Land* (Philadelphia: Jewish Publication Society of America, 1971), p. 15.

4. Baron, S.W., *Steeled by Adversity* (Philadelphia: Jewish Publication Society of America, 1971), pp. 107–111.

5. de Sola Pool, D., Reverend, "Hebrew Learning among the Puritans of New England Prior to 1700," *American Jewish*

Historical Quarterly, Vol. 19, (1910), pp. 32–45.

6. Goldman, Shalom, "Biblical Hebrew in Colonial America," *American Jewish Historical Quarterly*, Vol. 79, (1989–1990), pp. 193, 174–179.

7. Friedman, Lee M., "Judah Monis, First Instructor in Hebrew at Harvard University," *American Jewish Historical Quarterly*, Vol. 22, (1914), pp. 1–18.

8. Friedman, Lee M., *Early American Jews* (Cambridge, Mass.: Harvard University Press, 1934), pp. 23–38.

9. Meyer, Isadore S., "Hebrew at Harvard," *American Jewish Historical Quarterly*, Vol. 35, (1939), pp. 161–164.

10. Friedman, Lee M., "Some Further Notes on Judah Monis," *American Jewish Historical Quarterly*, Vol. 37, (1947), pp. 121–123, 134.

11. Lebeson, Anita, *Pilgrim People* (New York: Minerva Press, 1975), p. 5.

12. Baron, S.W., *Steeled by Adversity* (Philadelphia: Jewish Publication Society of America, 1971), p. 119.

13. Huhner, Leon, "The Jews of New England (Other than Rhode Island) Prior to 1800," *American Jewish Historical Quarterly*, Vol. 11, (1903), p. 77.

14. Marcus, J.R., *Early American Jewry* (Philadelphia: Jewish Publication Society of America, 1951–1955), pp. 106–117.

15. Friedman, Lee M., *Early American Jews* (Cambridge, Mass.: Harvard University Press, 1934), p. 4.

16. Friedman, Lee M., "Boston in American Jewish History," *American Jewish Historical Quarterly*, Vol. 42, (1953), pp. 334–335.

17. Huhner Leon, "The Jews of New England (Other than Rhode Island) Prior to 1800," *American Jewish Historical Quarterly*, Vol. 11, (1903), pp. 79–83.

18. Friedman, Lee M., "Rowland Gideon, an Early Boston Jew and His Family," *American Jewish Historical Quarterly*, Vol. 35, (1939), pp. 27–28.

19. Ibid., pp. 29–36.

20. St. John, Robert, *Jews, Justice and Judaism* (Garden City, N.Y.: Doubleday, 1969), pp. 12–14.

21. Schappes, Morris Y., *A Documentary History of the Jews* (New York: Schocken Books, 1971), p. 86.

22. Friedman, Lee M., *Early American Jews* (Cambridge, Mass.: Harvard University Press, 1934), pp. 5–6.

23. Friedman, Lee M., "Early Jewish Residents in Massachusetts," *American Jewish Historical Quarterly*, Vol. 24, (1916), pp. 73–81.

24. Blau, Joseph L., *The Jews of the United States* (New York: Columbia University Press, 1963), p. 18.

25. Marcus, J.R. *The Jew in the American World* (Detroit: Wayne State University Press, 1996), p. 37.

26. Friedman, Lee M., "Boston in American Jewish History," *American Jewish Historical Quarterly*, Vol. 43(4), (1933), p. 336.

27. Friedman, Lee M., *Early American Jews* (Cambridge, Mass.: Harvard University Press, 1934), pp. 9–38.

28. Lebowich, Joseph, "The Jews in Boston till 1875," *American Jewish Historical Quarterly*, Vol. 12 (1904), pp. 101–109.

29. de Sola Pool, D. Reverend, "Hebrew Learning among the Puritans of New England Prior to 1700," *American Jewish Historical Quarterly*, Vol. 19, (1910), pp. 45–58.

30. Friedman, Lee M., *Pilgrims in a New Land* (Philadelphia: Jewish Publication Society of America, 1948), p. 133.

31. Lebeson, Anita, *Pilgrim People* (New York: Minerva Press, 1971), pp. 13–15.

32. Baron, S.W., *Steeled by Adversity* (Philadelphia: Jewish Publication Society of America, 1971), p. 143.

33. Gutstein, Morris A., *The Story of the Jews of Newport* (New York: Bloch, 1936), p. 17.

34. Gutstein, Morris A., *History of the Jews in America* (New York: Bloch, 1936), p. 22.

35. Janowsky, Oscar I., ed., *The American Jew: A Composite Portrait* (New York and London: Harper Brothers, 1942), pp. 3–5.

36. Gutstein, Morris A., *The Story of the Jews of Newport* (New York: Bloch, 1936), p. 22.

37. Op. cit., "Roger Williams: Witness beyond Christendom," (1603–1683), p. 189.

38. Ibid., p. 214.

39. Ibid., "La Fantasie, Glenn W.: The Correspondence of Roger Williams," pp. 648–659.

40. Baron, S.W., *Steeled by Adversity* (Philadelphia: Jewish Publication Society of America, 1971), p. 86.

41. Ibid., p. 87.

42. Oppenheim, Samuel, "The First Settlement of Jews in Newport: Some New Matter on the Subject," *Publication of the American Jewish Historical Society*, Vol. 34 (1937), pp. 2–4, 42.

43. Faber, Eli, *A Time for Planting* (Baltimore: Johns Hopkins University Press, 1992), pp. 36–38.

44. Blau, Joseph L., *The Jews of the United States* (New York: Columbia University Press, 1963), pp. 65–68.

45. Ibid., pp. 71–73, 74, 76.

46. McLoughlin, William G., *Rhode Island* (New York: W.W. Norton, 1986), p. 75.

47. Daniels, Bruce C., *Dissent and Conformity on Narragansett Bay: The Colonial Rhode Island Town*, (Middleton, Conn.: Wesleyan University Press, 1983), p. 102.

48. Marcus, J.R., *The Jew in the American World* (Detroit: Wayne State University Press, 1996), p. 53.

49. Kohler, Max J., "The Jews in Newport," *American Jewish Historical Quarterly*, Vol. 5 (1897), pp. 38–39.

50. Ibid., pp. 70–74.

51. Ibid., p. 75.

52. Ibid., pp. 77–78.

53. Chyet, Stanley F., *Lopez of Newport: Colonial American Merchant Prince* (Detroit: Wayne State University Press, 1970), pp. 40–53.

54. Friedman, Lee M., *Pilgrims in a New Land* (Philadelphia: Jewish Publication Society of America, 1948), pp. 177–81.

55. Gay, Ruth, *Jews in America* (New York: Basic Books, 1965), p. 17.

56. Op, cit., pp. 193–94.

57. Kohler, Max J., "Judah Touro: Merchant and Philanthropist," *American Jewish Historical Quarterly*, Vol. 13 (1905), pp. 94–103.

58. Eisenbeg, A., and Goodman, H.G., eds., *Eyewitness to American Jewish History* (New York: Union of American Hebrew Congregations, 1976), p. 86.

59. Marcus, J.R., *Early American Jewry* (Philadelphia: Jewish Publication Society of America, 1951–1955), pp. 63–70.

60. Schappes, Morris Y., *A Documentary History of the Jews* (New York: Schocken Books, 1971), p. 100.

61. Marcus, J.R., *The Jew in the American World* (Detroit: Wayne State University Press, 1996), pp. 95, 109.

62. Baron, S.W., *Steeled by Adversity* (Philadelphia: Jewish Publication Society of America, 1971), p. 150.

63. Reznick, Samuel, *Unrecognized Patriots* (Westport, Conn.: Greenwood Press, 1975), p. 65.

64. Wiernik, Peter, *History of the Jews in America* (New York: Harmon Press, 1972), p. 74.

65. Faber, Eli, *A Time for Planting* (Baltimore: Johns Hopkins University Press, 1992), p. 45.

66. Blau, Joseph L., *The Jews of the United States* (New York: Columbia University Press, 1963), pp. 8–9.

67. Marcus, J.R., *The Jews in the American World* (Detroit: Wayne State University Press, Jewish Publication Society of America, 1996), pp. 91–92.

68. Willner, W., "Ezra Stiles and the Jews," *American Jewish Historical Quarterly*, Vol. 5 (1897), pp. 120–125.

69. Chiel, Arthur A., "Ezra Stiles: The Education of an 'Hebrician,'" *American Jewish Historical Society*, Vol. 60 (1970–1971), pp. 235–236.

70. Chiel, Arthur A., "The Rabbis and Ezra Stiles," *American Jewish Historical Quarterly*, Vol. 61 (1972), pp. 295–308.

71. Lewis, T.R., and Harmond, J.E., *Connecticut: A Geography* (Boulder: Westview Press, 1986), p. 61.

72. Dalen, D.G., and Rosenbaum, J., *Making a Life, Building a Community: A History of the Jews of Hartford* (New York and London: Holmes and Meier, 1997), p. 9.

73. Marcus, J.R., *Early American Jewry* (Philadelphia: Jewish Publication Society of America, 1951–1955), pp. 160–162.

74. Op. cit., pp. 7, 8.

75. Ibid., pp. 9, 10.

76. Huhner, Leon, "The Jews of New England (Other than Rhode Island) Prior to 1800," *American Jewish Historical Quarterly*, Vol. 11 (1903), pp. 83–87.

77. Marcus, J.R., *American Jewry: Documents—Eighteenth Century* (Cincinnati: Hebrew Union College Press, 1959), p. 1.

78. Marcus, J.R., "Light on Early Connecticut Jewry," *Critical Studies in American Jewish History from American Jewish Archives* (New York: KTAV Publishers, 1971), pp. 84–90.

79. Huhner, Leon, "The Jews of New England (Other than Rhode Island) Prior to 1800," *American Jewish Historical Quarterly*, Vol. 11 (1903), pp. 87–89.

80. Op. cit., p. 94.

81. Marcus, J.R., *Early American Jewry* (Philadelphia: Jewish Publication Society of America, 1951–1955), pp. 174–187.

82. Huhner, Leon, "The Jews of New England (Other than Rhode Island) Prior to 1800," *American Jewish Historical Quarterly*, Vol. 11 (1903), pp. 90–98.

83. Karp, A.J., "Jewish Experience in America," *Publication of the American Jewish Historical Society*, (Waltham, Mass.: 1969), p. 74.

84. Marchs, J.R., *Studies in Early American Jewish History* (Cincinnati: Hebrew Union College Press, 1969), pp. 54–57.

85. Marcus, J.R., "Light on Early Connecticut Jewry," *Critical Studies in American Jewish History from American Jewish Archives* (New York: KTAV, 1971), pp. 74–79.

86. Dalen, D.G., and Rosenbaum, J., *Making a Life, Building a Community: A History of the Jews of Hartford* (New York and London: Holmes and Meier, 1997), p. 10.

87. Marcus, J.R., *Early American Jewry* (Philadelphia: Jewish Publication Society of America, 1951–1955), pp. 191–210.

88. Ibid., pp. 220–222.

89. Joseph, Andrew C., "The Settlement of Jews in Canada," *American Jewish Historical Quarterly*, Vol. 1 (1892), pp. 117–119.

90. Marcus, J.R., *The Jew in the American World* (Detroit: Wayne State University Press, 1996), p. 189.

91. Rosenberg, Louis, "Some Aspects of the Historical Development of the Canadian Jewish Community," *American Jewish Historical Quarterly*, Vol. 50, (1960–1961), pp. 126, 130, 131.

Chapter 3

1. Hollander, J.H., "The Civil Status of the Jews in Maryland 1634–1776," *American Jewish Historical Quarterly*, Vol. 2, 1894, pp. 33–36.

2. Eitches, Edward, "Maryland's 'Jew Bill,'" *American Jewish Historical Quarterly*, Vol. 60, 1970-1971, pp. 258–261.

3. Lebeson, Anita, *Pilgrim People* (New York: Minerva Press, 1975), p. 33.

4. Hollander, J.H. "Some Unpublished Material Relating to Dr. Jacob Lumbrozo," *American Jewish Historical Quarterly*, Vol. 1, 1892, pp. 25–34.

5. Marcus, J. *The Jew in the American World* (Detroit: Wayne State University Press, 1996), pp. 40–42.

6. Harbogensis, B.H., "Unequal Religious Rights in Maryland Since 1776," *American Jewish Historical Quarterly*, Vol. 25, 1917, p. 93.

7. Eitches, Edward, "Maryland 'Jew Bill,'" *American Jewish Historical Quarterly*, Vol. 60, 1970-1971, pp. 261–265.

8. Rosenwaike, Ira, "The Jews of Baltimore to 1810," *American Jewish Historical Quarterly*, 64(4), 1975, pp. 301–308.

9. Harbogensis, B.H., "Unequal Religious Rights in Maryland Since 1776," *American Jewish Historical Quarterly*, Vol. 25, 1917, pp. 94–99.

10. Ibid., pp. 100–102.

11. Rosenwaike Ira, "The Jews of Baltimore to 1810," *American Jewish Historical Quarterly*, 64(4), 1975, pp. 204–224.

12. Eitches, Edward, "Maryland 'Jew Bill,'" *American Jewish Historical Quarterly*, Vol. 60, 1970-1971, p. 266.

13. Rosenwaike, Ira, "Simon M. Levy, West Point Graduate," *American Jewish Historical Quarterly*, Vol. 61, 1971-1972, pp. 69–72.

14. Rosenwaike, Ira, "The Jews of Baltimore to 1810," *American Jewish Historical Quarterly*, 64(4), 1975, pp. 313–320.

15. Kuhner, Leon, "The Jews of Virginia from the Earliest Time to the Close of the Eighteenth Century," *American Jewish Publications Quarterly*, Vol. 19, 1910, pp. 85–88.

16. Marcus, J.R. *The Colonial American Jew* (Detroit: Wayne State University Press, 1970), pp. 226.

17. Adler, Cyrus, "Jews in the American Plantations," *American Jewish Historical Quarterly*, Vol. 1, 1892, p. 22.

18. "Notes and Queries," *Virginia Magazine of History and Biography*, Vol. 1, 1893-1894, p. 467.

19. Marcus, J.R. *Early American Jewry* (Philadelphia: Jewish Publication Society of America, 1991–1995), p. 216.

20. Marcus, J.R., *Early American Jewry* (Philadelphia: Jewish Publication Society of America, 1951–1955, p. xi.

21. Ibid., pp. 165–173.

22. Marcus, J.R. *Early American Jewry* (Philadelphia: Jewish Publication Society of America, 1951–1955), pp. 214, 217.

23. Faber, Eli, *A Time for Planting* (Baltimore: Johns Hopkins University Press, 1992), p. 231.

24. Marcus, J.R., *American Jewry Documents: Eighteenth Century* (Cincinnati: Hebrew Union College Press, 1959, p. 144.

25. Blau, J.L., *The Jews of the United States* (New York: Columbia University Press, 1963), p. 81.

26. Marcus, J.R., *Early American Jewry* (Philadelphia: Jewish Publication Society of America, 1991–1995), pp. 177, 180, 186.

27. Kohler, Max J., "Phases in the History of Religious Liberty in America with Special Reference to the Jews," *American Jewish Historical Quarterly*, Vol. 11, 1903, pp. 60–62.

28. Fuchs, Lawrence H., *The Political Behavior of American Jews* (Glencoe, Ill.: Free Press, 1956), p. 244.

29. Marcus, J.R., *Early American Jewry* (Philadelphia: Jewish Publication Society of America, 1991–1995), p. 239.

30. Kuhner, Leon, "The Jews of Virginia from the Earliest Time to the Close of the Eighteenth Century," *American Jewish Publications Quarterly*, Vol. 19, 1910, pp. 100–104.

31. Gay, Ruth, *Jews in America* (New York: Basic Books, 1965), pp. 30, 31.

32. Ezekiel, Jacob, "The Jews of Richmond," *American Jewish Historical Publication*, Vol. 4, 1896, pp. 22–24.

33. Huhner, Leon, "The Jews of North Carolina Prior to 1800," *American Jewish Historical Quarterly*, Vol. 29, 1925, pp. 39–42.

34. Ibid., pp. 138–141.
35. Lefler, H.T., and Powell, W.S., *Colonial North Carolina: A History* (New York: Charles Scribner's Sons, 1973), p. 192.
36. Op. cit., pp. 146, 147.
37. Goodman, A.V., "South Carolina from Shaffesbury to Salvador," *Publication of the American Jewish Historical Society*, Vol. 29, 1931, p. 32.
38. Jones, H.G., *North Carolina Illustrated* (Chapel Hill: University of North Carolina Press, 1983), p. 126.
39. *American Jewish Historical Society*, Vol. 22, 1914, p. 183.
40. Marcus, J.R., *Early American Jewry* (Philadelphia: Jewish Publication Society of America, 1951–1955), p. 190.
41. Ibid., p. 202.
42. Dinnerstein, Leonard, *Jews in the South* (Baton Rouge: Louisiana University Press, 1973), p. 26.
43. Huhner, Leon, "The Struggle for Religious Liberty in North Carolina with Special Reference to the Jews," *American Jewish Historical Quarterly*, Vol. 16, 1907, pp. 38–52.
44. Fuchs, Lawrence H., *The Political Behavior of American Jews* (Glencoe, Ill.: Free Press, 1956), p. 183.
45. Huhner, Leon, "The Jews of South Carolina from the Earliest Settlement to the End of the American Revolution," *American Jewish Historical Quarterly*, Vol. 12, 1904, pp. 39, 40.
46. Ibid., p. 41.
47. Marcus, J., *The Jew in the American World* (Detroit: Wayne State University Press, 1996), p. 36.
48. Andrews, C. McLean, *Colonial Period of American History* (New Haven: Yale University Press, 1934), p. 51.
49. Marcus, J., *The Jew in the American World* (Detroit: Wayne State University Press, 1996), pp. 95–109.
50. Op. cit., p. 30.
51. Wright, Louis B., *South Carolina: A Bicentennial History* (New York: W.W. Norton, 1976).
52. Goodman, A.V., "South Carolina from Shaffesbury to Salvador," *Publication of the American Jewish Historical Society*, Vol. 29, 1931, p. 34.
53. Lebeson, Anita, *Pilgrim People* (New York: Minerva Press, 1975), pp. 84–86.
54. "South Carolina Commons—Assembly Journal, 1683, 1697," *Statutes of South Carolina II*:131, p. 34.
55. Weyl, Nathanael, *The Jew in America: Politics* (New Rochelle: Arlington House, 1968), p. 216.
56. Marcus, J.R., *The Colonial American Jew* (Detroit: Wayne State University Press,, 1970), p. 287.
57. Gutstein, M.A., *History of the Jews in America* (New York: Bloch, 1936), p. 32.
58. Friedman, Lee M., *Pilgrims in a New Land* (Philadelphia: Jewish Publication Society of America, 1948), pp. 151–155.
59. Huhner, Leon, "The Jews of South Carolina from the Earliest Settlement to the End of the American Revolution," *American Jewish Historical Quarterly*, Vol. 12, 1904, pp. 43, 44.
60. Faber, Eli, *A Time for Planting* (Baltimore: Johns Hopkins University Press, 1992), p. 111.
61. Engleman, U.Z., "Jewish Education in Charleston, South Carolina, During the Eighteenth and Nineteenth Centuries," *American Jewish Historical Quarterly*, Vol. 42, 1952-1953, p. 45.
62. Eisenberg, H., and Goodman, G.H., *Eyewitness to American Jewish History*, p. 3.
63. Edgar, Walter, *South Carolina: A History* (Columbia: University of South Carolina Press, 1998), pp. 43–62.
64. Huhner, Leon, "Francis Salvador," *American Jewish Publication Quarterly*, Vol. 9, 1901, pp. 108–114.
65. Blau, J.L., *The Jews of the United States* (New York: Columbia Press, 1963), p. 49.
66. Marcus, J.R., *Early American Jewry* (Philadelphia: Jewish Publication Society of America, 1951–1955), p. 242.
67. Selber, Mendel, "Americans in Hebrew Literature," *American Jewish Historical Quarterly*, Vol. 22, 1914, pp. 129–130.
68. Ibid., p. 136.
69. Coulter, E.M., *Georgia: A Short History* (Chapel Hill: University of North Carolina Press, 1933, 1947, 1960), p. 21.
70. Stern, M.H., "New Light on the Jewish Settlement of Savannah," *American Jewish Historical Quarterly*, Vol. 52, 1962-1963, pp. 72–74.
71. Karp, A.J., *Jewish Experience in America* (Waltham, Mass.: American Jewish Historical Society, 1969), pp. 221–224.
72. Coulter, E.M., *Georgia: A Short History* (Chapel Hill: University of North Carolina Press, 1933, 1947, 1960), p. 31.
73. Op. cit., pp. 242–243.
74. Feldstein, *The Land That I Show You* (New York: Anchor Press, 1978), p. 227.
75. Blau, J.L., *The Jews of the United States* (New York: Columbia University Press, 1963), pp. 35–36.
76. Ibid., pp. 47.
77. Coleman, Kenneth, *Colonial Georgia: A History* (New York: Charles Scribner's Sons, 1975), pp. 33, 34, 158.

78. Martin, Harold H., *Georgia: A Bicentennial History* (New York: W.W. Norton, 1977), p. 17.

79. Stern, M.H., "New Light on the Jewish Settlement of Savannah," *American Jewish Historical Quarterly*, Vol. 52, 1962-1963, p. 75.

80. Ibid., pp. 187–188.

81. Morgan, D.T., "The Sheftalls of Savannah," *American Jewish Historical Society*, Vol. 62, 1972-1973, pp. 349–353.

82. Gay, Ruth, *Jews in America* (New York: Basic Books, 1965), pp. 26–27.

83. Huhner, Leon, "The Jews of Georgia in Colonial Times," *American Jewish Historical Quarterly*, Vol. 10, 1902, pp. 71, 73, 76.

84. Stern, M.H., "New Light on the Jewish Settlement of Savannah," *American Jewish Historical Quarterly*, Vol. 52, 1962-1963, pp. 83–87.

85. Jones, Charles C., "The Settlement of the Jews in Georgia," *American Jewish Historical Quarterly*, Vol. 1, 1892, pp. 9–12.

86. Op. cit., pp. 80–82.

87. Ibid., pp. 192–193.

88. Harden, William, *A History of Savannah and South Georgia* (Atlanta: Cherokee, 1969), p. 48.

89. Marcus, J.R., *Early American Jewry* (Philadelphia: Jewish Publication Society of America, 1951–1955), p. xiii.

90. Sachar, H.M., *History of the Jews in America* (New York: Knopf, 1992), pp. 19–21.

91. Huhner, Leon, "The Jews of Georgia in Colonial Times," *American Jewish Historical Quarterly*, Vol. 10, 1902, pp. 92–94.

92. Marcus, J.R., *Early American Jewry* (Philadelphia: Jewish Publication Society of America, 1951–1955), p. 246.

93. Faber, Eli, *The Jewish People in America* (Baltimore: Johns Hopkins University Press, 1992), p. 234.

94. Morgan, D.T., "The Sheftalls of Savannah," *American Jewish Historical Society*, Vol. 62, 1972-1973, pp. 353–360.

95. Marcus, J.R., *Early American Jewry* (Philadelphia: Jewish Publication Society of America, 1951-1955), pp. 279–283.

96. Baron, S.W., *Steeled by Adversity* (Philadelphia: Jewish Publication Society of America, 1971), p. 99.

97. Op. cit., p. 297.

98. Huhner, Leon, "The Jews of Georgia in Colonial Times," *American Jewish Historical Quarterly*, Vol. 10, 1902, p. 95.

99. Faber, Eli, *A Time for Planting* (Baltimore: Johns Hopkins University Press, 1992), p. 253.

100. Morgan, D.T., "The Sheftalls of Savannah," *American Jewish Historical Society*, Vol. 62, 1972-1973, p. 361.

Chapter 4

1. Kohler, Max J., "The Jews and the American Anti-Slavery Movement," *American Jewish Historical Quarterly*, Vol. 4, 1896, p. 140.

2. Birmingham, S., *The Grandees* (New York: Harper and Row, 1971), pp. 101, 108, 110.

3. Hollander, J.H., "Documents Relating to the Attempted Departure of the Jews from Surinam," *American Jewish Historical Quarterly*, Vol. 5, 1897, pp. 9, 10, 17.

4. Chyet, S.F., *Lopez of Newport—Colonial American Merchant Prince* (Detroit: Wayne State University Press, 1970), pp. 66–71.

5. Birmingham, S., *The Grandees* (New York, Harper and Row, 1971), p. 116.

6. Marcus, J.R., *American Jewry Documents: Eighteenth Century* (Cincinnati: Hebrew Union College Press, 1959), pp. 446, 448.

7. Feingold, H.L., *A Midrash on American Jewish History* (Albany: University of New York Press, 1982), p. 15.

8. Marcus, J.R., *American Jewry Documents: Eighteenth Century* (Cincinnati: Hebrew Union College Press, 1959), p. 416.

9. "Massachusetts Historical Society Collections," *Commerce of Rhode Island*, Vol. 69, 1:96–97, p. 55.

10. Kohler, Max J., "Phases of Jewish Life in New York Before 1800," *American Jewish Historical Quarterly*, Vol. 2, 1894, p. 84.

11. Marcus, J.B., *Early American Jewry* (Philadelphia: Jewish Publication Society of America, 1951–1955), pp. 65, 65.

12. Blau, Joseph L., *The Jews of the United States* (New York: Columbia University Press, 1963), p. 104.

13. Marcus, J.R., *American Jewry Documents: Eighteenth Century* (Cincinnati: Hebrew Union College Press, 1959), p. 456.

14. Korn, B.W., "Jews and Negro Slavery in the Old South 1789-1865," *American Jewish Historical Quarterly*, Vol. 50, 1961, pp. 91–100.

15. Marcus, J.R., *American Jewry Documents: Eighteenth Century* (Cincinnati: Hebrew Union College Press, 1959), p. 80.

16. Korn, B.W., "Jews and Negro Slavery in the Old south 1789–1865," *American Jewish Historical Quarterly*, Vol. 50, 1961, pp. 152–157.

17. Ibid., pp. 101–117.

18. "New York Slave Insurrection 1741," *American Jewish Historical Quarterly*, Vol. 27, 1920, p. 384.

19. Wolf, E., II, and Whiteman, Maxwell, *A History of the Jews of Philadelphia* (Philadelphia: Jewish Publication Society of America, 1957), pp. 190–192.

20. Korn, B.W., "Jews and Negro Slavery in the Old South 1789-1865," *American Jewish Historical Quarterly*, Vol. 50, 1961, pp. 158-163.

21. Blau, Joseph L., *The Jews of the United States* (New York: Columbia University Press, 1963), p. 207.

22. Op. cit., pp. 164, 165.

23. Ibid., pp. 172, 173, 177, 180, 191.

24. Korn, B.W., "Jews and Negro Slavery in the Old South 1789-1865," *American Jewish Historical Quarterly*, Vol. 50, 1961, p. 116.

25. "Pennsylvania Journal January 4, 1786," *American Jewish Historical Quarterly*, Vol. 5, 1897, p. 22.

26. Marcus, J.R., *American Jewry Documents: Eighteenth Century* (Cincinnati: Hebrew Union College Press, 1959), pp. 158-159, 360.

27. Marcus, J.R., *American Jewry Documents: Eighteenth Century* (Cincinnati: Hebrew Union College Press, 1959), p. 419.

Chapter 5

1. Netanyahu, B., *The Origin of the Inquisition in Fifteenth-Century Spain* (New York: Random House, 1995), p. 106.

2. Johnson, Paul, *A History of the Jews* (New York: Harper and Row, 1987), pp. 134-136.

3. Sobel, B. Zui, "Jews and Christian Evangelization: The Anglo-American Approach," *American Jewish Historical Quarterly*, Vol. 58, 1968-1969), pp. 241-246.

4. Blau, Joseph L., *The Jews of the United States* (New York: Columbia University Press, 1963), pp. 9-11.

5. Johnson, Paul, *A History of the Jews* (New York: Harper and Row, 1987), pp. 259-273.

6. Marcus, J.R., *The American Jew 1585-1990: A History* (Brooklyn: Carlson, 1995), pp. 23-26.

7. Seeligman, Sigmund, "David Nassy of Surinam," *American Jewish Historical Quarterly*, Vol. 22, 1914, pp. 33-35.

8. "Notes: A Remarkable Verdict at Amsterdam 1/19/1690," *American Jewish Historical Quarterly*, Vol. 34, 1937.

9. Kohler, Max J., "The Doctrine That 'Christianity Is a Part of Common Law' and Its Recent Judicial Overthrow in England," *American Jewish Historical Quarterly*, Vol. 13, 1905, p. 110.

10. Kohler, Max J., "Phases in the History of Religions. Liberty in America with Particular Reference to the Jews," *American Jew-*

ish Historical Quarterly, Vol. 13, 1905, pp. 8-10.

11. Jews Voted in Election in Westchester," *American Jewish Historical Quarterly*, Vol. 66, 1976-1977, pp. 13-15.

12. Judah, George F., "The Jews' Future in Jamaica," *American Jewish Historical Society*, Vol. 18, 1909, pp. 149-157.

13. Friedenwald, Herbert, "Material for the History of Jews in the British West Indies," *American Jewish Historical Society*, Vol. 5, 1896, p. 55.

14. Ibid., pp. 57-60.

15. Oppenheim, Samuel, "The Early History of the Jews of New York 1654-1664," *American Jewish Historical Quarterly*, Vol. 18, 1909, pp. 3-6.

16. Kohler, Max J., "Beginnings of New York Jewish History," *American Jewish Historical Quarterly*, Vol. 1, 1892, pp. 46-48.

17. Op. cit., pp. 17-19.

18. Fishman, Priscilla, *The Jews of the United States* (New York: Quadrangle, 1973), pp. 5-6.

19. Schappes, Morris V., *A Documentary History of the Jews in the United States* (New York: Schocken Books, 1971), p. 27.

20. Friedman, Lee M., *Early American Jews* (Cambridge, Mass.: Harvard University Press, 1934), pp. 49-52.

21. Baron, S.W., *Steeled by Adversity* (Philadelphia: Jewish Publication Society of America, 1971), p. 29.

22. Marcus, J.R., *The Jew in the American World* (Detroit: Wayne State University Press, 1996), p. 32.

23. Friedman, Lee M., *Early American Jews* (Cambridge: Mass.: Harvard University Press, 1934), pp. 3-5.

24. Ibid., pp. 9-10.

25. Marcus, J.R., *American Jewry Documents: Eighteenth Century* (Cincinnati: Hebrew Union College Press, 1959), pp. 30-37.

26. Ibid., pp. 53-54.

27. Harden, William, *A History of Savannah and South Georgia* (Atlanta: Cherokee, 1969), pp. 44-46.

28. Friedman, Lee M., "Cotton Mather and the Jews," *American Jewish Historical Quarterly*, Vol. 26, 1918, pp. 201-205.

29. Schappes, Morris V., *A Documentary History of the Jews* (New York: Schocken books, 1971), p. 110.

30. Marcus, J.R., *American Jewry Documents: Eighteenth Century* (Cincinnati: Hebrew Union College Press, 1959), p. 17.

31. Fishman, Priscilla, *The Jews of the United States* (New York: Quadrangle, 1973), pp. 13-14.

32. Harap, Louis, "Image of the Jew in American Drama 1794–1823," *American Jewish Historical Quarterly*, Vol. 60, 1970-1971, pp. 242–243.

33. Marcus, J.R., *American Jewry Documents: Eighteenth Century* (Cincinnati: Hebrew Union College Press, 1959), pp. 374–375.

34. Schappes, Morris V., *A Documentary History of the Jews* (New York: Schocken Books, 1971), p. 100.

35. Marcus, J.R., *The American Jew: A History* (Brooklyn: Carlson, 1995), p. 34.

36. Birmingham, Stephen, *The Grandees* (New York: Harper and Row, 1971), pp. 238–240.

37. Blau, Joseph L., *The Jews of the United States* (New York: Columbia University Press, 1963), p. xix.

38. Marcus, J.R., *American Jewry Documents: Eighteenth Century* (Cincinnati: Hebrew Union College Press, 1959), p. 295.

39. Samuel, John, "Some Cases in Pennsylvania Wherein Rights Claimed by Jews Are Affected," *American Jewish Historical Quarterly*, Vol. 5, 1896, pp. 35–37.

40. Feldstein, *The Land That I Show You* (New York: Anchor Press, 1978), p. ii.

41. Cohen, Naomi W., *Jews in Christian America* (New York: Oxford University Press, 1992), pp. 18, 19.

42. Welsh, R., and Fox. W.L., eds. *Maryland: A History 1632–1974* (Baltimore: Maryland Historical Society, 1974), pp. 102–103, 257–259.

43. Fein, Isaac M., *The Making of an American Jewish Community* (Philadelphia: Jewish Publication Society of America, 1971), pp. 48–50.

44. Bordon, M., *Jews, Turks and Infidels* (Chapel Hill and London: University of North Carolina Press, 1984), p. 14.

45. Op. cit., pp. 31–42.

46. Fuchs, M.H., *The Political Behavior of American Jews* (Glencoe, Ill.: Free Press, 1956), p. 28.

47. Bordon, M., *Jews, Turks and Infidels* (Chapel Hill and London: University of North Carolina Press, p. 12.

48. Ibid.

49. Ibid., p. 13.

50. Marcus, J.R., *The Jew in the American World* (Detroit: Wayne State University Press, 1996), pp. 127–130.

51. Ibid., pp. 212–214.

52. Baron, S.W., *Steeled by Adversity* (Philadelphia: Jewish Publication Society of America, 1971), pp. 92, 93.

53. Faber, Eli, *A Time for Planting* (Baltimore: Johns Hopkins University Press, 1992), p. 101.

54. Bordon, M., *Jews, Turks and Infidels* (Chapel Hill and London: University of North Carolina Press, 1992), p. 11.

55. Ibid.

56. Marcus, J.R., *The Jew in the American World* (Detroit: Wayne State University Press, 1996), p. 218.

57. Cohen, Naomi W., *Jews in Christian America* (New York: Oxford University Press, 1992), pp. 27–29.

58. Op. cit., p. 224.

59. Bordon, M., *Jews, Turks and Infidels* (Chapel Hill and London: University of North Carolina Press, 1984), pp. 187–190.

60. Kohler, Max J., "Phases in the History of Religious Liberty in America with Special Reference to the Jews," *American Jewish Historical Quarterly*, Vol. 11, 1903, pp. 54–64.

61. Cohen, Naomi W., *Jews in Christian America* (New York: Oxford University Press, 1992), pp. 25–26.

62. Sachar, H.M., *History of the Jews in America* (New York: Knopf, 1992), p. 38.

63. Berman, Myron, *Richmond's Jewry* (Charlottesville: University Press of Virginia, 1979), pp. 32, 33.

64. Fishman, Priscilla, *The Jews in the United States* (New York: Quadrangle Press, 1973), pp. vi, viii, x.

65. Cohen, Naomi W., *Jew in a Christian World* (New York: Oxford University Press, 1992), p. 20.

66. Ibid., p. 3.

67. Janowsky, Oscar I., *The American Jew: A Composite Portrait* (New York: Harper and Row, 1942), p. 12.

68. Bordon, M., *Jews, Turks and Infidels* (Chapel Hill and London: University of North Carolina Press, 1984), pp. 14–21.

69. Schappes, Morris V., *A Documentary History of the Jews* (New York: Schocken Books, 1971), pp. 102–105.

70. Marcus, J.R., *The Jew in the American World* (Detroit: Wayne State University Press, 1996), p. 133.

71. Bordon, M., *Jews, Turks and Infidels* (Chapel Hill and London: University of North Carolina Press, 1984), pp. 5–11.

72. Ibid., pp. 38–50.

73. Faber, Eli, *A Time for Planting* (Baltimore: Johns Hopkins University Press, 1992), p. 100.

74. Ibid., p. 101.

75. Bordon, M., *Jews, Turks and Infidels* (Chapel Hill and London: University of North Carolina Press, 1984), pp. 84–87.

76. Sterm, M.H., "New Light on the Jewish Settlement of Savannah," *American Jewish Historical Quarterly*, Vol. 52, 1962-1963, pp. 78–79.

77. Ibid., p. 82.
78. Faber, Eli, *A Time for Planting* (Baltimore: Johns Hopkins University Press, 1992), p. 140.
79. Schappes, Morris V., "Anti-Semitism and Reaction 1795–1800," *American Jewish Historical Quarterly*, Vol. 38, 1948-1949, p. 114.
80. Ibid., pp. 131-136.
81. Kohler, Max J., "Beginnings of New York Jewish History," *American Jewish Historical Quarterly*, Vol. 1, 1892, p.87.
82. Marcus, J.R., *Early American Jewry* (Philadelphia: Jewish Publication Society of America, 1951–1955), p. 174.
83. Faber, Eli, *A Time for Planting* (Baltimore: Johns Hopkins University Press, 1992), pp. 96–99.
84. Hertzberg, A., *The Jews in America* (New York: Simon and Schuster, 1989), p. 75.
85. Scharf, J.T., and Westcott, T., *History of Philadelphia, 1609–1884* (Philadelphia: L.H. Everts, 1884), p. 642.
86. Marcus, J.R. *Early American Jewry* (Philadelphia: Jewish Publication Society of America, 1951–1955), p. 128.
87. Lemmon, S.M., ed., *The Pettigrew Papers Vol. 1, 1685–1818* (Raleigh: State Department of Archives and History, 1971), p. 399.
88. Smith, J.M., "The Aurora and the Alien and Sedition Laws Parts 1 and 2," *The Pennsylvania Magazine of History and Biography*, Vol. 77, 1953, pp. 3–23, 123–55.
89. Faber, Eli, *A Time for Planting* (Baltimore: Johns Hopkins University Press, 1992), pp. 134–137.
90. "Notes: Disgraceful Acts of a Mob at a Jewish Funeral in New York 1743," *American Jewish Historical Society*, 31(90) (1928), p. 240.
91. Huhner, Leon, *The Jews of New England (Other Than Rhode Island) Prior to 1800* (Philadelphia: Jewish Publication Society of America, 1946), footnote, p. 84.
92. Dexter, F.B., ed., *The Literary Diary of Ezra Stiles* (New York: C. Scribner's Sons, 1901), p. 13.
93. Marcus, J.R., *American Jewry Documents: Eighteen Century* (Cincinnati: Hebrew College Press, 1959), p. 136.
94. Dabney, Virginius, *Virginia: The New Dominion* (Garden City, N.Y.: Doubleday, 1971), p. 179.
95. Fuchs, M.H., *The Political Behavior of American Jews* (Glencoe, Ill.: Free Press, 1956), p. 25.
96. Healey, R.M., "Jefferson on Judaism and the Jews—Divided We Stand, United We Fall," *American Jewish Historical Quarterly*, Vol. 73, 1983-1984, pp. 360–364.

97. Kohler, Max J., "Unpublished Correspondence Between Thomas Jefferson and Some American Jews," *American Jewish Historical Quarterly*, Vol. 19, 1910, pp. 21, 24.
98. Ibid., pp. 12, 14, 17.
99. "Notes: Jefferson Looks for Attorney-General," *American Jewish Historical Quarterly*. 19(161) (1910), p. 161.
100. Blau, Joseph L., *The Jews of the United States* (New York: Columbia University Press, 1963), pp. 82, 87, 88, 90.
101. Faber, Eli, *A Time for Planting* (Baltimore: Johns Hopkins University Press, 1992), p. 84.

Chapter 6

1. Marcus, J.R., *Early American Jewry* (Philadelphia: Jewish Publication Society of America, 1951–1955), pp. 45–48.
2. Marcus, J.R., *American Jewry Documents: Eighteenth Century* (Cincinnati: Hebrew Union College Press, 1959), p. 311.
3. Marcus, J.R., *The Colonial American Jew* (Detroit: Wayne State University Press, 1940), Vol. II, pp. 17–22.
4. Ibid., pp. 34–35.
5. Marcus, J.R., *Early American Jewry* (Philadelphia: Jewish Publication Society of America, 1951–1955), p. 314.
6. Marcus, J.R., *American Jewry Documents: Eighteenth Century* (Cincinnati: Hebrew Union College Press, 1959), pp. 323–325.
7. Ibid., p. 332.
8. Marcus, J.R., *Early American Jewry* (Philadelphia: Jewish Publication Society of America, 1951–1955), p. 324.
9. Marcus, J.R., *American Jewry Documents: Eighteenth Century* (Cincinnati: Hebrew Union College Press, 1959), p. 344.
10. Ibid., p. 48.
11. Ibid., p. 215.
12. Feingold, Henry, *A Midrash on American Jewish History* (Albany: State University of New York Press, 1982), pp. 17, 23, 24.
13. Lebeson, Anita, *Pilgrim People* (New York: Minerva Press, 1975), p. 189.
14. Karp, A.J., *Jewish Experience in America* (Waltham, Mass.: American Jewish Historical Society, 1969), pp. 31–34.
15. Heineman, D.E., "The Startling Experience of a Jewish Trader During Pontiac's Siege of Detroit in 1763," *American Jewish Historical Quarterly*, Vol. 24, 1916, pp. 28–32.
16. Dublin, F., "Jewish Colonial Enterprise in Light of the Amherst Papers," *American Jewish Historical Quarterly*, Vol. 25, 1939, pp. 16–19.

17. Ibid., pp. 6–8.
18. Eisenberg, A., and Goodman, H.G., eds., *Eyewitness to American Jewish History* (New York: Union of American Hebrew Congregations, 1976), pp. 46–48.
19. Marcus, J.R., *American Jewry Documents: Eighteenth Century* (Cincinnati: Hebrew Union College Press, 1959), pp. 88–91.
20. Sachar, H.M., *History of the Jews in America* (New York: Knopf, 1992), p. 222.
21. Fuch, L.H., *The Political Behavior of American Jews* (Glencoe, Ill.: Free Press, 1956), p. 24.
22. Reznick, Samuel, *Unrecognized Patriots* (Westport, Conn. and London: Greenwood Press, 1975), p. 1.
23. Cohen, N.W., *Jews in Christian America* (New York: Oxford University Press, 1992), p. 22.
24. Sarna, Jonathan D., ed., *American Jewish Experience* (New York: Holmes and Maier, 1986), pp. 214–216.
25. Wiernik, Peter, *History of the Jews in America* (New York: Harmon Press, 1972), pp. 280–287.
26. Reznick, Samuel, *Unrecognized Patriots* (Westport, Conn. and London, Greenwood Press, 1975), p. 248.
27. No author, "Documents Relating to the Career of Colonel Isaac Franks," *American Jewish Publication Quarterly*, Vol. 5, 1896, pp. 32–33.
28. Op. cit., p. 7.
29. Huhner, Leon, "Some Additional Notes on the History of the Jews of South Carolina," *American Jewish Historical Quarterly*, Vol. 19, 1910, pp. 151–152.
30. Pessin, Deborah, *History of the Jews in America* (New York: United Synagogue Commission, 1957), p. 17.
31. Reznick, Samuel, *Unrecognized Patriots* (Westport, Conn. and London: Greenwood Press, 1975), p. 4.
32. Op. cit., pp. 49–50.
33. Blau, J.L., *The Jews of the United States* (New York: Columbia University Press, 1963), 70–72.
34. Reznick, Samuel, *Unrecognized Patriots* (Westport, Conn. and London: Greenwood Press, 1975), p. 36.
35. Huhner, Leon, "The Jews of South Carolina from the Earliest Settlement to the End of the American Revolution," *American Jewish Historical Quarterly*, Vol. 12, 1904, pp. 49–52.
36. Marcus, J.R., *Early American Jewry* (Philadelphia: Jewish Publication Society of America, 1951–1955), pp. 282–284.
37. Sheftall, Mordecai, *American Jewish Historical Quarterly*, Vol. 67 (1977-1978), pp. 77–78.

38. Marcus, J.R., *The American Jew* (Brooklyn: Carlson, 1995), pp. 294–298.
39. Sheftall, Mordecai, *The Jewish Encyclopedia* (New York and London: Funk & Wagnalls Co., 1905), p. 643.
40. Abrahams, E.H., "Some Notes on the Early History of the Sheftalls of Georgia," *American Jewish Historical Quarterly*, Vol. 17, 1908, pp. 176–179.
41. Op. cit., p. 648.
42. Huhner, Leon, "The First Jew to Hold Office of Governor of One of the United States," *American Jewish Historical Quarterly*, Vol. 17, 1808, pp. 188–193.
43. Huhner, Leon, "The Jews of South Carolina from the Earliest Settlement to the End of the American Revolution," *American Jewish Historical Quarterly*, Vol. 12, 1904, pp. 54–55.
44. Marcus, J.R., *The Colonial American Jew* (Detroit: Wayne State University Press, 1970), Vol. III, p. 88.
45. *American Jewish Historical Quarterly*, Vol. 27, 1920, pp. 184–185.
46. Hertzberg, A., *The Jews in America* (New York: Simon and Schuster, 1989), pp. 62–65.
47. Kohler, Max, "Incidents Illustrative of American Jewish Patriotism," *American Jewish Historical Quarterly*, Vol. 4, 1896, pp. 87–97.
48. Ibid., pp. 103–105.
49. Marcus, J.R., *The American Jew* (Brooklyn: Carlson, 1995), pp. 275–279.
50. Rosenback, A.S.W., "Documents Relative to Major David S. Franks While Aide-de-Corp to General Arnold," *American Jewish Historical Quarterly*, Vol. 5, 1896, pp. 158–171.
51. Reznick, Samuel, *Pilgrim People* (Westport, Conn., Greenwood Press, 1975), pp. 189–192.
52. Marcus, J.R., *American Jewry Documents: Eighteenth Century* (Cincinnati: Hebrew Union College Press, 1959), pp. 274–275.
53. Blau, J.L., *The Jews of the United States* (New York: Columbia University Press, 1963), pp. 40–42.
54. Ibid., pp. 50–56.
55. Marcus, J.R., *Early American Jewry* (Philadelphia: Jewish Publication Society of America, 1951–1955), pp. 257–260.
56. Wolf, E., II, and Whiteman, M., *History of the Jews of Philadelphia* (Philadelphia: Jewish Publication Society of America, 1957), pp. 84–92.
57. Reznick, Samuel, *Unrecognized Patriots* (Westport, Conn. and London: Greenwood Press, 1975), p. 6.

58. Friedman, Lee, *Pilgrims in a New Land* (Philadelphia: Jewish Publication Society of America, 1948), pp. 85–89.

59. Marcus, J.R., *The Colonial American Jew* (Detroit: Wayne State University Press, 1970), Vol. III, p. 214.

60. Birmingham, S., *The Grandees* (New York: Harper and Row, 1971), p. 4.

61. *American Jewish Historical Quarterly*. 3/27/1903, p. 41.

62. Reznick, Samuel, *Unrecognized Patriots* (Westport, Conn. and London: Greenwood Press, 1975), p. 64.

63. Huhner, Leon, "Jews Interested in Privateering in America During the Eighteenth Century," *American Jewish Historical Quarterly*, Vol. 24, 1916, pp. 169–176.

64. Rosen, G., ed., *Jewish Life in America* (New York, KTAV, 1978), pp. 86–88.

65. Huhner, Leon, "Jews Interested in Privateering in America During the Eighteenth Century," *American Jewish Historical Quarterly*, Vol. 24, 1916, pp. 165–169.

66. "Letter by Offspring of Moses Family to the *New York Times* re: Privateer Activity of Isaac Moses and Others," *American Jewish Historical Quarterly*, Vol. 4, 1895, p. 23.

67. Schappes, Morris, *A Documentary History of the Jews in the United States* (New York: Schocken Books, 1971), pp. 121–124.

68. Marcus, J.R., *American Jewry Documents: Eighteenth Century* (Cincinnati: Hebrew Union College Press, 1959), p. 346.

69. Friedman, Lee, "Aaron Lopez: Long Deferred *Hope*," *American Jewish Historical Quarterly*, Vol. 37, 1947, pp. 103–113.

70. Lebeson, Anita, *Pilgrim People* (New York: Minerva Press, 1975), pp. 211–212.

71. Polcross, D.R., "Excerpts from Robert Morris' Diaries in the Office of Finance 1781–1784 Referring to Haym Salomon and Other Jews," *American Jewish Historical Quarterly*, Vol. 68, 1977-1978, pp. 3–6.

72. Levy, L.E., ed., *The American Jews as Patriot Soldier and Citizen* by Simon Wolf (Philadelphia, Levytype, 1895), pp. 164–168.

73. Gutstein, M.A., *History of the Jews in America* (New York: Bloch, 1936), p. 49.

74. Adams, H.B., "A Sketch of Haym Salomon," *American Jewish Historical Quarterly*, Vol. 2, 1894, pp. 7–14.

75. Schappes, M.V., "Excerpts from Robert Morris' Diaries in the Office of Finance Referring to Haym Salomon and Other Jews," *American Jewish Historical Quarterly*, Vol. 67, 1977-1978, pp. 14–27.

76. Kaganoff, M.M., "The Business Career of Haym Salomon as Reflected in His Newspaper Advertisements," *American Jewish His-*

torical *Quarterly*, Vol. 66, 1976–1977, pp. 35–41.

77. Wolfe, E., II, and Whiteman, M., *History of the Jews of Philadelphia* (Philadelphia: Jewish Publication Society of America, 1957), pp. 101–108.

78. Polcross, D.R., "Excerpts from Robert Morris' Diaries in the Office of Finance (1781–1784) Referring to Haym Salomon and Other Jews," *American Jewish Historical Quarterly*, Vol. 68, 1977-1978, p. 10.

79. Friedenwald, H., "Some Newspaper Advertisements of the Eighteenth Century," *American Jewish Historical Quarterly*, Vol. 5, 1897, pp. 50–52.

80. Birmingham, S., *The Grandees* (New York: Harper and Row, 1971), pp. 5–9.

81. "Robert Morris' Diary in the Office of Finance, Vol. II," *American Jewish Historical Quarterly*, Vol. 68, 1977-1978, pp. 47–51.

82. Birmingham, S., *The Grandees* (New York, Harper and Row, 1971), pp. 150–154.

83. Grenstein, H.B., "A Haym Salomon Letter to Rabbi David Tevde Schiff, London, 1784," *American Jewish Historical Quarterly*, Vol. 34, 1937, pp. 115–116.

84. Friedman, L., *Pilgrims in a New Land* (Philadelphia: Jewish Publication Society of America, 1948), pp. 67–70.

85. Gay, Ruth, *Jews in America* (New York: Basic Books, 1965), p. 36.

86. No author, "Manuscript of the Treasury Department," *American Jewish Historical Quarterly*, Vol. 27, 1920, p. 174.

87. Levy, L.E., ed., *The American Jews as Patriot Soldier and Citizen* by Simon Wolf, (Philadelphia: Levytype, 1895), pp. 188–192.

88. Friedenwald, H., "Some Newspaper Advertisements of the Eighteenth Century," *American Jewish Historical Quarterly*, Vol. 5, 1897, p. 52.

89. Karp, A.J., *The Role of the Jews in the American Revolution: A Historical Perspective* (Waltham, Mass.: American Jewish Historical Society, 1969), pp. 316–319.

90. Marcus, J.R., *Early American Jewry* (Philadelphia: Jewish Publication Society of America, 1951–1955), pp. 304–307.

91. Friedman, L., *Pilgrims in a New Land* (Philadelphia: Jewish Publication Society of America, 1948), pp. 216–219.

92. Ibid., pp. 59–63.

93. Birmingham, S., *The Grandees* (New York: Harper and Row, 1971), pp. 109–112.

94. Adams, H.B., "A Sketch of Haym Salomon," *American Jewish Historical Quarterly*, Vol. 2, 1894, pp. 15–16.

95. Levy, L.E., ed., *The American Jews as Patriot Soldier and Citizen* by Simon Wolf

(Philadelphia: Levytype, 1895), pp. 281–287.

96. Scharf, J.T., and Westcott, T., *History of Philadelphia 1609–1884* (Philadelphia, L.H. Everts, 1884), p. 473.

97. Marcus, J.R., *Early American Jewry* (Philadelphia: Jewish Publication Society of America, 1951–1955), p. 99.

Chapter 7

1. Kohler, M.J., "Jewish Activity in American Colonial Commerce," *American Jewish Historical Quarterly*, Vol. 10, 1902, pp. 48–54.

2. Marcus, J.R., *The Jew in the American World* (Detroit: Wayne State University Press, 1996), p. 52.

3. Marcus, J.R., *American Jewry Documents: Eighteenth Century* (Cincinnati: Hebrew Union College Press, 1959), pp. 340–341.

4. Fein, I.M., *The Making of an American Jewish Community* (Philadelphia: Jewish Publication Society of America, 1971), pp. 12–14.

5. Hertzberg, Arthur, *The Jews in America* (New York: Simon and Schuster, 1989), pp. 58–59.

6. Kohler, M.J., "A Memorial of Jews to Parliament Concerning Jewish Participation in Colonial Trade," *American Jewish Historical Quarterly*, Vol. 18, 1909, pp. 83, 123, 124.

7. "Ad in Rivington's *Royal Gazette*—New York, November 3, 1779, Page 58," *American Jewish Historical Quarterly*, Vol. 5, 1887, p. 58.

8. Kohler, M.J., "Phases of Jewish Life in New York Before 1800," *American Jewish Historical Quarterly*, Vol. 2, 1894, pp. 37–39.

9. "Jewish Owners of Ships Registered in the Port of Philadelphia 1730–1775, Page 235," *American Jewish Historical Quarterly*, Vol. 26, 1918, p. 235.

10. Chyet, S.F., "Aaron Lopez, a Study in Buenafama," *American Jewish Historical Quarterly*, Vol. 66, 1976-1977, p. 14.

11. Marcus, J.R., *American Jewry Documents: Eighteenth Century* (Cincinnati: Hebrew Union College Press, 1959), p. 273.

12. Ibid., p. 383.

13. Ibid., p. 461.

14. Ibid., p. 406.

15. Oppenheim, Samuel, "The Question of the Kosher Meat Supply in New York in 1813," *American Jewish Historical Quarterly*, Vol. 25, 1917, pp. 31, 32, 41–43.

16. Marcus, J.R., *American Jewry Documents: Eighteenth Century* (Cincinnati: Hebrew Union College Press, 1959), p. 93.

17. Gutstein, M.A., *The Story of the Jews in Newport* (New York: Bloch, 1936), pp. 142–146.

18. Hershkowitz, L., "Some Aspects of the New York Jewish Merchant Community," *American Jewish Historical Quarterly*, Vol. 66, 1976-1977, pp. 19–27.

19. Wolf, E., II, and Whiteman, Maxwell, *The History of the Jews in Philadelphia* (Philadelphia: Jewish Publication Society of America, 1957), p. 25.

20. "Letter of Philip Cuyler to David Franks, insurance broker," *American Jewish Historical Quarterly*, Vol. 26, 1918, p. 269.

21. Wolf, E., II, and Whiteman, Maxwell, *The History of the Jews in Philadelphia* (Philadelphia: Jewish Publication Society of America, 1957), p. 68.

22. Neuman, J.N., "Some Eighteenth Century American Jewish Letters," *American Jewish Historical Society*, Vol. 34, 1937, p. 80.

23. Op. cit., p. 134.

24. Newman, J.N., "Some Eighteenth Century American Jewish Letters," *American Jewish Historical Quarterly*, Vol. 34, 1937, pp. 81–84.

25. Wolf, E., II, and Whiteman, Maxwell, *The History of Jews in Philadelphia* (Philadelphia: Jewish Publication Society of America, 1957), pp. 66–78.

26. Schappe, M.V., *A Documentary History of the Jews in the United States* (New York: Schocken Books, 1971), p. 86.

27. Marcus, J.R., *American Jewry Documents: Eighteenth Century* (Cincinnati: Hebrew Union College Press, 1959), pp. 438–439.

28. "Note: P119, David Franks, William Murray and John Campbell 1774," *American Jewish Historical Quarterly*, Vol. 25, 1917, note p. 119.

29. Schappes, M.V., "Excerpts from Robert Moses' Diary in the Office of Finance," *American Jewish Historical Quarterly*, Vol. 67, 1977-1978, pp. 77–78.

30. Marcus, J.R., *American Jewry Documents: Eighteenth Century* (Cincinnati: Hebrew Union College Press, 1959), p. 325.

31. Ibid., p. 443.

32. Ibid., pp. 399–400.

33. Marcus, J.R., *The American Jew: A History* (Brooklyn: Carlson, 1995), pp. 60–66.

34. Hershkowitz, L., "Some Aspects of the New York Jewish Merchant Community," *American Jewish Historical Quarterly*, Vol. 66, 1976-1977, p. 38.

35. "Jonas Philips Vendue Store—September 19, 1897," *American Jewish Historical Society*, Vol. 5, 1897, p. 47.

36. New, I.D., "The Jewish Business-women in America," *American Jewish His-*

torical Quarterly, Vol. 66, 1976-1977, pp. 137–140.

37. Marcus, J.R., *American Jewry Documents: Eighteenth Century* (Cincinnati: Hebrew Union College Press, 1959), p. 3.

38. Ibid., p. 474.

39. Schappes, M.V., *A Documentary History of the Jews of the United States* (New York: Schocken Books, 1971), p. 271.

40. Hertzberg, Arthur, *The Jews in America* (New York: Simon and Schuster, 1989), pp. 53–57.

41. Baron, S.W., *Steeled by Adversity* (Philadelphia: Jewish Publication Society of America, 1971), p. 97.

42. Schappes, M.V., *A Documentary History of the Jews of the United States* (New York: Schocken Books, 1971), p. 289.

43. "Notes: 'A Massive Silver Tureen Made in New York City circa 1760 by Myer Myers,'" *American Jewish Historical Quarterly,* Vol. 28, 1922, pp. 236–237.

44. Fishman, Priscilla, *The Jews of the United States* (New York: Quadrangle, 1973), pp. 9, 10.

45. Marcus, J.R., *American Jewry Documents: Eighteenth Century* (Cincinnati: Hebrew Union College Press, 1959), p. 380.

46. "Items Related to the Jews of Newport," *American Jewish Historical Quarterly,* Vol. 27, 1920, p. 137.

47. Gutstein, M.A., *The Story of the Jews of Newport* (New York: Bloch, 1936), pp. 157–158.

48. McLoughlin, W.G., *Rhode Island* (New York: W.W. Norton, 1978), p. 65.

49. Marcus, J.R., *American Jewry Documents: Eighteenth Century* (Cincinnati: Hebrew Union College Press, 1959), p. 393.

50. Ibid., p. 329.

51. Blau, J.L., *The Jews of the United States* (New York: Columbia University Press, 1963), p. 103.

52. Sachar, H.M., *History of the Jews in America* (New York: Knopf, 1992), pp. 30–32.

53. Feldstein, S., *The Land That I Show You* (Garden City, N.Y.: Anchor Press, 1978), p. 270.

54. Birmingham, S., *The Grandees* (New York: Harper and Row, 1971), pp. 94–97.

55. Gutstein, M.A., *The Story of the Jews of Newport* (New York: Bloch, 1936), pp. 53–56.

56. Wolf, E., II, and Whiteman, Maxwell, *The History of the Jews of Philadelphia* (Philadelphia: Jewish Publication Society of America, 1957), pp. 59–61.

57. Ibid., pp. 167–175.

58. Marcus, J.R., *The American Jew: A History* (Brooklyn: Carlson, 1995), pp. 60, 63.

59. Op. cit., pp. 175, 178.

60. Marcus, J.R., *American Jewry Documents: Eighteenth Century* (Cincinnati: Hebrew Union College Press, 1959), p. 302.

61. Kohler, M.J., "Phases of Jewish Life in New York Before 1800," *American Jewish Historical Quarterly,* Vol. 2, 1894, pp. 111, 114.

62. Kohler, M.J., "Unpublished Correspondence Between Thomas Jefferson and Some American Jews," *American Jewish Historical Quarterly,* Vol. 19, 1910, pp. 18–20.

63. Sachar, H.M., *History of the Jews in America* (New York: Knopf, 1992), pp. 22, 23.

64. Huhner, L., "The Jews of South Carolina from the Earliest Settlement to the End of the Revolution," *American Jewish Historical Quarterly,* Vol. 12, 1904, p. 145.

65. Marcus, J.R., *The American Jew: A History* (Brooklyn: Carlson, 1995), pp. 21–26.

66. Berman, M., *Richmond's Jewry* (University Press of Virginia, 1978), p. 80.

67. Marcus, J.R., *American Jewry Documents: Eighteenth Century* (Cincinnati: Hebrew Union College Press, 1959), p. 148.

68. Gratz, Mordecai, "Notice of Jacob Mordecai, Founder and Proprietor from 1809–1818 of the Warrenton, N.C., Female Seminary," *American Jewish Historical Quarterly,* Vol. 5, 1897, p. 89.

69. Jones, H.G., *North Carolina Illustrated* (Chapel Hill: University of North Carolina Press, 1983), p. 183.

70. Hanft, Sheldon, "Mordecai's Female Academy," *American Jewish History,* Vol. 79, 1989-1990, pp. 73–89.

71. Marcus, J.R., *American Jewry Documents: Eighteenth Century* (Cincinnati: Hebrew Union College Press, 1959), pp. 90–99.

72. Ibid., p. 441.

73. Kohler, M.J., "Phases of Jewish Life in New York Before 1800," *American Jewish Historical Quarterly,* Vol. 2, 1894, pp. 85–89.

74. Korn, H., "Receipt Book of Judah and M. Hays Commencing January 12, 1763 and Ending July 18, 1776," *American Jewish Historical Quarterly,* Vol. 28, 1922, pp. 225–229.

75. "Receipt Book of Isaac Moses," *American Jewish Historical Society Quarterly,* Vol. 2, 1903, p. 27.

76. Faber, E., *A Time for Planting* (Baltimore: Johns Hopkins University Press, 1992), pp. 112–113.

77. Blau, J.L., *The Jews of the United States* (New York: Columbia University Press, 1963), pp. 110–111.

78. Huhner, L., "Jews in the Legal and Medical Professions in America Prior to 1800," *American Jewish Historical Quarterly,* Vol. 22, 1914, pp. 147–153.

79. Marcus, J.R., *American Jewry Docu-*

ments: Eighteenth Century (Cincinnati: Hebrew Union College Press, 1959), pp. 465–466.

80. Marcus, J.R., *Early American Jewry* (Philadelphia: Jewish Publication Society of America, 1951–1955), p. 79.

81. Marcus, J.R., *American Jewry Documents: Eighteenth Century* (Cincinnati: Hebrew Union College Press, 1959), p. 69.

82. Huhner, L., "Jews in Connection with the Colleges of the 13 Original States Prior to 1800," *American Jewish Historical Quarterly*, Vol. 19, 1910, pp. 119–123.

83. "Commencement Address of Sampson Simson in Hebrew from Columbia College 1800," *American Jewish Historical Quarterly*, Vol. 27, 1920, pp. 373–375.

84. Marcus, J.R., *The American Jew: A History* (Brooklyn: Carlson, 1995), pp. 67–73.

85. Marcus, J.R., *A Jew in the American World* (Detroit: Wayne State University Press, 1996), pp. 45, 77.

86. Oppenheim, S., "The Jews and Masonry in the United States Before 1810," *American Jewish Historical Quarterly*, Vol. 19, 1910, pp. 73–75.

87. Huhner, L., "Jews in Connection with the Colleges of the 13 Original States Prior to 1800," *American Jewish Historical Quarterly*, Vol. 19, 1910, pp. 114–116.

88. "An Advertisement in Dunlap's *American Daily Advertiser* June 4, 1793, Page 281," *American Jewish Historical Quarterly*, Vol. 35, 1939, p. 281.

89. "Advertisement in the Pennsylvania *Gazette*—February 16, 1769—Page 266," *American Jewish Historical Quarterly*, Vol. 34, 1937, p. 266.

90. Faber, E., *A Time for Planting* (Baltimore: Johns Hopkins University Press, 1992), pp. 85, 93, 95.

91. Daniels, D.G., "Colonial Jewry Religion Domestic and Social Relations," *American Jewish Historical Quarterly*, Vol. 66, 1977, pp. 381–399.

92. Rosenwaike, I., "An Estimate and Analysis of the Jewish Population of the United States in 1790," *American Jewish Historical Quarterly*, Vol. 50, 1960-1961, pp. 23–25.

93. Werblowsky, R.J., "What's in a Name—The Sephardim. The Origin of Their Name and Their Liturgical Customs," *American Jewish History*, Vol. 12, 1982, pp. 165–171.

94. Blau, J.L., *The Jews of the United States* (New York: Columbia University Press, 1963), pp. 16–18.

95. Cohen, N.W., *Jews in Christian America* (New York: Oxford University Press, 1992), pp. 11–13.

96. Marcus, J.R., *The Colonial American Jew* (Detroit: Wayne State University Press, 1970), p. 13.

97. Baron, S.W., *Steeled by Adversity* (Philadelphia: Jewish Publication Society of America, 1971), pp. 130–131.

98. Blau, J.L., *The Jews of the United States* (New York: Columbia University Press, 1963), pp. 67–69.

99. Feldstein, S., *The Land That I Show You* (Garden City, N.Y.: Anchor Press, 1978), p. 221.

100. Gay, R., *Jews in America* (New York: Basic Books, 1965), pp. 13–15.

101. Faber, E., *A Time for Planting* (Baltimore: Johns Hopkins University Press, 1992), pp. 59–65.

102. Marcus, J.R., *American Jewry Documents: Eighteenth Century* (Cincinnati: Hebrew Union College press, 1959), p. 143.

103. Ibid., p. 44.

104. Ibid., p. 187.

105. "Certificate of Conversion of Jacob Bar Abraham Abiner, Page 231," *American Jewish Historical Quarterly*, Vol. 27, 1920, p. 231.

106. Marcus, J.R., *American Jewry Documents: Eighteenth Century* (Cincinnati: Hebrew Union College Press, 1959), p. 19.

107. Wolf, E., II, and Whiteman, Maxwell, *The History of the Jews in Philadelphia* (Philadelphia: Jewish Publication Society of America, 1957), p. 200.

108. Hartogensis, B.H., "Rhode Island and Consanguineous Marriages," *American Jewish Historical Quarterly*, Vol. 19, 1910, pp. 137–139.

109. "*Ketubah* of Levy Solomons and Katherine Manuel, Page 172," *American Jewish Historical Quarterly*, Vol. 27, 1920, p. 172.

110. Wolf, E., II, and Whiteman, Maxwell, *The History of Jews in Philadelphia* (Philadelphia: Jewish Publication Society of America, 1957), pp. 199–200.

111. Marcus, J.R., *American Jewry Documents: Eighteenth Century* (Cincinnati: Hebrew Union College Press, 1959), pp. 138–141.

112. Ibid., p. 107.

113. "*Society Gemilut Hasadim* (Mutual Benefit Society) Page 254," *American Jewish Historical Quarterly*, Vol. 27, 1920, pp. 254–255.

114. Marcus, J.R., *The American Jew: A History* (Brooklyn: Carlson, 1995), pp. 174–180.

115. Faber, E., *A Time for Planting* (Baltimore: Johns Hopkins University Press, 1992), pp. 318–320.

116. Hershkowitz, L., "Powdered Tin and Rose Petals: Myer Myers Goldsmith and Peter Middleton Physician," *American Jewish History*, Vol. 70, 1981, pp. 462–467.

117. Marcus, J.R., *American Jewry Documents: Eighteenth Century* (Cincinnati: Hebrew Union College Press, 1959), p. 172.

118. "Regulations of Shearith Israel, Pages 117–128," *American Jewish Historical Quarterly*, Vol. 21, 1913, pp. 116–118.

119. Wiernik, P., *History of the Jews in America* (New York: Hermon Press, 1972), p. 407.

120. Op. cit., pp. 112–113.

121. Faber, Eli, "The Formative Era of American Jewish History," *American Jewish Historical Quarterly*, Vol. 81, 1993–1994, pp. 9–10.

122. "The Earliest Extant Minute Book of the Spanish and Portuguese Congregation Shearith Israel in New York 1728–1760," *American Jewish Historical Quarterly*, Vol. 21, 1912, pp. 1, 2, 3.

123. "Items Relating to Congregation Shearith Israel, New York, Pages 2–17," *American Jewish Historical Quarterly*, Vol. 27, 1920, pp. 2–7.

124. Faber, E., *A Time for Planting* (Baltimore: Johns Hopkins University Press, 1992), pp. 117–131.

125. Godfrey, St. J., "The King vs. Moses Gomez et al.: Opening the Prosecutor's File Over 200 Years Later," *American Jewish Historical Quarterly*, Vol. 80, 1991, pp. 397–401.

126. Marcus, J.R., *American Jewry Documents: Eighteenth Century* (Cincinnati: Hebrew Union College Press, 1959), pp. 148–161.

127. "Statement of Friends of the Synagogue, 1803, Pages 72–73," *American Jewish Historical Quarterly*, Vol. 27, 1920, pp. 72–73.

128. Ibid., p. 130.

129. Wiernik, P., *History of the Jews in America* (New York: Hermon Press, 1972), p. 217.

130. Marcus, J.R., *American Jewry Documents: Eighteenth Century* (Cincinnati: Hebrew Union College Press, 1959), pp. 94–95.

131. Wolf, E., II, and Whiteman, Maxwell, *The History of the Jews of Philadelphia* (Philadelphia: Jewish Publication Society of America, 1957), pp. 114–141.

132. Smith, Robert C., "A Portuguese Naturalist in Philadelphia 1799," *The Pennsylvania Magazine of History and Biography*, Vol. 78, 1954, pp. 71–107.

133. Gutstein, M.A., *The Story of the Jews in Newport* (New York: Bloch, 1936), pp. 80–98.

134. Faber, Eli, "The Formative Era of American Jewish History," *American Jewish*

135. "Dimensions of Inside the Synagogue (Touro)," *American Jewish Historical Quarterly*, Vol. 27, 1920, pp. 404–407.

136. Eisenberg, A., and Goodman, H.G., eds., *Eyewitness to American Jewish History* (New York: Union of American Hebrew Congregations, 1976), p. 276.

137. Faber, Eli, "The Formative Years of American Jewish History," *American Jewish Historical Quarterly*, Vol. 81, 1993–1994, pp. 17–19.

138. Huhner, L., "The Jews of South Carolina from the Earliest Settlement to the End of the American Revolution," *American Jewish Historical Quarterly*, Vol. 12, 1904, pp. 57–60.

139. Marcus, J.R., *The American Jew: A History* (Brooklyn: Carlson, 1995), pp. 85–86.

140. Faber, Eli, "The Formative Era of American Jewish History," *American Jewish Historical Quarterly*, Vol., 81, 1993–1994, pp. 20–21.

141. Harden, W., *A History of Savannah and South Georgia* (Atlanta: Cherokee, 1969), pp. 50–52.

142. Berman, Myron, *Richmond Jewry* (Virginia University Press, 1979), pp. 38–40, 64–65.

143. Marcus, J.R., *A Jew in the American World* (Detroit: Wayne State University Press, 1996), p. 131.

144. "A Case in the Superior Court of the City of New York," *American Jewish Historical Quarterly*, Vol. 27, 1920, pp. 382–383.

145. Marcus, J.R., *American Jewry Documents: Eighteenth Century* (Cincinnati: Hebrew Union College Press, 1959), p. 288.

146. Sokohen, Samuel, "The Simson-Hirsch Letter to the Chinese Jews 1795," *American Jewish Historical Quarterly*, Vol. 49, 1959–1960, p. 39.

147. Marcus, J.R., *American Jewry Documents: Eighteenth Century* (Cincinnati: Hebrew Union College Press, 1959), pp. 167–169.

148. Scharf, I.T., and Westcott, T., *History of Philadelphia from 1600 to 1884* (Philadelphia: L.H. Everts, 1884), p. 563.

149. Fuchs, M.H., *The Political Behavior of American Jews* (Glencoe, Ill.: Free Press, 1956), p. 283.

150. Grasso, C., *A Speaking Aristocracy* (Chapel Hill and London: University of North Carolina Press, 1999), pp. 36, 37, 73, 131, 132, 254, 255.

Historical Quarterly, Vol. 81, 1993–1994), p. 11.

Bibliography

Abrahams, E.H., "Some Notes on the Early History of the Sheftalls of Georgia," *American Jewish Historical Quarterly*, Vol. 17, (1908).

"Ad in Rivington's *Royal Gazette*—New York, November 3, 1779, page 58," *American Jewish Historical Quarterly*, Vol. 5, 1887.

Adams, H.B., "A Sketch of Haym Salomon," *American Jewish Historical Quarterly*, Vol. 2, 1894.

Adler, Cyrus, "Jews in the American Plantations," *American Jewish Historical Quarterly*, Vol. 1, 1892.

"Advertisement in Dunlap's *American Daily Advertiser*, June 4, 1793, page 281," *American Jewish Historical Quarterly*, Vol. 35, 1939.

"Advertisement in the Pennsylvania *Gazette*—February 16, 1769—page 266," *American Jewish Historical Quarterly*, Vol. 34, 1937.

Andrews, C. McLean, *Colonial Period of American History* (New Haven: Yale University Press, 1934).

Andrews, M.P., *History of Maryland, Province & State* (Hatboro, Penn.: Tradition Press, 1965).

Auerbach, Jerold S., *Rabbis and Lawyers—The Journey from Torach to Constitution* (Bloomington: Indiana University Press, 1990).

Baron, S.W., *Steeled by Adversity* (Philadelphia: Jewish Publication Society of America, 1971).

Berman, Myron, *Richmond's Jewry* (Charlottesville: University Press of Virginia, 1979).

Birmingham, Stephen, *The Grandees* (New York: Harper and Row, 1971).

Blau, Joseph L., and Baron, S.W., eds., *The Jews of the United States 1790–1840* (New York and London: Columbia University Press, 1963).

Bordon, M., *Jews, Turks and Infidels* (Chapel Hill and London: University of North Carolina Press, 1984).

Bronner, Edwin B., and Fraser, David, eds., *The Papers of William Penn*, Volume 5, (Philadelphia: University of Pennsylvania Press, 1986).

Byars, William V., "The Gratz Papers," *American Jewish Historical Quarterly*, Vol. 23, 1915.

"Case in the Superior Court of the City of New York," *American Jewish Historical Quarterly*, Vol. 27, 1920.

Census 1790—"Joel and Amelia Henry and Jacob in Carteret County, North Carolina."

Certificate 12/15/1779—"Concerning the Service of Benjamin Nones Under General Pulaski," *American Jewish Historical Quarterly*, Vol. 27, 1920.

"Certificate of Conversion of Jacob Bar Abraham Abiner, Page 231," *American Jewish Historical Quarterly*, Vol. 27, 1920.

Chiel, Arthur A., "Ezra Stiles, the Education of an 'Hebrician,'" *American Jewish Historical Society*, Vol. 60, 1970-1971.

_____, "The Rabbis and Ezra Stiles," *American Jewish Historical Quarterly*, Vol. 61, 1972.

Chyet, Stanley F., "Aaron Lopez, a Study in Buenafama," *American Jewish Historical Quarterly*, Vol. 66, 1976-1977.

_____, *Lopez of Newport, Colonial American Merchant Prince* (Detroit: Wayne State University Press, 1970).

Cohen, Naomi W., *Jew in a Christian World* (New York: Oxford University Press, 1992).

_____, *Jews in Christian America* (New York: Oxford University Press, 1992).

Coleman, Kenneth, *Colonial Georgia—A History* (New York: Charles Scribner's Sons, 1975).
_____, ed., *A History of Georgia*, 2d ed. (Athens and London: University of Georgia Press, 1977, 1991).
Colonial Records of Pennsylvania: Minutes of the Supreme Executive Council of Pennsylvania, Vol. 15 1781–1783 (Philadelphia: Theo Fenn, 1853).
"Commencement Address of Sampson Simson in Hebrew from Columbia College 1800," *American Jewish Historical Quarterly*, Vol. 27, 1920.
Coulter, E. M., *Georgia, a Short History* (Chapel Hill: University of North Carolina Press, 1933, 1947, 1960).
Dabney, Virginius, *Virginia, the New Dominion* (Garden City: New York, Doubleday, 1971).
Dalen, D.G., and Drosenbaum, J., *Making a Life, Building a Community: A History of the Jews of Hartford* (New York and London: Holmes and Meier, 1997).
Daniels, Bruce C., *Dissent and Conformity on Narragansett Bay—The Colonial Rhode Island Town* (Middleton, Conn.: Wesleyan University Press, 1983).
Daniels, Doris G., "Colonial Jewry Religion Domestic and Social Relations," *American Jewish Historical Quarterly*, Vol. 66, 1977.
de Sola Pool, D., Reverend, "Hebrew Learning Among the Puritans of New England Prior to 1700, *American Jewish Historical Quarterly*, Vol. 19, 1910.
Dexter, F.B., ed., *The Literary Diary of Ezra Stiles* (New York: C. Scribners' Sons, 1901).
"Dimensions of Inside the Synagogue (Touro)," *American Jewish Historical Quarterly*, Vol. 27, 1920.
Diner, Hasia R., "Jewish Self Governance, American Style," *American Jewish Historical Quarterly*, Vol. 81, 1983-1984.
Dinnerstein, Leonard, "A Neglected Aspect of Southern Jewish History," *American Jewish Historical Quarterly*, Vol. 61, 1971-1972.
_____, and Pateson, Mary Dale, eds., *Jews in the South* (Baton Rouge: Louisiana University Press, 1973).
"Documents Relating to the Career of Colonel Isaac Franks," *American Jewish Publication Quarterly*, Vol. 5, 1896.
Dublin, F., "Jewish Colonial Enterprise in Light of the Amherst Papers," *American Jewish Historical Quarterly*, Vol. 35, 1939.
Dunn, Mary M., and Dunn, Richard Z., eds., *The Papers of William Penn*, 1644–1679, Vol. 1 (Philadelphia: University of Pennsylvania Press, 1981), pp. 91, 226, 43, Vol. V.
Dyer, A.M., "Points in the First Chapter of New York Jewish History," *American Jewish Historical Quarterly*, Vol. 3, 1895.
"Earliest Extant Minute Book of the Spanish and Portuguese Congregation Shearith Israel in New York 1728–1760," *American Jewish Historical Quarterly*, Vol. 21, 1912.
Edgar, Walter, *South Carolina, a History* (Columbia: University of South Carolina Press, 1998).
Eisenberg, A., and Goodman, H.G., eds., *Eyewitness to American Jewish History* (New York: Union of American Hebrew Congregations, 1976).
Eitches, Edward, "Maryland's 'Jew Bill,'" *American Jewish Historical Quarterly*, Vol. 60, 1970–1971.
Engleman, U.Z., "Jewish Education in Charleston, South Carolina During the Eighteenth and Nineteenth Centuries," *American Jewish Historical Quarterly*. Vol. 42, 1952-1953.
Ezekiel, Jacob, "The Jews of Richmond," *American Jewish Historical Publication*, Vol. 4, 1896.
Faber, Eli, "The Formative Era of American Jewish History," *American Jewish Historical Quarterly*, Vol. 81, 1993-1994.
_____, *The Jewish People in America*, Vol. I, "A Time for Planting. The First Migration 1654–1820" (Baltimore: Johns Hopkins University Press, 1992).
Fein, Isaac M., *The Making of an American Jewish Community* (Philadelphia: Jewish Publication Society of America, 1971).
Feingold, Henry I., *Zion in America* (Albany: State University of New York Press, 1986).
_____, *A Midrash on American Jewish History* (Albany: State University of New York Press, 1982).
Feldstein, Stanley, *The Land That I Show You* (Garden City, N.Y.: Anchor Press/Doubleday, 1978).
Fishman, Priscilla, *The Jews of the United States*, "Striking Roots" (New York: Quadrangle Press, 1973).
Friedenberg, Albert M., "The Jews of New Jersey from the Earliest Times to 1850," *American Jewish Historical Quarterly*, Vol. 17, 1908.
Friedenwald, Herbert, "Material for the History of the Jews in the British West Indies," *American Jewish Historical Quarterly*, Vol. 4, 1896.

_____, "Material for the History of the Jews in the British West Indies," *American Jewish Historical Society*, Vol. 5, 1896.

_____, "Some Newspaper Advertisements of the Eighteenth Century," *American Jewish Historical Quarterly*, Vol. 5, 1897.

Friedman, Lee M., "Boston in American Jewish History," *American Jewish Historical Quarterly*, Vol. 42, 1953.

_____. *Early American Jews* (Cambridge: Harvard University Press, 1934).

_____. "Early Jewish Residents in Massachusetts," *American Jewish Historical Quarterly*, Vol. 24, 1916.

_____, "Rowland Gideon, an Early Boston Jew and His Family," *American Jewish Historical Quarterly*. Vol. 35, 1939.

_____, "Aaron Lopez: Long Deferred *Hope*," *American Jewish Historical Quarterly*, Vol. 37, 1947.

_____, "Cotton Mather and the Jews," *American Jewish Historical Quarterly*, Vol. 26, 1918.

_____, "Judah Monis, First Instructor in Hebrew at Harvard University," *The American Jewish Historical Quarterly*, Vol. 22, 1914.

_____, *Pilgrims in a New Land* (Philadelphia: Jewish Publication Society of America, 1948).

_____, "Some Further Notes on Judah Monis," *American Jewish Historical Quarterly*, Vol. 37, 1947.

Fuchs, Lawrence, H., *The Political Behavior of American Jews* (Glencoe, Ill.: Free Press, 1956).

Gay, Ruth, *Jews in America* (New York: Basic Books, 1965).

Godfrey, St. J., "The King vs. Moses Gomez et al: Opening the Prosecutor's File Over 200 Years Later," *American Jewish Historical Quarterly*, Vol. 80, 1991.

Goldman, Shalom, "Biblical Hebrew in Colonial America," *American Jewish Historical Quarterly*, Vol. 79, 1989-1990.

Goodman, A.V., "Jewish Elements in Brown's Early History," *American Jewish Historical Society*, Vol. 37, 1947.

_____, "South Carolina from Shaffesbury to Salvador," *American Jewish Historical Society*, Vol. 29, 1931.

Grasso, C., *A Speaking Aristocracy* (Chapel Hill and London: University of North Carolina Press, 1999).

Gratz, Mordecai, "Notice of Jacob Mordecai, Founder and Proprietor from 1809 to 1818 of the Warrenton, N.C., Female Seminary," *American Jewish Historical Quarterly*, Vol. 5, 1897.

Grenstein, H.B., "A Haym Salomon Letter to Rabbi David Tevde Schiff; London, 1784," *American Jewish Historical Quarterly*, Vol. 34, 1937.

Gutstein, Linda, *History of the Jews in America* (Edison, N.J.: Chartwell Books, 1988).

Gutstein, Morris A., *The Story of the Jews of Newport* (New York: Bloch, 1936).

_____, "Roger Williams—Witness beyond Christendom," 1603–1683.

_____, *History of the Jews in America* (New York: Bloch, 1938).

Hanft, Sheldon, "Mordecai's Female Academy," *American Jewish History*, Vol. 79, 1989–1990.

Harbogensis, Benjamin H., "Rhode Island and Consanguineous Marriages," *American Jewish Historical Quarterly*, Vol. 19, 1910.

_____, "Unequal Religious Rights in Maryland Since 1776," *American Jewish Historical Quarterly*, Vol. 25, 1917.

Harap, Louis, "Image of the Jew in American Drama 1794–1823," *American Jewish Historical Quarterly*, Vol. 60, 1970–1971.

Harden, William, *A History of Savannah and South Georgia* (Atlanta: Cherokee, 1969).

Hart, Gustavio, "Notes on Myer Hart and Other Jews of Easton, Pennsylvania," *American Jewish Historical Quarterly*, Vol. 5, 1897.

Healey, R.M., "Jefferson on Judaism and the Jews—Divided We Stand, United We Fall," *American Jewish Historical Quarterly*, Vol. 73, 1983–1984.

Heineman, D.E., "The Starling Experience of a Jewish Trader during Pontiac's Siege of Detroit in 1763," *American Jewish Historical Quarterly*, Vol. 24, 1916.

Herrwitz, Samuel J. and Edith, "The New World Sets an Example for the Old," *American Jewish Historical Quarterly*, Vol. 55, September 1965-1966:1.

Hershkowitz, Leo, "Powdered Tin and Rose Petals: Myer Myers Goldsmith and Peter Middleton Physician," *American Jewish History*, Vol. 70, 1981.

_____, "Some Aspects of the New York Merchant Community," *American Jewish Historical Quarterly*, 1976–1977.

_____, "Wills of Early New York Jews (1704–1740), *American Jewish Historical Quarterly*, Vol. 55, 1965–1966.

Hertzberg, Arthur, *The Jews in America* (New York: Simon and Schuster, 1989).
Hollander, J.H., "The Civil Status of the Jews in Maryland 1634–1776," *American Jewish Historical Quarterly*, Vol. 2, 1894.
_____, "Documents Relating to the Attempted Departure of the Jews from Surinam," *American Jewish Historical Quarterly*, Vol. 5, 1897.
_____, "The Naturalization of Jews in the American Colonies Under the Act of 1740," *American Jewish Historical Quarterly*, Vol. 4, 1896.
_____, "Some Unpublished Material Relating to Dr. Jacob Lumbrozo," *American Jewish Historical Quarterly*, Vol. 1, 1892.
Hufnagle, G.W., "An Account of the House at Germantown," *American Jewish Historical Quarterly*, Vol. 5, 1896.
Huhner, Leon, "The First Jew to Hold Office of Governor of One of the United States," *American Jewish Historical Quarterly*, Vol. 17, 1908.
_____, "Jews in Connection with the Colleges of the 13 Original States Prior to 1800," *American Jewish Historical Quarterly*, Vol. 19, 1910.
_____, "Jews in the Legal and Medical Professions in American Prior to 1800," *American Jewish Historical Quarterly*, Vol. 22, 1914.
_____, "Jews in the War of 1912," *American Jewish Historical Quarterly*, Vol. 9, 1901.
_____, "Jews Interested in Privateering in American During the Eighteenth Century," *American Jewish Historical Quarterly*, Vol. 24, 1916.
_____, "The Jews of Georgia in Colonial Times," *American Jewish Historical Quarterly*, Vol. 10, 1902.
_____, "The Jews of New England (Other than Rhode Island) Prior to 1800," *American Jewish Historical Quarterly*, Vol. 11, 1903.
_____, "The Jews of North Carolina Prior to 1800," *American Jewish Historical Quarterly*, Vol. 29, 1925.
_____, "The Jews of South Carolina from the Earliest Settlement to the End of the American Revolution," *American Jewish Historical Quarterly*, Vol. 12, 1904.
_____, "The Jews of Virginia from the Earliest Time to the Close of the Eighteenth Century," *American Jewish Publications Quarterly*, Vol. 19, 1910.
_____, "Asser Levy," *American Jewish Historical Quarterly*, Vol. 5, 1897.
_____, "Francis Salvador," *American Jewish Publication Quarterly*, Vol. 9, 1901.
_____, "Some Additional Notes on the History of the Jews of South Carolina," *American Jewish Historical Quarterly*, Vol. 19, 1910.
_____, "The Struggle for Religious Liberty in North Carolina with Special Reference to the Jews," *American Jewish Historical Quarterly*, Vol. 16, 1907.
_____, "Whence Came the First Jewish Settlers of New York?" *American Jewish Historical Quarterly*, Vol. 9, 1901.
"Items Related to the Jews of Newport," *American Jewish Historical Quarterly*, Vol. 27, 1920.
"Items Relating to Congregation Shearith Israel, New York, Page 2–17," *American Jewish Historical Quarterly*, Vol. 27, 1920.
Janowsky, Oscar I., *The American Jew, a Composite Portrait* (New York: Harper and Brothers, 1942).
Jastrow, Morris, Jr., "Documents Relating to the Career of Colonel Isaac Franks," *American Jewish Historical Quarterly*, Vol. 4, 1896.
Jenkins, Howard M., ed., *Pennsylvania—Colonial and Federal, a History 1608–1903* (Philadelphia: Pennsylvania Historical Publishing Association, 1903).
"Jew Bill," *American Jewish Historical Quarterly*, Vol. 26, 1918.
"Jewish Owners of Ships Registered in the Port of Philadelphia 1730–1775, Page 235," *American Jewish Historical Quarterly*, Vol. 26, 1918.
"Jews Voted in Election in Westchester," *American Jewish Historical Quarterly*, Vol. 66, 1976–1977.
Johnson, Paul, *A History of the Jews* (New York: Harper Perennial Press, 1987).
"Jonas Philips Vendue Store—September 19, 1897," *American Jewish Historical Society*, Vol. 5, 1897.
Jones, Charles C., "The Settlement of the Jews in Georgia," *American Jewish Historical Quarterly*, Vol. 1, 1892.
Jones, H.G., *North Carolina Illustrated* (Chapel Hill: University of North Carolina Press, 1983).
Joseph, Andrew C., "The Settlement of Jews in Canada," *American Jewish Historical Quarterly*, Vol. 1, 1892.
Judah, George F., "The Jews' Future in Jamaica," *American Jewish Historical Society*, Vol. 18, 1909.

Kaganoff, M.M., "The Business Center of Haym Salomon as Reflected in His Newspaper Advertisements," *American Jewish Historical Quarterly*, Vol. 66, 1976–1977.

Karp, A.J., "Jewish Experience in America," *American Jewish Historical Society* (Waltham, Mass., 1969).

_____, *The Role of the Jews in the American Revolution: A Historical Perspective* (Waltham, Mass., American Jewish Historical Society, 1969).

Kelley, Joseph J., Jr., *Pennsylvania—The Colonial Years, 1681–1775* (New York: Doubleday, 1980).

"*Ketubah* of Levy Solomons and Katherine Manuel, Page 172," *American Jewish Historical Quarterly*, Vol. 27, 1920.

Kohler, Max J., "Beginnings of New York Jewish History," *American Jewish Historical Quarterly*, Vol. 1, 1892.

_____, "Civil Status of the Jews in Colonial New York," *American Jewish Historical Quarterly*, Vol. 5, 1897.

_____, "The Doctrine That 'Christianity Is a Part of Common Law' and Its Recent Judicial Overthrow in England," *American Jewish Historical Quarterly*, Vol. 13.

_____, "Incidents Illustrative of American Jewish Patriotism," *American Jewish Historical Quarterly*, Vol. 4, 1896.

_____, "Jewish Activity in American Colonial Commerce," *American Jewish Historical Quarterly*, Vol. 10, 1902.

_____, "The Jews and the American Anti-Slavery Movement," *American Jewish Historical Quarterly*, Vol. 4, 1896.

_____, "The Jews and the Anti-Slavery Movement," *American Jewish Historical Quarterly*, Vol. 5, 1897.

_____, "The Jews in Newport," *American Jewish Historical Quarterly*, Vol. 5, 1897.

_____, "Judah Touro, Merchant and Philanthropist," *American Jewish Historical Quarterly*, Vol. 13, 1905.

_____, "A Memorial of Jews to Parliament Concerning Jewish Participation in Colonial Trade," *American Jewish Historical Quarterly*, Vol. 18, 1909.

_____, "Phases in the History of Religious Liberty in American with Special Reference to the Jews," *American Jewish Historical Quarterly*, Vol. 11, 1903.

_____, "Phases in the History of Religions. Liberty in America with Particular Reference to the Jews," *American Jewish Historical Quarterly*, Vol. 13, 1905.

_____, "Phases of Jewish Life in New York before 1800," *American Jewish Historical Quarterly*, Vol. 2, 1894.

_____, "Unpublished Correspondence Between Thomas Jefferson and Some American Jews," *American Jewish Historical Quarterly*, Vol. 19, 1910.

Korn, B.W., "Jews and Negro Slavery in the Old South 1789–1865," *American Jewish Historical Quarterly*, Vol. 50, 1961.

Korn, H., "Receipt Book of Judah and M. Hays Commencing January 12, 1763 and Ending July 18, 1776," *American Jewish Historical Quarterly*, Vol. 28, 1922.

Kull, Irving S., ed., *New Jersey: A History* (New York, American Historical Society, Inc., 1930).

La Fantasie, Glenn W., "The Correspondence of Roger Williams" (Brown University Press/University Press of New England, Hanover/London, 1988).

Lebeson, Anita, *Pilgrim People* (New York, Minerva Press, 1975).

Lebowich, Joseph, "The Jews in Boston Till 1875," *American Jewish Historical Quarterly*, Vol. 12, 1904.

Lefler, H.T., and Powell, W.S., *Colonial North Carolina, A History*, (New York: Charles Scribner's Sons, 1973).

Lemmon, S.M., ed., *The Pettigrew Papers 1683–1818*, Vol. 1 (Raleigh: State Department of Archives and History, 1971).

"Letter by Offspring of Moses Family to the *New York Times*: re: Privateer Activity of Isaac Moses and Others," *American Jewish Historical Quarterly*, Vol. 4, 1895.

"Letter of Philip Cuyler to David Franks, Insurance Broker," *American Jewish Historical Quarterly*, Vol. 26, 1918.

Levy, L.E., ed., *The American Jews as Patriot Soldier and Citizen* by Simon Wolf (Philadelphia: Levytype, 1895).

Lewis, T.R., and Harmond, J.E., *Connecticut: A Geography* (Boulder: Westview Press, 1986).

"Manuscript of the Treasury Department," *American Jewish Historical Quarterly*, Vol. 27, 1920.

Marcus, Jacob R., *The American Jew 1585–1990: A History* (Brooklyn: Carlson, 1995).

_____, *American Jewry Documents: Eighteenth Century* (Cincinnati: Hebrew Union College Press, 1959).

_____, *The Colonial American Jew* (Detroit: Wayne State University Press, 1970), Vols. I–III.

_____, *Early American Jewry* (Philadelphia: Jewish Publication Society of America, 1951–1955), Vols. I and II.

_____, *The Jew in the American World* (Detroit: Wayne State University Press, 1996).

_____, "Light on Early Connecticut Jewry," *Critical Studies in American Jewish History from American Jewish Archives* (New York: KTAV Publishers, 1971).

_____, *Studies in Early American Jewish History* (Cincinnati: Hebrew Union College Press, 1969).

_____, *U.S. Jewry 1776–1965*, Vol. 1 (Detroit: Wayne State University Press, 1989).

Martin, Harold H., *Georgia: A Bicentennial History* (New York: W.W. Norton, 1977).

Maslin, Simeon J., "1732–1982 in Curaçao," *American Jewish Historical Quarterly*, Vol. 72, 1882-1883.

"Massachusetts Historical Society Collections," *Commerce of Rhode Island*, Vol. 69, 1:96–97.

McAllister, W.J., "Pioneer Days in Allegheny County," *Virginia Magazine of History and Biography*, Vol. 10, 1902-1903, #2.

McLoughlin, W.G., *Rhode Island* (New York: W.W. Norton, 1978).

Meyer, Isadore S., "Hebrew at Harvard," *American Jewish Historical Quarterly*, Vol. 35, 1939.

Mischnitzer, Rachel, "Ezra Stiles and the Portrait of Menassah Ben Israel," *American Jewish Historical Quarterly*, Vol. 51, 1961-1962.

Morais, Sabato, "Mickvé Israel Congregation of Philadelphia," *American Jewish Historical Quarterly*, Vol. 1, 1892.

Morgan, D.T., "The Sheftalls of Savannah," *American Jewish Historical Society*, Vol. 62, 1972-1973.

Munroe, John A., *Colonial Delaware—A History* (New Jersey: KTO Press, 1978).

Necarsulmer, Henry, "Early Jewish Settlement at Lancaster, Pennsylvania," *American Jewish Historical Quarterly*, Vol. 9, 1901.

Netanyahu, B., *The Origin of the Inquisition in Fifteenth Century Spain* (Random House: 1995).

Neuman, J.N., "Some Eighteenth Century American Jewish Letters," *American Jewish Historical Society*, Vol. 34, 1937.

New, I.D., "The Jewish Businesswomen in America," *American Jewish Historical Quarterly*, Vol. 66, 1976–1977.

"New York Slave Insurrection 1741," *American Jewish Historical Quarterly*, Vol. 27, 1920.

"Note: David Franks, William Murray and John Campbell 1774," *American Jewish Historical Quarterly*, Vol. 25, 1917.

Notes *American Jewish Historical Quarterly*, 3/27/1903.

Notes *American Jewish Historical Quarterly*, Vol. 27, 1920.

Notes *American Jewish Historical Quarterly*, Vol. 28, 1922.

Notes *American Jewish Historical Society*, Vol. 22, 1914.

"Notes and Queries," Virginia Magazine of History and *Biography*, Vol. 1, 1893-1894.

"Notes: Disgraceful Acts of a Mob at a Jewish Funeral in New York 1743," *American Jewish Historical Society*, Vol. 31:90 (1928).

"Notes: Jefferson Looks for Attorney-General," *American Jewish Historical Quarterly*, Vol. 19: 161 (1910).

"Notes: 'A Massive Silver Tureen Made in New York City circa 1760 by Myer Myers," *American Jewish Historical Quarterly*, Vol. 28, 1922.

"Notes on Early Jews in Middlesex County, New Jersey," *American Jewish Historical Society*, Vol. 33, 1934.

"Notes: A Remarkable Verdict at Amsterdam 1/19/1690," *American Jewish Historical Quarterly*, Vol. 34, 1937.

Oppenheim, Samuel, "The Early History of the Jews of New York 1654–1664," *American Jewish Historical Quarterly*, Vol. 18, 1909.

_____, "The First Settlement of Jews in Newport: Some New Matter on the Subject," *Publication of the American Jewish Historical Society*, Vol. 34, 1937.

_____, "The Jews and Masonry in the United States before 1810," *American Jewish Historical Quarterly*, Vol. 19, 1910.

_____, "The Question of the Kosher Meat Supply in New York in 1813," *American Jewish Historical Quarterly*, Vol. 25, 1917.

_____, "Will of Nathan Simpson, a Jewish Merchant of New York," *American Jewish Historical Quarterly*, Vol. 25, 1917.

Pennsylvania Archives First Series—Vol. X, 1783–1788 (Philadelphia: Joseph Severns, 1854).

"Pennsylvania Journal January 4, 1786," *American Jewish Historical Quarterly*, Vol. 5, 1897.

Pessin, Deborah, *History of the Jews in America* (New York: United Synagogue Commission, 1957).

Phillips, N. Taylor, "The Congregation *Shearith Israel*," *American Jewish Historical Quarterly*, Vol. 5, 1897.

_____. "Family History of the Reverend Daniel Mendez Machado," *American Jewish Historical Quarterly*, Vol. 2, 1894.

Polcross, D.R., "Excerpts from Robert Morris' Diaries in the Office of Finance 1781–1784, Referring to Haym Salomon and Other Jews," *American Jewish Historical Quarterly*, Vol. 68, 1977-1978.

"Receipt Book of Isaac Moses," *American Jewish Historical Society Quarterly*, Vol. 2, 1903.

"Regulations of Shearith Israel, Page 117–128," *American Jewish Historical Quarterly*, Vol. 21, 1913.

Reiss, Oscar, *Medicine and the American Revolution* (Jefferson, N.C., McFarland & Co., Inc., Publishers, 1998).

Reznick, Samuel, *Pilgrim People* (Westport, Conn. and London: Greenwood Press, 1975).

_____, *Unrecognized Patriots* (Westport, Conn.and London: Greenwood Press, 1975).

"Robert Morris' Diary in the Office of Finance—Vol. II," *American Jewish Historical Quarterly*, Vol. 68, 1977-1978.

Rosen, G., ed., *Jewish Life in America* (New York: KTAV Publishing House, Inc., 1978).

Rosenbach, Abraham S. W., "Documents Relative to Major David S. Franks while Aide-de-Corp to General Arnold," *American Jewish Historical Quarterly*, Vol. 5, 1896.

_____, "Notes on the First Settlement of Jews in Pennsylvania, 1655–1703," *American Jewish Historical Quarterly*, Vol. 5, 1896.

Rosenberg, Louis, "Some Aspects of the Historical Development of the Canadian Jewish Community," *American Jewish Historical Quarterly*, Vol. 50, 1960-1961.

Rosendale, Simon W., "An Early Ownership of Real Estate in Albany, New York, by a Jewish Trader, *American Jewish Historical Quarterly*, Vol. 3, 1895.

Rosenwaike, Ira, "An Estimate and Analysis of the Jewish Population of the United States in 1790," *American Jewish Historical Quarterly*, Vol. 50, 1960-1961.

_____, "Further Light on Jacob Henry," *Statutes—South Carolina II 232F.*

_____, "The Jews of Baltimore to 1810," *American Jewish Historical Quarterly*, Vol. 64, 1975:4.

_____, "Simon M. Levy, West Point Graduate," *American Jewish Historical Quarterly*, Vol. 61, 1971-1972.

Roth, Cecil, "A Jewish Voice for Peace in the War of American Independence," *American Jewish Historical Quarterly*, Vol. 3, 1928.

Sachar, H.M., *A History of the Jews in America* (New York: Knopf, 1992).

Samuel, John, "Some Cases in Pennsylvania Wherein Rights Claimed by Jews Are Affected," *American Jewish Historical Quarterly*, Vol. 5, 1896.

Sarna, Jonathan D., ed., *American Jewish Experience* (New York: Holmes and Maier, 1986).

Schappes, Morris V., "Anti-Semitism and Reaction 1795–1800," *American Jewish Historical Quarterly*, Vol. 38, 1948-1949.

_____, *A Documentary History of the Jews in the United States* (New York: Schocken Books, 1971).

_____, "Excerpts from Robert Morris' Diaries in the Office of Finance Referring to Haym Salomon and Other Jews," *American Jewish Historical Quarterly*, Vol. 67, 1977-1978.

Scharf, J. Thomas, and Westcott, Thompson, *History of Philadelphia, 1609–1804* (Philadelphia: L.H. Everts, 1884); *Freeman's Journal* (Philadelphia) 1/21/1784.

Seeligman, Sigmund, "David Nassy of Surinam," *American Jewish Historical Quarterly*, Vol. 22, 1914.

Selber, Mendel, "Americans in Hebrew Literature," *American Jewish Historical Quarterly*, Vol. 22, 1914.

Sharfman, I. Harold, *Jews on the Frontier* (Chicago: Henry Regnery Co., 1977).

Sheftall, Mordecai, *American Jewish Historical Quarterly*, Vol. 67, 1977-1978.

_____, *The Jewish Encyclopedia* (New York and London: Funk and Wagnalls Co., 1905).

Smith, J.M., "The Aurora and the Alien and Sedition Laws, Part 1 & 2," *The Pennsylvania Magazine of History and Biography*, Vol. 77, 1953.

Smith, Robert C., "A Portuguese Naturalist in Philadelphia 1799," *The Pennsylvania Magazine of History and Biography*, Vol. 78, 1954.

Sobel, B. Zui, "Jews and Christian Evangelization, the Anglo-American Approach," *American Jewish Historical Quarterly*, Vol. 58, 1968-1969.

"*Society Gemilut Hasadim* (Mutual Benefit Society) Page 254," *American Jewish Historical Quarterly*, Vol. 27, 1920.

Sokohen, Samuel, "The Simson-Hirsch Letter to the Chinese Jews 1795," *American Jewish Historical Quarterly*, Vol. 49, 1959-1960.

Solis-Cohen, Solomon, "Note Concerning David Hays and Esther E. Hays, His Wife," *American Jewish Historical Quarterly*, Vol. 2, 1894.

"South Carolina Commons—Assembly Journal, 1683, 1697," *Statutes of South Carolina II*: 131.

St. John Robert, *Jews Justice and Judaism* (Garden City, N.Y.: Doubleday, 1969).

"Statement of Friends of the Synagogue, 1803, Pages 72–73," *American Jewish Historical Quarterly*, Vol. 27, 1920.

Stern, M. H., "New Light on the Jewish Settlement of Savannah," *American Jewish Historical Quarterly*, Vol. 52, 1962-1963.

Swetschinski, Daniel M., "Conflict and Opportunity in Europe's Other Sea. The Adventure of Caribbean Jewish Settlement." *American Jewish Historical Quarterly*, December 1982.

Theberties, Charles, "Duke of York—Takes New York," *American Jewish Historical Society*, Vol. 4, 1895.

Tinall, F., David, N.D., and Friedenberg, A.M., "Documents Relating to the History of the Jews in Jamaica and Barbados in the Time of William III," *American Jewish Historical Quarterly*, Vol. 24, 1916.

Vater, Manasseh, "Naturalization Roll of New York (1740–1859)," *American Jewish Historical Quarterly*, Vol. 37, 1947.

Welsh, R., and Fox, W.L., eds., *Maryland, a History 1632–1974* (Baltimore: Maryland Historical Society, 1974).

Werblowsky, R.J., "What's in a Name—the Sephardim. the Origin of Their Name and Their Liturgical Customs," *American Jewish History*, Vol. 12, 1982.

Weyl, Nathaniel, *The Jew in America—Politics* (New Rochelle, Arlington House, 1968).

Wiernik, Peter, *History of the Jews in America* (New York, Harmon Press, 1972).

Willner, W., "Ezra Stiles and the Jews," *American Jewish Historical Quarterly*, Vol. 5, 1897.

Winkel, Peter, "Naturalization in Colonial New Jersey," *New Jersey History*, Vol. 109, 1–2, 1991.

Wolf, Edwin, "The First Book of Jewish Authorship Printed in America," *American Jewish Historical Quarterly*, Vol. 60, 1970-1971.

Wolf, Edwin, II, and Whiteman, Maxwell, *The History of the Jews of Philadelphia* (Philadelphia: Jewish Publication Society of America, 1957).

Wolf, Simon, *The American Jew as Patriot Citizen Soldier* (Philadelphia: Levytype, 1895).

Wright, Louis B., *South Carolina, a Bicentennial History* (New York, W.W. Norton, 1976).

"Yellow Fever Epidemic of Philadelphia 1793," *American Jewish Historical Quarterly*, Vol. 35, 1939.

Yerushalmi, Yosef Haym, "Between Amsterdam and New Amsterdam," *American Jewish History*, LXXII:2 (December 1982).

Index